Writing

Winning

Business

Proposals

Third Edition

RICHARD C. FREED

JOSEPH D. ROMANO

SHERVIN FREED

New York Chicago San Francisco Lisbon London Madrid Mexico City
Milan New Delhi San Juan Seoul Singapore Sydney Toronto

For Julie, Sarah, Adele, Bruce, Marcia,
Renee, Terese, and Amara

1 2 3 4 5 6 7 8 9 10 11 12 13 14 15   DOC/DOC   1 9 8 7 6 5 4 3 2 1 0

ISBN   978-0-07-174232-0
MHID   0-07-174232-8

This publication is designed to provide accurate and authoritative information in regard to the subject matter covered. It is sold with the understanding that neither the author nor the publisher is engaged in rendering legal, accounting, securities trading, or other professional services. If legal advice or other expert assistance is required, the services of a competent professional person should be sought.
>   —*From a Declaration of Principles Jointly Adopted by a Committee of the*
>   *American Bar Association and a Committee of Publishers and Associations*

Library of Congress Cataloging-in-Publication Data

Freed, Richard C., 1946–
        Writing winning business proposals / by Richard C. Freed, Shervin Freed, Joseph D. Romano.—3rd ed.
            p.   cm.
        Includes index.
        ISBN 978-0-07-174232-0 (alk. paper)
        1. Proposal writing in business.   2. Business report writing.   I. Freed, Shervin.   II. Romano, Joseph D.   III. Title.

        HF5718.5.F74   2011
        808'.06665—dc22
                                                                    2010026599

Interior design by Think Book Works

McGraw-Hill books are available at special quantity discounts to use as premiums and sales promotions or for use in corporate training programs. To contact a representative, please e-mail us at bulksales@mcgraw-hill.com.

This book is printed on acid-free paper.

Contents

Preface

This book is written for business people who prepare proposals (and for business people who evaluate them). If you are a consultant who owns your own business or who works for a firm of one or one thousand, if you are an internal consultant who "sells" services to your own organization, if you are a business executive who "sells" ideas to your management, you will benefit greatly from this book.

If you are like most people, you probably find selling your services or ideas in a proposal both demanding and difficult. Your proposals not only take too long to prepare, they are often written when you least want to write them—at night or on weekends, because during the day you are occupied with everything else that you do: conducting projects, furthering relationships, developing people. Proposal writing often seems like extra work, additional but necessary effort to get selected to perform projects so that you can be successful in your intensely competitive business.

Perhaps equally frustrating is the margin of difference between winning and losing. Hundreds of people consulting in the private sector have told me the same thing: the difference between winning and coming in second is very small, often just two to five points on a hundred-point scale. Those who place a close second never get back the upfront costs of proposal development. What they do get is second place. The situation in the public sector is similar. For a recent proposal to manage a $30 million project for a U.S. government agency, the difference between the winner and the second-place also-ran was five points out of one thousand—one-half of 1 percent!

What accounts for this difference? Sometimes it's price, of course, sometimes your particular methodology or your qualifications. But all too often, it's something much less tangible and rarely part of the evaluation criteria, whether those criteria are written down or in the buyers'[1] heads. That something has to do with relationships, with the buyers' feeling that you are *right*, that you *understand*, that you are *compatible*. So, yes, price is frequently a consideration, as is expertise. But someone is always or can always be less costly, and the world is full of experts. Price and expertise get you in the running, but they don't ensure that you'll win.

The goal of this book is twofold:

1. Specifically, to get you the additional two to five points necessary to win
2. Generally, to increase your win rate, your hit rate

By how much? That's impossible to say, of course, though some data suggest that it might be considerable. The concepts in *Writing Winning Business Proposals* (*WWBP*) are the same ones taught in a two-day program that has been offered to organizations large and small in more than 25 countries on five continents over the last 20 years. The largest organization tracked over one year the performance of those who had taken the two-day program and those who hadn't. Following are the results. (See Figure P.1.)

When you calculate the number of proposals won by the number of proposals submitted, the participants' hit rate percentage (proposals won divided by proposals submitted) was 30 points higher. More interesting is that when hit rate was weighted using the monetary value of the proposals won compared to the total value submitted, the hit rate percentage more than doubled, suggesting that participants were able to sell higher-value work than those who had not taken the program. As you read the contents of *WWBP*, you'll clearly understand why.

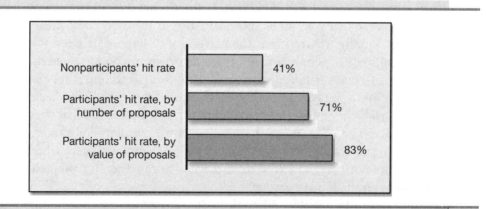

FIGURE P.1   Those who completed the two-day training program based on this book's concepts had more than double the hit rate of those who did not.

This Edition

In its first two editions, *Writing Winning Business Proposals* sold 50 percent more copies than its nearest "competitor" and almost four times the number of copies that publishers normally consider a bestseller—not for novels, of course, but for books of its kind. Those figures attest to the relatively wide readership *WWBP* has enjoyed. More important, the book's sales have made possible this third edition and therefore the opportunity to continue to improve on the previous two.

Specifically, this third edition includes four kinds of improvements:

1. **The chapters have been considerably revised**, not so much to change the overall content but to improve how that content is delivered—how it teaches you to think about and develop your proposals. During the eight years between editions, the slide deck used in the training program has been revised a dozen times. Although the concepts did not change, the slides themselves changed considerably, helping participants to understand those concepts more quickly and to apply them more strategically. *WWBP* has been similarly revised. For example, those who have read (or have taught from) the previous edition will note that the visuals in Chapter 9 now clearly indicate how a background section can be quickly constructed from the cells of the Logics Worksheet.

2. Related to the above, **every visual has been redrawn**, again to provide additional clarity about the concepts and how they fit together during the proposal-development process.[2]

3. **Two new appendices have been added.** Appendix G, "Reading RFPs," discusses important strategies for responding to Requests for Proposals. Appedix H, "A Worksheet for Qualifying Your Lead," includes criteria for determining your positioning and, based on that positioning, a forecast of your prospects for winning.

4. **Substantial learning materials are now available for download** that heretofore could be obtained only through the two-day training course. To access these downloads, visit: http://web.me.com/rfreed/Writing_Winning _Business_Proposals/Home.html. As of this writing, the downloads include:
   - The Logics, Psychologics, and Themes Development Worksheets, which should be printed in landscape in 11″ × 17″ or A4 (or larger—for example, poster size, which is ideal for team use). The previous edition contained only the individual cells of the Logics and Psychologics Worksheets; this download includes the complete worksheets.
   - A handbook for completing every cell on every worksheet
   - Guidelines for conducting Red Team Reviews
   - A discussion of deliverables and benefits and the differences between them
   - A glossary listing all the key terms in this book

- A small Excel application that includes criteria for determining your positioning with the potential client and, based on that positioning, a forecast of your prospects for winning
- An elaboration on the content in Appendix D that discusses the differences between proposals and recommendation (or final) reports and provides strategies for composing the latter
- A discussion of Stakeholder Matrices, which can be used during proposal development, the engagement, and account planning to improve your positioning

Acknowledgments

One doesn't write a book like this in isolation, and over the course of many years on this effort, I have numerous people to thank:

- Consultants from ECS Limited in New Delhi and KPMG in Chicago, who were helpful in providing opportunities to test my initial concepts, and the hundreds of consultants from A. T. Kearney's and IMS Consulting's American, European, and Asia-Pacific offices, who helped me refine those concepts
- The many graduate students at Iowa State University, who have served as a laboratory to develop my ideas, as well as the university itself, which provided release time so that the project could be completed
- Mike Hora, pricer and negotiator extraordinaire, whose insights about pricing were helpful in composing Chapter 13
- Barbara Minto for her work in what she calls the Minto Pyramid Principle, which forms the conceptual basis for Chapter 5 as well as the discussion in Chapter 11 and Appendix D
- David Maister, whose ideas about the professional-services firm and the selling of professional services saturate this and former editions
- The large team of McGraw-Hill editors, designers, and proofreaders—especially our project editor, Susan Moore, whose tireless efforts have significantly contributed to the quality of the book

—Richard Freed (richardfreed@gmail.com)
Ames, Iowa

Introduction

I am your potential client, and I'd like to introduce myself. Whether you are a consultant (either on your own or working for a consulting firm), an internal consultant, or a project-oriented employee working within my own firm, I am a reader of your proposal and/or a viewer of your proposal presentation. You are trying to sell me a service, and I will decide, singly or in concert with others, whether you, someone else, or no one will get the work you desire. Likewise, if you are an employee with an idea to sell, I am also a reader of your proposal and/ or a viewer of your proposal presentation. You are trying to sell me an idea, and I will decide, singly or with others, whether it is valid or workable or serviceable or fundable. In all of these cases, your job is to persuade me to engage you.

Regardless of your situation, your relationship with me is far different from my relationship to you. You are courting me; I am testing you. You are wooing me; I am assessing you—your abilities, insights, perspicacity, personal characteristics, and desire to support me. I know what you want from me—my agreement that your service or idea is worthwhile and, in many cases, more worthwhile than someone else's. But I'm not so certain that you know where I'm coming from or what I want from you. So I'll tell you.

If you're an outsider, engaging you as a consultant (at least initially) is often viewed by me and my colleagues as a sign of weakness. If I am at all typical of other potential clients I know, many of us share this perception. In my mind, hiring you frequently indicates—or at least suggests—my inability to do my job entirely by myself within my organization. I know all the reasons why outside support makes sense and should add value. At the same time, however, when

I'm really honest with myself, I'm not excited by the prospect of engaging you. Rather, I feel worried, threatened, impatient, and even at times suspicious.

I'm worried by the implication that potential changes you propose will indicate that I haven't been doing my job, or at least not doing it as well as I should. I'm threatened by the possibility of losing control to you, the outsider, and how this could make my position—my power base—vulnerable within my organization. I'm impatient because I've tried for some time to address the issue we're discussing, didn't seek outside support when the symptoms initially occurred, and now have a need for rapid response. I'm suspicious of your ability to help me because I've been burned before, have heard all your promises, and have compared them to the eventual results. You all talk a good game. Not all of you perform as well as you talk. So when I discuss my situation with you, I want you to understand me and what makes my situation unique. It may not be unique to you, but it is to me. I'm looking for assurance that your involvement will make me and my organization significantly better and more competitive.

Therefore, if you are a consultant, I believe that your responsiveness and interest in the proposal-development stage indicate the kind of service you'll provide if you are selected. As a result, I want you to demonstrate your desire to serve me, your knowledge of my industry and organization, your understanding of my priorities, and your ability to listen, to challenge, and to understand my situation, my needs, and my desired benefits. I want you to prepare thoroughly for your meetings with me, go out of your way to show me how good you are, be specific about how you will help me, share your knowledge and experience from similar situations, and make me feel that this proposed project is important to you and your firm. I want you to begin providing "service" early in the process by offering advice, ideas, and perspective, even if I don't request them.

When I do make a request, especially one that is obviously a test of your responsiveness, I want you to respond quickly and thoroughly. In short, during the early stages of our courtship, I want to learn, and I want you to establish a sound relationship by providing value. I want you to act as if my situation is the most important one you are addressing. You offer a professional service, and I need to know that you'll serve me professionally—that is, provide value for my proposed expenditure.

If you do all that, especially over time as we develop a closer relationship, you might not even have to write a proposal, and, of course, you really don't want to. Proposals take a lot of time, often a huge investment in time. And let's be honest: Even when they're well written, proposals frequently don't win jobs so much as they clinch or lose them.

But the plain truth is that we don't always have a close relationship and you can't always sell a job up front. Therefore you need to write a proposal, and you need to learn to write a good one. Hence this book. I've written it because I and other potential clients like me have read hundreds of your proposals and heard just as many of your presentations, and although a few are outstanding, most of them aren't.

Many offend with cut-and-paste boilerplate, miss important opportunities to provide value, suffer from poor logic and organization, and focus more on you than on me and my organization. Although some do a few things well, some don't do much well at all. All can be improved, and I guarantee that I can help you improve them.

I'm not saying your proposal will always win. That I can't guarantee. But I do promise that you'll prepare better proposals—because you'll think more strategically about how to write and present them. Getting you to think and write more strategically, particularly from my point of view, is one of the major goals of this book.

So what do I as a potential client, either outside or within your organization, want from your proposal? Nothing that should surprise you. From my perspective, I want to feel that you and your team can best meet my objectives and achieve my desired results from engaging you. Therefore, I desire:

- Agreement on my question, i.e., on the specific question or questions that must be answered to move my organization from our current situation to our desired result
- A clear understanding of the benefits I will receive by your answering that question—benefits I will gain during, by the end of, and beyond the proposed project
- Clarity on how you propose to answer the question and the way we will work together as you do so
- Confidence in and comfort with you and your proposed team
- Return on my investment from my actual and/or anticipated benefits

To help you address these desires, I've developed the proven proposal-development process summarized in Figure I.1. Although preparing effective and persuasive proposals involves far more than Figure I.1 illustrates (and this book covers much more than the process shown), the following five steps will provide you with a road map for the journey we'll take through much of this book.

1. **Understand the baseline logic.** Every proposal situation involves a real or perceived discrepancy between where I and my organization are and where we want to be—between, that is, our current situation (let's call it S_1) and our desired result (S_2). The project or ideas you propose will achieve or get us closer to achieving that desired result and therefore begin to or entirely remove that discrepancy. Consequently, benefits (B) will accrue to us. At its fundamental level, your proposal must clearly express the relationship between my current situation, my desired result, and the benefits of my achieving that result. I call this the proposal's "baseline logic," represented by the formula $S_1 \rightarrow S_2 \rightarrow B$. Your proposal (and your project, if you win) stands little chance of success if these elements aren't clearly identified, logically related, and agreed to. I discuss this relationship in Chapter 2 and Chapter 3.

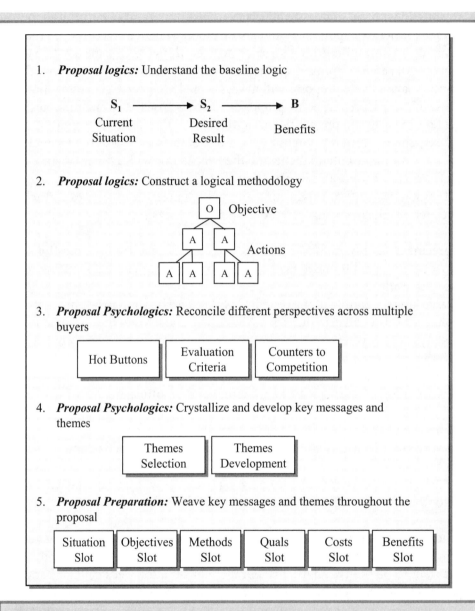

FIGURE I.1   A very brief overview of the proposal-development process

2. Construct a logical methodology. To move me from S_1 to S_2, your document
   or presentation proposes a series of actions, a methodology, that must clearly
   and logically communicate how you'll help me and my organization achieve
   our objective and desired result. In Chapter 5, I show you a logical framework

that will help you thoughtfully develop, organize, and sequence the actions necessary to achieve our objective.

Part 1 of this book, then, focuses on what I call the "logics" of proposals: the logical relationship among the current situation, desired result, and benefits; and the logically constructed methodology you will use to help remove the discrepancy between where I and my organization are and where we want to be.

The Preface of this book mentions that the difference between winning and coming in second is often only two to five points on a hundred-point scale, and understanding proposal logics may get you only some of the points you need to win. Why not all? Because I and others buy for psychological as well as for logical reasons. Accordingly, Part 2 focuses on what I call the "psychologics" of proposals. The next two steps in my proposal-development process address these psychologics.

3. **Reconcile different perspectives across multiple buyers.** *Writing Winning Business Proposals* assumes that most of your proposal situations involve what is called a "complex sale." A complex sale exists when you sell to multiple buyers, each of whom may play a different role in evaluating your proposal. Each may have a different perception—sometimes slight, sometimes significant—of the problem or opportunity and of the benefits that will accrue to their organization, collectively, and to them, individually, from solving that problem or realizing that opportunity.

Too often, proposals are unsuccessful because the writers assume they are selling to organizations rather than to individuals. Although an organization can be in a problematic situation, different people within the organization often have different points of view of the current situation. What to one person is eroding profits might be a lack of productivity to a second and poor customer service to a third. Each "buyer," in short, has a different agenda, a different critical issue, or at least a different slant on the issue that must be considered. I'll help you explore these persons as individuals who play different roles on the consultant-evaluation committee and have different buying criteria. I discuss these roles in Chapter 6.

Once you've understood the individual players in the selling situation, you need to create a framework, a mosaic, a collage, to understand their similarities and differences. A successful proposal has to address these differences in one document or in one presentation. Addressing different perceptions is a major challenge. You need, for example, to know each buyer's hot buttons: their individual desires and concerns that must be addressed during the project. You need to understand the benefits that will accrue to each, once the proposed objectives are achieved. But, just as important, you need to understand how each buyer's hot buttons complement or conflict with the desires and concerns of other buyers. In Chapter 7, I discuss these matters as well as proposal evaluation criteria and counters to the competition.

4. **Crystallize and develop key proposal messages and themes**. To be most effective, your proposal (spoken or written) needs to communicate several essential messages that clearly differentiate it from competitors' proposals and convince me and the other buyers that you have heard and understood the issues from our respective points of view. These messages, which characterize our story and our needs, are called "themes." They come from your analysis of our individual hot buttons and our collective evaluation criteria and from your counters to your competition. Once you have identified your themes and developed them, you will have generated much of the persuasive content to incorporate into your proposal. In Chapter 7, I discuss themes and the themes-development process in detail.

5. **Weave the messages and themes throughout the proposal.** All the logical and psychological strategy must be applied, of course, and the chapters in Part 3 address this application. Just as Beethoven repeated his musical themes throughout his symphonies, you want to "play" your themes throughout your proposal. By weaving your web of persuasion, you can communicate why you, and not someone else, can best support me to achieve my desired result. In Chapter 10, I discuss the important concept of persuasion slots, those parts of your proposal that contain your themes and other selling points. Chapters 9 to 13 discuss major parts of the proposal where you discuss your understanding of my situation, your proposed method for addressing it, the benefits to the buyers of your doing so, and the like.

Each of this book's chapters introduces you to important concepts and strategies, which are then applied in a work session. I've written the work sessions from your point of view, so that you can see how the strategies are applied as you develop your proposal step-by-step. That is, the work sessions (which are based on a real-life case) allow you to experience and practice the concepts laid out step-by-step in the chapter preceding it. I can't tell you how important this is: *Do not skip the work sessions; they bring the concepts to life.*

Before we begin our journey together, I have to let you in on a little secret. *There are no rules for writing; there are only strategies.* No rules. Not even that subjects and verbs should always agree. Not even that sentences (like this and the previous two) shouldn't be fragments.

Rule-bound writers are limited writers. Having been told never to begin a sentence with *but*, they never do. "*But* why not do so?" I ask, if the situation suggests that you should. Consequently, rule-bound writers have fewer options to choose from, fewer possibilities to consider, fewer arrows in their quiver or weapons in their arsenal. Your challenge now is to persuade me, your potential client, using all the tools and techniques at your disposal.

Writing always involves choices, always decisions among options, and the more options you consider, the better your chance of selecting the most appropriate one for a given situation. Even the rule-bound writer has made a decision, but what I call a "nondecision decision," an unconsidered one. I'll show you how to make better decisions, thoughtful ones, considered ones. And remember that what worked well in one situation will not necessarily work as well in another. Even if the questions are identical. Even if the industry issues are identical. If preparing winning proposals were that easy, there'd be no need for this book.

I'm willing to teach you if you're willing to learn. I challenge you to think hard about the concepts presented. Some of them will make almost immediate sense because they will provide guidelines for what you already know, and these frameworks will allow you to use your knowledge more consistently and effectively. Other concepts will be more difficult to master, because proposals are difficult to master. I've spent over 30 years trying to master this beast called proposals. I'm closer to doing so than I used to be, and, if you work with me, I'll help you get far closer than you've ever been.

Let our journey begin!

Proposal Logics

As your potential client, one thing that amazes and even at times upsets me about your proposals is that, although you are obviously well educated, intelligent, and thoughtful, your documents and presentations often do not convey your ideas logically. I cannot comprehend a well-thought-out logical argument about my situation and how you might help me improve it if you don't present that argument.

At the beginning of Part 1, I provide the framework to help you do so. Then I share my desire for your having and communicating in your proposal document or presentation an orientation toward measurable substantive results in whatever type of support you propose to me and my organization. Finally, I discuss how to construct a logical methodology that will answer my key questions, achieve my objectives, and therefore move me and my organization from one condition to another, from our less-than-ideal current situation to a better place, our desired results. You are writing your proposal because we have this gap, and your methodology must clearly and logically explain how you propose to bridge it. You have the knowledge and expertise to help us bridge that gap, but based on the hundreds of proposals I've evaluated, I can only conclude that you don't know how to communicate that knowledge to me clearly and logically. You will by the end of Part 1.

CHAPTER 1

Understanding Generic Structure Logic

Like most people, I like stories, so let me begin by telling you a very short story—after which I'll ask you several questions.

Paula was hungry. After she entered and ordered a pastrami sandwich, it was served to her quickly. She left the waitress a big tip.

- Where was Paula?
- What did she eat?
- Who made the sandwich?
- Who took the order?
- Who served the sandwich?
- Why did Paula leave a big tip?

How is it that you could answer those questions rather easily even though nothing in the story explicitly provides the information necessary for your answers? Because you have a schema for the concept of "restaurant."

Schemas are knowledge structures that you have built and stored in your memory as patterns, as analytical frameworks. Schemas represent generic concepts such as restaurant or airplane or house. Each schema has "slots" that exist in a network of relations. Your schema for restaurant may have slots for "ordering," "eating," "tipping," and "paying." Your schema for house may contain slots for "family room," "kitchen," "living room," and "bathroom." A slot for "home office" is also possible, but probably not for "boardroom" or "conference room," since such spaces typically are not found in residences. Therefore, you don't expect to find a boardroom or a conference room in someone's house.

You also have schemas for different kinds of texts, and these schemas create expectations. In a novel, for example, you expect character and plot and setting. In a particular type of novel, such as a spy novel, you may expect that the hero will be betrayed and captured, only to escape and triumph. In a eulogy, you expect some account of the deceased person's character and accomplishments; in a personal letter, some account of your friend's life and feelings; in a sermon, some moral based on a religious belief. If the sermon consisted solely of an analysis of price-earnings ratios or bills of materials or various strategies for penetrating new markets, your expectations would be denied, and you'd be suspicious of the speaker's competence and reliability, maybe even his or her sanity.

Proposals and other business documents also carry with them schemas and sets of expectations. If I asked you to submit a proposal to me, I'd be surprised if the document contained findings, conclusions, and recommendations. These are slots I'd expect in a report, not a proposal.[1] Potential clients like me, then, have certain expectations, and as a writer, you're at some risk if you don't meet those expectations. If your reader is in a proposal-reading situation, you'd better deliver a document that fits your reader's proposal schema, not the schema for a report or a eulogy or a novel.

Your schema for a proposal also has slots, and those slots make up what I call a proposal's generic structure. No matter how different one proposal may be from another, something generic makes them both proposals, and that something is their generic structure.

The Slots in a Proposal's Generic Structure

Most of your proposal opportunities exist because I, your potential client, have an unsolved problem or an unrealized opportunity. Therefore, your primary task is to convince me, both logically and psychologically, that you can help me address my problem or opportunity and, in competitive situations, that you'll do so better than anyone else.

Your entire proposal needs to communicate that message in one seamless argument (which may happen to be divided into sections or even volumes for my convenience). Your argument is suggested by the following propositions, each of which is preceded by the proposal slot that contains it. (See Figure 1.1.)

Situation. This is our understanding of your problem or opportunity.
Objectives. Given that problem or opportunity, these are our objectives for addressing it.
Methods. Given those objectives, these are our methods for achieving them.
Qualifications. Given those methods, these are our qualifications for performing them.
Costs (or Fees). Given those qualifications and methods, this is how much it will cost.
Benefits. Given our efforts and their associated costs, these are the benefits or value you will receive.

FIGURE 1.1   The generic structure of proposals

Slots Speaking to Slots

Although the preceding statements might suggest that your proposal's argument flows only one way—from top to bottom—the argument should be so tight that the logic also can flow from bottom to top:

> These are the *benefits* or value you will receive
> considering the *costs* you will incur
> given our *qualifications*
> for performing these *methods*
> that will achieve your *objectives*
> and therefore improve your *situation*.

Now, I've never seen a proposal organized that way, but however the proposal is organized, every generic structure slot needs to "speak" to all the others. No slot exists in isolation: Each contributes to your communicating the proposal's primary message. In later chapters, I'll show you specific techniques for assuring that each slot in your proposal speaks to every other one.

Slots Are Not Necessarily Sections

You've probably noticed that I've been referring to OBJECTIVES, METHODS, BEN-EFITS, and so on, as "slots," even though many proposals might designate those parts of the proposal by using section headings of the same name.[2] I've been calling these elements slots rather than sections because in any given proposal it is possible that:

- **No slot could be used as a section heading.** That's the case if you don't use headings in your document or if your headings are different from the slot names. The situation slot could be called "Background" or "Business Issues" or "Our Understanding of Your Situation." The methods slot could be named "Approach" or "Methodology" or "Study Strategy."
- **Two or more slots could be combined into one section.** You could combine SITUATION and OBJECTIVES into one section. Or OBJECTIVES and METHODS.
- **One slot could be split into two or more sections.** METHODS could be divided among "Approach," "Workplan," and "Deliverables." QUALIFICATIONS could be split among "Project Organization," "Qualifications," "References," and "Résumés."

All Slots Should Be Filled or Accounted For

Every proposal you write or present contains six slots, but these slots are not necessarily organized into corresponding sections or presented in predetermined or fixed order. Nevertheless, whether they are combined, split, or not named at all, each slot should be filled or accounted for. On some occasions, you don't have to fill slots in the proposal document or presentation because they've already been "filled" in prior discussions with me, your potential client, and therefore accounted for during the proposal process. We all know that proposal development itself is often only one part of the selling process, and actions, good or bad, that occur before the actual document is submitted affect the proposal's content, organization, tone, and the like.

If before you submit the proposal you have already convinced me that you thoroughly understand my problem or opportunity, you've already filled much of the situation slot and may not need to fill it (or fill it very much) in the proposal. If you and your team previously have done a good deal of commendable work for me, you've filled much of the qualifications slot, and loading the document with résumés and references may be not only unnecessary but strategically unwise and perhaps even annoying. Remember, there are no rules, only strategies. And effective strategies are driven by the specifics of the situation, by the context of the selling process.

●　●　●

By understanding the schema for house, you know what kind of rooms can exist in a house; therefore, you expect rooms such as a kitchen, a bathroom, and a bedroom. You also have some sense of the relationship among those rooms and, to some degree, their placement. For example, in a two-story house, you would expect a first-floor kitchen; in a two-story house with only one bath, you might expect a second-floor bathroom; in a house with more than one bath, you would not be surprised to find the second one adjoined to a master bedroom. Similarly, by understanding generic structure—the schema for proposals—you understand an important logical element of proposals. You know that proposals, to be proposals, also have certain kinds of rooms or slots, and you know the relationship among those rooms. You know, for example, that one slot explains the problem or opportunity, another explains a method for addressing the problem or capitalizing on the opportunity, and yet another argues the benefits of doing so. Throughout much of this book, I will build upon the concept of generic structure. In fact, the next two chapters focus on the three proposal slots—SITUATION, OBJECTIVES, and BENEFITS—that make up what I call "the baseline logic."

CHAPTER 1 REVIEW

Understanding Generic Structure Logic

1. All proposals have the same generic structure, which contains the following six slots:
   - **Situation:** What is the problem or opportunity?
   - **Objectives:** Given that problem or opportunity, what are your objectives for solving or realizing it?
   - **Methods:** Given those objectives, how will you achieve them?
   - **Qualifications:** Given those methods, how are you qualified to perform them?
   - **Costs:** Given the methods and qualifications, how much will it cost?
   - **Benefits:** Given those costs, what benefits and/or value will accrue?

2. Generic structure is not a matter of organization. That is, a proposal is not necessarily sequenced according to the slots as they are ordered above.

3. The slots do not necessarily correspond to sections. One section could contain two or more slots. A single slot could be distributed among two or more sections.

4. The extent to which the slots should be filled in the proposal presentation or document depends upon how much they were filled in preproposal meetings or prior working relationships.

WORK SESSION 1: Proposal Opportunity at the ABC Company, a Division of Consolidated Industries

See Figure 1.2 for the instructions for this chapter's work session.

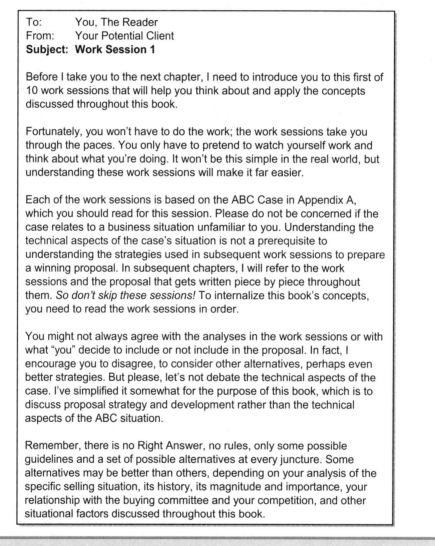

To: You, The Reader
From: Your Potential Client
Subject: Work Session 1

Before I take you to the next chapter, I need to introduce you to this first of 10 work sessions that will help you think about and apply the concepts discussed throughout this book.

Fortunately, you won't have to do the work; the work sessions take you through the paces. You only have to pretend to watch yourself work and think about what you're doing. It won't be this simple in the real world, but understanding these work sessions will make it far easier.

Each of the work sessions is based on the ABC Case in Appendix A, which you should read for this session. Please do not be concerned if the case relates to a business situation unfamiliar to you. Understanding the technical aspects of the case's situation is not a prerequisite to understanding the strategies used in subsequent work sessions to prepare a winning proposal. In subsequent chapters, I will refer to the work sessions and the proposal that gets written piece by piece throughout them. *So don't skip these sessions!* To internalize this book's concepts, you need to read the work sessions in order.

You might not always agree with the analyses in the work sessions or with what "you" decide to include or not include in the proposal. In fact, I encourage you to disagree, to consider other alternatives, perhaps even better strategies. But please, let's not debate the technical aspects of the case. I've simplified it somewhat for the purpose of this book, which is to discuss proposal strategy and development rather than the technical aspects of the ABC situation.

Remember, there is no Right Answer, no rules, only some possible guidelines and a set of possible alternatives at every juncture. Some alternatives may be better than others, depending on your analysis of the specific selling situation, its history, its magnitude and importance, your relationship with the buying committee and your competition, and other situational factors discussed throughout this book.

FIGURE 1.2   Instructions for work session 1

CHAPTER 2

Understanding the Baseline Logic

A lot of people (and I'm one of them) think that too many proposals try to make the simple complex, when in fact what I and many other buyers want them to do is to make the complex simple. So let me simplify what proposals do, or at least what I'd like them to do from my potential client's perspective. Let's concentrate on just three things (which, we'll see in Chapter 3, are related to three of the generic structure slots—SITUATION, OBJECTIVES, and BENEFITS). Figure 2.1 depicts your proposed project (with examples from the ABC case) in a nutshell.

In the beginning is my organization, which is in a condition, a current "state of health," a current situation—call it S_1. This current situation is what is happening today. Perhaps we don't like this situation because we have a problem that needs addressing or solving. Or perhaps we would like another situation better because we have an opportunity on which we might capitalize. In either case, we desire to change. Or we might be uncertain about whether we like or should like our current situation, and we'd like to know whether we ought to like it or dislike it.

In each of these cases, an actual or possible discrepancy exists between where we are and where we want to be. Therefore, we are willing to consider engaging a consultant to help us, to propose a project at the end of which we will have closed the gap and be in a different, improved state—call it S_2—which is what I call my desired result. At that point, our problem will be solved (or on its way to a solution), or our opportunity

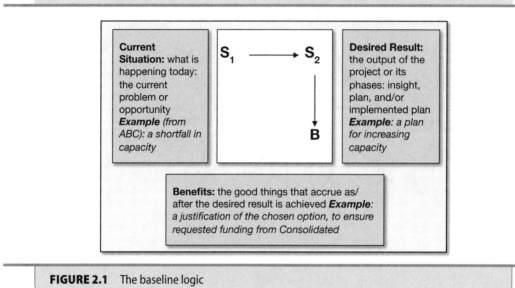

FIGURE 2.1   The baseline logic

will be realized (or at least closer to its realization), or we will know whether we even have a problem or an opportunity. In each case, we will have or know something more than we had or knew before. And we will be better off because of it; we will benefit and gain value from reaching our desired result, S_2, by the end of your proposed project.

We are here, we want to be over there, and we'll benefit when we get there. That simple idea needs to function as the baseline of your proposal—and of your thinking about your proposal to me. That idea has a logic to it, a fundamental logic, a baseline logic. And that idea, that baseline logic, needs to drive the argument of your proposal: "You are here, and we understand that 'here' is or might not be desirable. You want to be somewhere else instead, which is more desirable. Once we help you to be that somewhere else, you will enjoy the benefits of being there."

Although all this certainly isn't rocket science, only a minority of proposal writers understand this logic, and far fewer know how to test for and apply it. Most proposals are illogical at their core because the writers don't understand the baseline logic, and even when they do, they don't know how to convey that understanding clearly to me. They don't know how to take advantage of that logic to increase the persuasiveness of their presentations and documents. Illogical thinking reduces your probability of winning, and, if you should win, it dramatically reduces your likelihood of conducting a successful engagement. This baseline logic—or, if you prefer, this problem definition or analytical framework—is the basis for a meaningful and persuasive exchange of ideas.

Here I should express two cautionary notes. First, there are times when I, your potential client, am not clear about this baseline logic. I'm not clear about my current situation or about where I want to be at the end of your proposed project. When this occurs, and you do not help me achieve clarity, you and I are in a potential lose-lose situation. In this situation, you probably will write a proposal without clear objectives, without clearly defining my desired result, S_2, at the end of your project. I might even accept that proposal, but we might both pay a price, often a significant price, during the project. You may not satisfy me, possibly incur a cost overrun, and not develop the long-lasting relationship we both desire.

To avoid this situation and to ensure that your proposal is fundamentally sound, the rest of this chapter, as well as the next, will build on the concept of the baseline logic, show you how to test for it, and demonstrate how you can use it to your advantage.

The second cautionary note: Although I remarked at the beginning of this chapter that I want you to make the complex simple, I have to admit that the relatively simple concept of the baseline logic often is not easy to understand. Accordingly, this chapter on understanding the baseline logic and the next chapter on aligning the baseline logic are not easy going. At times, the reading will be laborious. Sometimes it will even appear redundant because I want constantly to reinforce important points that will help you use the baseline logic, in this chapter and those that follow, to:

- Challenge the depth of my thinking
- Clarify my overriding question(s)
- Clarify your project's objective(s)
- Articulate and generate benefits
- Communicate a measurable-results orientation
- Construct your methodology
- Define the magnitude of your proposed effort
- Identify your necessary qualifications
- Make better go/no-go decisions about deciding to bid
- Demonstrate your ability to address thoughtfully what—to me, anyway—is a complex issue

These substantial benefits will accrue to you only after you have mastered the concept of the baseline logic. Although mastery of anything is difficult, it's essential that you understand the baseline logic. Everything else in Part 1 of this book (and a good deal in Part 2 and Part 3) depends on this understanding, which provides the foundation you will need to win—to gain the additional two to five points, as the preface suggests, that are often the difference between winning and being a close second. So hang in there: I'm going to give you the key that unlocks the mystery of thinking about and writing winning business proposals.

The Three Kinds of Current Situations, Desired Results, and Objectives

As shown in the first row of the three boxes near the top of Figure 2.2, my current situation can be one of only three conditions. These are the three possible S_1 situations that can serve as a starting point for your efforts:

1. I and my organization don't know if we should change because (a) we're not certain that we have a problem or (b) we sense that a problem exists but are unsure of its nature, scope, or severity. That is, we *lack insight* about our situation.
2. We know we should change but we don't know how, because although we do *have insight*, we *lack a plan* to act on that insight.
3. We know we should change and we know how, but even though we do *have insight* and we *have a plan*, we don't have the time or resources to *implement* that plan.

In Figure 2.2, each of the three possible S_1 conditions corresponds to one of three desired results (the lowest row of three boxes near the bottom), and each

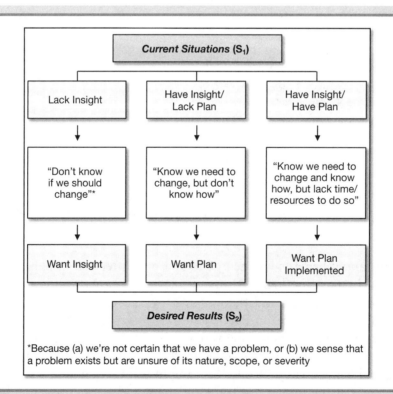

FIGURE 2.2 The relationship among current situations and desired results

of these desired results is related to three types of projects you could propose: insight, planning, or implementation. In an Insight Project (the left column of Figure 2.2), I don't know if my organization should change, so I may desire a competitive assessment or an identification of potential opportunities. Market surveys, benchmarking studies, and audits fall into this category, and your project's objective could include words such as *assess, compare, determine, evaluate, understand,* and *identify*. You provide me insight, which has value because it makes me and my organization smarter and provides a basis for learning whether we need to change.

In a Planning Project (the middle column of Figure 2.2), I already know that I need to change, because I have insight but don't know how to change, so I may desire a plan detailing how my organization should change. Your project's objective could begin with words such as *develop, determine, define,* or *recommend*.

In an Implementation Project (the right column of Figure 2.2), I know that I want to change and I know how to change because I have a plan, but I need additional resources or expertise to implement the change. Therefore, your project's objective could be *to implement, to increase or improve,* or *to decrease or reduce* some specific operational parameter by definable measures.

How many objectives your project will have depends on what my current situation is (lack insight, have insight, or have plan) and where I want to be at the end of your proposed project. For example, assume that my S_1 state is characterized by lack of insight: I don't know if we should enter a particular market. Assume that my desired result is to gain such insight. In this instance, you would move me one step, and therefore your study would have only one objective: to provide insight about whether I should enter that market. As Figure 2.3 illustrates, there are three possible combinations of S_1 and S_2 states that involve a movement of one step and therefore involve only one objective.

In some cases, I might want your efforts to move me two or more steps. Assume again that my current situation is characterized by lack of insight: I don't know if we should enter a particular market. My desired result, however, might involve more than just insight—I might also want a plan for entering my target market. In this instance, you will move me two steps, and therefore your project will have two objectives. First, you will determine the feasibility of entering the market; second, if entering appears attractive, you will develop a plan for doing so. Here, then, you would propose a two-step project, and a single objective would govern each step. As Figure 2.4 illustrates, there are two possible combinations of S_1 and S_2 that involve a movement of two steps and a third combination that involves all three steps.

Your proposal's objective(s) expresses the major outcome(s) of your project. Therefore, it must clearly indicate how far you will take me. As you'll see in Chapter 5, this clarity is essential if your proposal is to have a logical base on which to build your methodology.

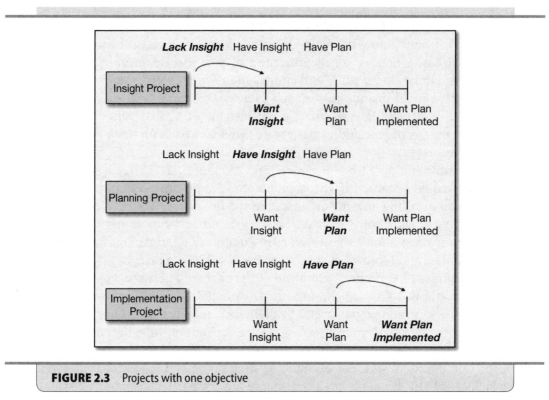

FIGURE 2.3   Projects with one objective

While all this might appear straightforward, let me reinforce the point that I, your potential client, don't always make it easy for you. I am often unclear in my own mind about what we are trying to do and therefore might unintentionally confuse you. But we're not here to debate right and wrong. And we're not here to become better mind readers. We're here to get agreement on the specific issues to be addressed so that your services will be of the greatest value to me and my organization.

Let's take the ABC case as an example. Many experienced consultants would believe that ABC's problem requires a combination study: insight and planning. These consultants would argue that ABC may not need to add capacity in the near term because new equipment and technology, better utilization of current equipment and space, outsourcing, and the like could allow ABC to produce enough product to meet forecasted demand. These consultants would believe, therefore, that two objectives should drive the ABC study: First, determine the feasibility of better utilizing existing capacity. (That's the insight piece.) Second, if additional capacity is needed, develop a plan for adding it. (That's the planning piece.) Note the decision point here. If no additional capacity is needed, the second objective may become

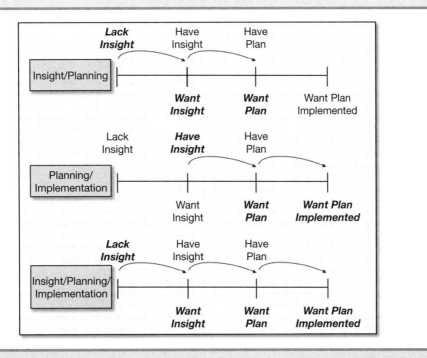

FIGURE 2.4 Projects with multiple objectives

unnecessary to achieve. If additional capacity is necessary, the second objective needs to be addressed. Combination studies can have such decision points, which occur after a former objective is achieved and before a subsequent one is addressed.

Based on my reading of the case, I don't believe that ABC is expecting an insight *and* planning study, and if I were the potential client at ABC, I'd be surprised by a document that proposed one. I might even be suspicious, thinking that the consultants were trying to sell me more than I'd asked for. Of course, the consultants could be correct in their assessment that I need both insight and a plan. If that's the case, however, they better convince me in our discussions before submitting the proposal. If they don't, my perception of my desired result will not be aligned with theirs. Those who have had the greatest success with me, both during the business-development process and while conducting the actual project, have made certain that clear alignment exists between my perception of my desired result or results and their own. This alignment is one example of the mutual benefit that should occur during the business-development process.

Understanding the Baseline Logic

1. Proposals contain a baseline logic expressed by $S_1 \rightarrow S_2 \rightarrow B$:
  - S_1 refers to the current situation. That situation always involves a discrepancy between what is and what could be. Therefore, S_1 is characterized by a problem or opportunity and by a lack of benefits. S_1 is discussed in the situation slot.
  - S_2 refers to the endpoint(s) of the project or phases of the project. S_2 is defined in the objectives slot, since your project's objective(s) is the expression of S_2.
  - B refers to the benefits that accrue to us from achieving our desired result(s). Benefits are identified in the benefits slot.

2. The desired result(s) expressed by the proposal's objective(s) defines the project's type, of which there are three and only three (excluding combinations):
  - **Insight** (e.g., audits, market research, or benchmarking projects). Potential client says: "We don't know if we should change because (a) we're not certain that we have a problem or (b) we sense that a problem exists but are unsure of its nature, scope, or severity." That is, we lack insight about our situation.
  - **Plan.** Potential client says: "We want to change, because we know we have a problem or opportunity or we sense that we do, but we don't know how to change."
  - **Implementation.** Potential client says: "We want to change, because we know we have a problem or opportunity or we sense that we do, and we know how to change, because we already have a plan, but we need help to implement that plan."

If the project combines two or more of the previous elements (e.g., insight and planning), a decision point might exist necessitating a phased study.

CHAPTER 3

Aligning the Baseline Logic

This is the most difficult, perhaps the longest, and arguably the most important chapter in the book. If you skip this chapter, you won't understand fully most of the book's subsequent content. So find some blocks of time during which you're not distracted, and forge on.

Why is this the most important chapter? First, because the baseline logic, introduced in Chapter 2, is the foundation of your proposal, and more than 95 percent of the proposals I've read, over the course of 30 years, have serious flaws in the baseline logic, causing serious cracks in their foundations. Second, this chapter demonstrates how you can fully align the baseline logic, as shown in Figure 3.1, and thereby:

- Identify substantial content for your proposal that you would otherwise miss
- Assess the clarity (or lack of clarity) in *your* thinking
- Understand the clarity (or lack of clarity) in *my* thinking
- Recognize where you and I view matters differently as a first step in having serious conversations about your proposed approach, scope, and projected outcomes

Note two things about Figure 3.1. First, all the new material is just an expansion of what we've already discussed: S_1 (the current situation), S_2 (the desired results), and B (the benefits). On the left side of Figure 3.1 are aspects of the current situation. That's where you and your firm will begin the change process I desire. On the right side are major project outcomes, including the results I desire and the benefits my organiza-

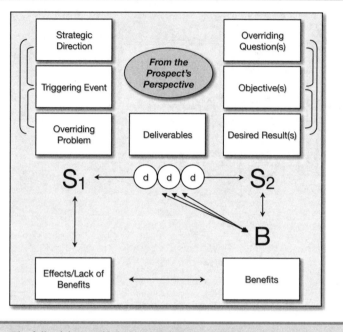

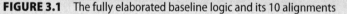

FIGURE 3.1   The fully elaborated baseline logic and its 10 alignments

tion and I will enjoy. In the middle are the deliverables, those smaller outcomes you will provide along the way as you help us move from one state to the other.

Second, as you enter content related to these elements into the worksheets (and as you watch the elements entered in this chapter's work session) you must express the content from the potential client's point of view, i.e., from *my* point of view. To help you enter that content, you will want to have next to you all six Logics Worksheet cells, which you can copy from Appendix B. Alternately, you can download and print out those cells as well as the complete Logics Worksheet from http://web.me.com/rfreed/Writing_Winning_Business_Proposals/Home.html.

What happens if your point of view differs from mine? What happens if my point of view differs from that of other members of the selection committee? What happens if your point of view differs from that of others on your own team? What happens if any of the baseline logic is not aligned? What happens if you don't know the content to enter on the worksheet or aren't certain about its accuracy?

The answer to all these questions is the same: You mark that difference, that discrepancy in understanding, with a red flag, which as the downloadable glossary indicates, signals "a weakness, vulnerability, gap in information, or, generally, something you don't like." Why should you begin by phrasing the content from my point of view? Because if you don't, you'll express *your* point of view and likely miss mine altogether. Start with me, your potential client, and remember this: You don't invent red flags; they exist. Red flags don't express your weaknesses. They signal an opportunity for resolving possible differences, so that, ideally, by the time you write your proposal, your understanding matches mine, and my team's, and your team's. Even if you can't resolve a red flag by the time you need to submit your proposal, you will at least recognize that it exists and make, not a nondecision decision, but a strategic decision based on the flag's existence.

What follows are crucial questions you need to ask yourself to help you fully align the various elements in Figure 3.1. Below these questions are subsections that discuss each question in some detail:

- Are the potential client's strategic direction, triggering event, overriding problem, and effects/lack of benefits aligned?
- Are the overriding question(s), objective(s), and desired result(s) aligned?
- Is the overriding problem aligned with the overriding question(s)?
- Are the deliverables aligned with the desired result(s)?
- Are the deliverables and desired result(s) aligned with the benefits?
- Are the benefits aligned with the effects/lack of benefits?

Are the Potential Client's Strategic Direction, Triggering Event, Overriding Problem, and Effects/Lack of Benefits Aligned? (Logics Worksheet, Cells 1 and 2)

Regarding the left side of Figure 3.1, the current situation, you need to understand four vital elements and their alignments.

Strategic Direction

Why strategic direction? Because if you want to have a rich relationship with me, as opposed to just a "one-off" engagement, you want to work on projects that will help my firm achieve our strategic direction. In such projects, your fees will likely be greater (because such projects are more valuable to me), and you will be working at higher levels of my organization, with the very people with whom you wish to develop solid relationships. Accordingly, you want the overriding problem you will address to align with our strategic direction. If it doesn't, red flag it.

Triggering Event

As defined in the downloadable glossary, the triggering event is that event (in some cases, events) that brought to our consciousness the existence of the overriding problem (or opportunity). A triggering event could be external (e.g., the entrance of a new competitor into my market) or internal (e.g., a change in top management that initiates a whole series of new agendas). Consider the ABC case in Appendix A. What brought to ABC's consciousness the existence of their imminent shortfall in capacity? Probably Marcia Collins's market forecast. That forecast triggered, brought to ABC's consciousness, the need to take action to address the projected shortfall in capacity. If you don't know the triggering event, you should place a red flag next to that phrase in Cell 2. If the triggering event and overriding problem are not aligned, use a red flag to signal that lack of alignment.

Overriding Problem

"Overriding" means at the highest level, and it means a *single* problem. My organization has lots of problems, just like yours. For your project with me, however, you need to identify not the major problems but the main one, the single highest-level problem your engagement will address or solve. In expressing that problem in Cell 2, be certain that you phrase the problem *as* a problem, rather than (as is all too typical) a question. And make certain that it is a single problem rather than "lack of X *and* insufficient Y." Assuming that one of those is the overriding problem, the other is likely a cause or an effect. If you don't know the overriding problem or are uncertain about *any* aspect of it, use a red flag.

Effects of the Overriding Problem

Problems create further problems. These are the problem's effects, and your discussion of them in your proposal can be compelling, since we usually sense a problem's severity by the effects it produces. (I might have the problem of a broken ankle, for example, but I really experience that problem as a result of its effects: pain, immobility, etc.) Use red flags to indicate any lack of alignment between the overriding problem and any of the effects. Also flag any effects that you believe exist but haven't been confirmed by me.

Are the Overriding Question(s), Objective(s), and Desired Result(s) Aligned? (Logics Worksheet, Cells 4 and 5)

The overriding problem is the beginning point of your project; the three elements on the upper right of Figure 3.1 are the end points, where you will have answered my overriding question(s), achieved the project objective(s), and provided me my desired result(s). These three elements are three facets of the same diamond: They express the same content, differing only in their phrasing, as shown in Figure 3.2.

	Overriding Question	Engagement Objective	Desired Result
Phrasing	A question	A statement (beginning with verb)	A statement (beginning with noun)
Example (from ABC)	How can we increase our manufacturing capacity to meet projected product demand?	Develop a plan to increase our manufacturing capacity to meet projected product demand	A plan to increase our manufacturing capacity to meet projected product demand

FIGURE 3.2 The overriding question, engagement objective, and desired result contain the same content, differently phrased.

I can't tell you how important it is to get the overriding question right. Several years ago, I was playing the role of coach for a team of consultants submitting a proposal to my organization. Before we identified *the* single overriding question, we listed 24 possible versions, given that I, my colleagues, and the consulting team all had different agendas and conceptions of the overriding problem. Figure 3.3 should give you a good idea of what might happen if the overriding question is wrong. If it is, then the objective will be wrong. If the objective isn't correct, as we'll see in Chapter 5, the methodology will be wrong. See if you can answer correctly the question in Figure 3.3.

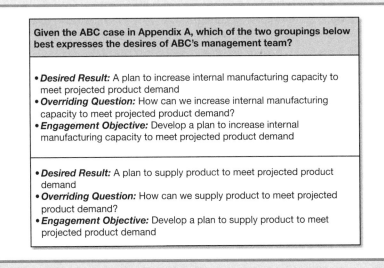

Given the ABC case in Appendix A, which of the two groupings below best expresses the desires of ABC's management team?

- **Desired Result:** A plan to increase internal manufacturing capacity to meet projected product demand
- **Overriding Question:** How can we increase internal manufacturing capacity to meet projected product demand?
- **Engagement Objective:** Develop a plan to increase internal manufacturing capacity to meet projected product demand

- **Desired Result:** A plan to supply product to meet projected product demand
- **Overriding Question:** How can we supply product to meet projected product demand?
- **Engagement Objective:** Develop a plan to supply product to meet projected product demand

FIGURE 3.3 The engagement objective depends upon the overriding question.

If your answer is the first grouping, then you have closely read the case in Appendix A. ABC wants to increase its manufacturing capacity. It does not wish to do so in part by outsourcing some of its components. The latter objective would require a project of greater scope because it would involve an extra deliverable: determination of the feasibility of outsourcing. I can think of two of ABC's responses to the latter objective: first, "You haven't listened"; second, "You are proposing a more expensive study than what we have asked for." It's possible, of course, that ABC could have a positive response: "That's an interesting objective that we hadn't considered; perhaps we ought to consider increasing capacity by outsourcing some components rather than making them in-house." But if you are going to propose the second objective, you had better be certain that, before the proposal has been submitted, you have obtained the required buy-in to avoid the negative responses.

Please note one final aspect concerning desired results, overriding questions, and project objectives. I have defined desired results as "the outcome of the engagement *or its phases.*" Depending on the type of project (i.e., insight, planning, implementation, or the various combinations) that you circle in the Logics Worksheet, Cell 3, there can be one, or more than one, overriding question and desired result.[1,2] As we have already discussed and as is illustrated in Figure 3.4, single-step projects have one of each. As illustrated in Figure 3.5, multiple-step projects have two or more.

Is the Overriding Problem Aligned with the Overriding Question(s)? (Logics Worksheet, Cells 2 and 4)

If you and I don't agree on the overriding problem and the overriding question(s), we will disagree about where you should begin and where you should end, and we will

Kind of Study	Overriding Question	Objective	Desired Result
Insight	Is it feasible to enter the Asia/ Pacific market?	Determine the feasibility of entering Asia/ Pacific	Determination of the feasibility of entering Asia/ Pacific
Planning	How best can we enter the Asia/ Pacific market?	Develop a plan for entering Asia/ Pacific	A plan for entering Asia/ Pacific
Implemen- tation	none[1]	Enter the Asia/ Pacific market	Entrance into Asia/Pacific

FIGURE 3.4   Overriding questions, objectives, and desired results for single-step engagements

Kind of Study	Overriding Questions	Objectives	Desired Results
Insight and Planning	• Is it feasible to enter the Asia/Pacific market? • Assuming feasibility, how best can we enter Asia/Pacific?	• Determine the feasibility of entering Asia/Pacific • Develop a plan for entering Asia/Pacific	• Determination of the feasibility of entering Asia/Pacific • A plan for entering Asia/Pacific
Planning and Implementation	• How best can we enter the Asia/Pacific Market? • none[1]	• Develop a plan for entering Asia/Pacific • Enter the Asia/Pacific market	• A plan for entering Asia/Pacific • Entrance into Asia/Pacific
Insight, Planning, and Implementation	• Is it feasible to enter the Asia/Pacific Market? • Assuming feasibility, how best can we enter Asia/Pacific? • none[1]	• Determine the feasibility of entering Asia/Pacific • Develop a plan for entering the Asia/Pacific market • Enter the Asia/Pacific market	• Determination of the feasibility of entering Asia/Pacific • A plan for entering Asia/Pacific • Entrance into Asia/Pacific

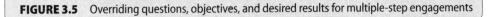

FIGURE 3.5 Overriding questions, objectives, and desired results for multiple-step engagements

likely disagree about where you are at every point in the project. This is the territory not just of red flags but of blood-red flags. If you don't know the overriding problem, that's a red flag. If you don't know the overriding question(s), that's a red flag. If you know neither, you and I are in for a bloodbath. (By the way, this need for alignment is one reason that generic or boilerplate proposals are recipes for disaster.)

And even if you know both, they had better be aligned. Their lack of alignment causes more cost overruns (on your part) and more dissatisfied clients (on my part) than perhaps any other aspect of business development.

Are the Deliverables Aligned with the Desired Result(s)? (Logics Worksheet, Cell 5)

I have defined deliverables as the outcomes you produce along the way toward achieving my desired result, and since many people have trouble understanding what deliverables are, here's an example.[3] Assume that your child is a college student in her senior year and that she wants to attend graduate school. Like any good parent, you decide to do an insight study for her. Your desired result is a determination of the best graduate school. This desired result reflects your "study's" objective: to determine the best graduate school for her to attend. Before you can achieve that objective and that desired result, before you can make that determination, you may desire other information along the way: the cost of tuition and fees; the percentage of graduates who obtain jobs in her academic area; ethnic and religious characteristics of the student body; the kind, availability, safety, and cost of housing; the school's proximity to cultural activities; the cost and convenience of traveling home; and the like. These are deliverables, the outcomes of your study that you will produce along the way to achieving your desired result.

Of course, some of these deliverables might be important to your daughter and not to someone else who, for example, might not care about cultural activities or ethnic affiliations. And some of these deliverables might be more important to you (or your daughter) than others. Nevertheless, for your and your daughter's situations, the deliverables must constitute that set of outcomes, no more and no less, that will achieve S_2. In other words, the deliverables must be aligned with the desired result.

The project you did for your daughter was an insight study, and, as a result, the deliverables you identified were insight deliverables. It should come as no surprise that there are also planning and implementation deliverables:

- **Insight deliverables** are, generally, something tangible, something you can hold in your hand, such as:
  - learning objectives for a training program
  - the results of a competitive assessment
  - forecasts
  - specifications
  - validated assumptions
- **Planning deliverables** include the wide range of outcomes necessary for producing a conceptual or implementable plan, such as:
  - arrangements made to conduct a training program
  - resource requirements
  - implementation timetables
- **Implementation deliverables** are something you can readily witness or observe, often capable of being measured and evaluated, such as:
  - a program for training consultants
  - trained consultants (or sales forces, etc.)
  - improved targeting efforts on the part of a sales force

Are the Deliverables and Desired Result(s) Aligned with the Benefits? (Logics Worksheet, Cells 5 and 6)

As the simplified baseline logic illustrates (Figure 3.6), benefits come from two elements: deliverables and desired result(s). Accordingly, benefits are the good things that accrue (1) *while the project's objectives are being achieved* (that is, those generated from deliverables) and (2) *after the project's objectives have been achieved* (that is, the direct result of achieved objectives).

Benefits flow from my desired result because once you have moved me from a less desirable state to a more desirable state, I am better off than I was before. Benefits flow from deliverables because at each juncture along the transition from one state to another, I am relatively better off than I was before. As an example, let's consider the story about "your" daughter. Assume that (1) she is attending undergraduate school at home, where she has many friends, (2) she has a close relationship with you and would want to come home from graduate school during major holidays and school vacations, and (3) she has a medical condition that could require unexpected hospitalization. Clearly, a deliverable such as "cost and convenience of traveling home" would be important, and its existence would provide you and your daughter with many benefits in terms of knowledge, comfort, and the ability to plan appropriately. Every deliverable is beneficial. Each deliverable should generate at least one benefit. If it doesn't, then why are you even including it in your project?

Benefits are usually of three kinds:

- **An insight benefit** is usually something you hold in your head—for example, understanding, awareness, or knowledge (unlike an insight deliverable, which you can often hold in your hand). An example is the benefit derived from a forecast (a deliverable) that allows me and my organization to determine the

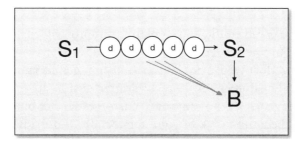

FIGURE 3.6 The simplified baseline logic

likely revenue for a new drug and, therefore, the level of investment justified for launching that pharmaceutical product.

- **A planning benefit** (which also can often involve understanding or knowledge) can be:
  - ○ **An enabler for achieving a result**—for example, "a road map for . . . ," "an understanding of the magnitude of the effort," "direction . . . ," and so on. An example is the benefit of a revised call and targeting plan that allows me to know how much of the sales force needs to be deployed when and where.
  - ○ **Group buy-in**—for example, "commitment," "consensus," or "confirmation." An example is the benefit from training my sales force in the value of a revised customer-targeting program, so they both believe in it and execute it fully, rather than continuing to call on their existing and familiar contacts.
- **An implementation benefit** often is a measurable or tangible result—for example, a change in my organization's business performance—and should be quantified whenever possible to help determine the basis for calculating return on consulting investment (ROCI). Examples include the ROCI achieved from a higher value on a drug for which I am executing a licensing deal; a more productive sales force; a greater return on promotional spend through better target marketing.

In general, deliverables are more specific than benefits (implementation benefits sometimes excepted), but that doesn't mean they are more important. In fact, deliverables are only instrumental. A list of specifications, such as in the graduate school example, is only useful and relevant if it leads to something more important, like knowledge or understanding, which is ultimately what I pay you for.

In proposal after proposal that I have read (and, possibly, in some of the proposals you have written), the benefits are not aligned with the deliverables and desired result, as is the case with the following two examples.

For the first example, assume that I know that my customer service levels are too low to be competitive. That's my current situation, my S_1 state. What I have is insight; I know I have a problem. What I don't have, but desire, is a plan for acting on that insight.

Therefore, my desired result, S_2, is a plan for improving customer service, and your objective would be related to developing that improvement plan. The benefits to me in this effort would not be those advantages accruing from achieving improved levels of customer service. My desired result, at least for now, at the completion of this project, is not improved customer service but a plan to improve it. Therefore, the benefits to me of your support are those advantages related to my having the plan you propose to develop. Those benefits, of course, could be considerable. At the beginning of your involvement, I had a problem that I didn't know how to fix. At the end of your efforts, I have a plan for fixing it. I now know how to improve the levels of my organization's customer service.

In proposal situation after proposal situation, I have asked for a plan (e.g., to improve customer service) only to get a proposal filled with benefits related to improved customer service. These are benefits I'd receive only *after* the plan was implemented. In specifying implementation benefits from a Planning Project, the consultants placed themselves in considerable jeopardy. Because the proposal is a contract, I could have made them deliver those "promised" implementation benefits by requiring an implementation phase at a cost to them of several hundred thousand dollars or more.

Now, as we'll see in the next chapter, your proposal could—and probably should—discuss the benefits related to *subsequent* implementation, especially if you can estimate those benefits. For example: "Subsequent to implementation, we expect your customer service to improve by X percent, thereby enabling you to do good things 1, 2, and 3." But if those implementation benefits are the only ones you discuss, you are missing significant opportunities to persuade me of the advantages of your developing the plan itself. These advantages—learning what we need to do better or faster, assessing our current organization's capabilities, selling the capital requirements to corporate management, evaluating our probability of success, training our people—provide me and my organization with significant benefits. With this plan, we can compare our options and decide to implement, wait, or whatever else may be appropriate given our resources and all the other plans we are considering in areas beyond the one you are studying.

Here's a second example of misalignment. Assume again that I know my customer service is less effective than is desirable. Again, what I have is insight. In this case, however, assume that what I desire is not only a plan but also an implemented plan that actually improves my customer service.

Therefore, your project's desired results and objectives (note the plural) need to express both your developing that plan and implementing it. Likewise, the benefits you express need to be those related both to my having the kind of plan you develop and to having that plan implemented. Again and again, in proposal situations like this one, the proposals indicate only the benefits of having the plan implemented. What they fail to do, or at least to communicate to me, is that the quality of the implementation often depends on the quality of the plan. Therefore, they miss important opportunities to persuade. They fail to indicate the benefits aligned with the first objective: developing the plan itself.

To test your understanding of the alignment between the desired result(s) and the benefits, I'd like you to evaluate the six situations found in Figures 3.7 through 3.12. Each table takes information from a different proposal I've had presented to me. Each table summarizes the current situation, the desired result(s), and the benefits as they were defined in the proposal. In the S_1 column, I've included the three possible current situations; in the S_2 column, the three possible desired results; in the Benefits column, the three kinds of benefits: insight, planning, and implementation. The checked boxes in each column indicate which current situation, desired result(s), and benefits are being described. By comparing those boxes, you should be able to detect misalignments. The bottom of each table explains whether the desired results and benefits are aligned or misaligned.

Are the Benefits Aligned with the Effects/Lack of Benefits? (Logics Worksheet, Cells 2 and 6)

By answering this question, you will not only assure alignment; you will also be able to generate additional possible benefits and additional possible effects that characterize and broaden your and my understanding of my current situation. The process of aligning benefits with the effects/lack of benefits is suggested by the graphic in the Logic Worksheet's second and sixth cells and in Figure 3.13, on page 40.

Here's an example of how you can use this process. Assume that yours is a pro-active lead with my organization. That is, you haven't received an RFP (request for proposal) from us, and you haven't been asked in any way to submit a proposal: You have initiated the lead.

1. Aligned or Misaligned?		
Project objective: Benchmark Sales and Marketing's effectiveness		
S_1 (Current Situation)	S_2 (Desired Result)	B (Benefits)
A leading small appliance manufacturer with a direct sales organization calling on retail outlets doesn't know if its sales and marketing organization is as effective as its competitors'.	The level of effectiveness of Sales and Marketing as compared to competitors	Knowledge of the magnitude of the gap and the level of urgency to improve the sales force's effectiveness
They: ☑ lack insight ☒ have insight ☒ have plan	They want: ☑ insight ☒ plan ☒ implemented plan	They will receive: ☑ insight benefits ☒ planning benefits ☒ implementation benefits
Answer: Aligned. The organization desires to move one step, from no insight to insight. Accordingly, there is one desired result, related to insight. The benefits are related to insight.		

FIGURE 3.7   Aligned or misaligned?

2. Aligned or Misaligned?		
Project objective: Determine the feasibility of entering a market		
S_1 (Current Situation)	S_2 (Desired Result)	B (Benefits)
A manufacturer of automotive products selling mainly to OEMs is uncertain about its ability to market its products through repair shops and about competitors' strategies, capabilities, and vulnerabilities.	Identification of market dynamics, customer-service requirements, and opportunities to increase sales in the aftermarket	Revenue growth from $9M to more than $70M within seven years in this new market
They: ☑ lack insight ☒ have insight ☒ have plan	They want: ☑ insight ☒ plan ☒ implemented plan	They will receive: ☒ insight benefits ☒ planning benefits ☑ implementation benefits
Answer: Misaligned. The organization desires to move one step, from no insight to insight. Accordingly, there is one desired result, related to insight. The benefits noted, however, are related to implementation.		

FIGURE 3.8   Aligned or misaligned?

3. Aligned or Misaligned?		
Project objective: Develop a marketing and logistics plan to improve competitive position		
S_1 (Current Situation)	S_2 (Desired Result)	B (Benefits)
A large paperback book publisher has problems related to its complex distribution system, including high warehousing and transportation costs.	A new marketing and logistics strategy to achieve competitive advantage	Significantly higher revenues, cost savings of approximately 20%, and logistics linked throughout the organization
They: ☒ lack insight ☑ have insight ☒ have plan	They want: ☒ insight ☑ plan ☒ implemented plan	They will receive: ☒ insight benefits ☒ planning benefits ☑ implementation benefits
Answer: Misaligned. The organization desires to move one step, from insight to plan. Accordingly, there is one desired result, related to developing a plan. The benefits, however, are not those related to having a plan; they are related to the plan's subsequent implementation.		

FIGURE 3.9   Aligned or misaligned?

4. Aligned or Misaligned?		
Project objective: Develop a facilities strategy related to product quality		
S_1 (Current Situation)	S_2 (Desired Result)	B (Benefits)
A metals processor anticipating an imminent plant capacity constraint knows that higher product quality expected in some key markets is not attainable from existing facilities.	A strategic plan for building a new facility with the capability of improving the quality of the product	By specifying required resources, the ability to compare the proposed action with other strategic options
They: ☒ lack insight ☑ have insight ☒ have plan	They want: ☒ insight ☑ plan ☒ implemented plan	They will receive: ☒ insight benefits ☑ planning benefits ☒ implementation benefits
Answer: Aligned. The organization desires to move one step, from insight to plan. Accordingly, there is one desired result, related to developing a plan. The benefits are related to having one.		

FIGURE 3.10 Aligned or misaligned?

5. Aligned or Misaligned?		
Project objectives: Develop and implement a plan to improve competitiveness		
S_1 (Current Situation)	S_2 (Desired Result)	B (Benefits)
A large agricultural products company has not adjusted to changes in its livestock and agricultural markets, having an obsolete strategy, organization, and control system.	A plan and an implemented plan to achieve competitive advantage and increased financial returns	Increased market share, $2M in improvements already gained, and $3M in additional improvements to be realized in one year
They: ☒ lack insight ☑ have insight ☒ have plan	They want: ☒ insight ☑ plan ☑ implemented plan	They will receive: ☒ insight benefits ☒ planning benefits ☑ implementation benefits
Answer: Misaligned. The organization desires to move two steps, from insight through planing to implementation. Accordingly, there are two desired results: one related to developing a plan and another related to implementing it. The benefits, however, are related to implementation only. The benefits should also include those related to having a plan.		

FIGURE 3.11 Aligned or misaligned?

Project objectives: Assess fit with North American market and develop and implement a plan for entering		
S₁ *(Current Situation)*	S₂ *(Desired Result)*	B *(Benefits)*
A major European manufacturer wants to acquire a North American company but doesn't understand NA market dynamics, segmentation, and distribution channels.	Insight about the market as well as a plan and an implemented plan to enter that market as a first step to becoming a dominant global player	A specific positioning and entry strategy in the NA market
They: ☑ lack insight ☒ have insight ☒ have plan	*They want:* ☑ insight ☑ plan ☑ implemented plan	*They will receive:* ☒ insight benefits ☑ planning benefits ☒ implementation benefits
Answer: Misaligned. The organization desires to move three steps, from no insight (about the market it desires to enter) all the way to implementation (i.e., to *being* in the market). Accordingly, there are three desired results: one related to providing insight, another related to developing a plan based on that insight, and a third related to implementing that plan. The benefits, however, are related only to having a plan, and these benefits aren't benefits at all: they are really the second desired result. Also included should be benefits related to having insight and having the plan implemented. These are critical because such benefits could be important at key management decision points during the project.		

FIGURE 3.12   Aligned or misaligned?

Step 1: List

Along with your team:

- You used the Logics Worksheet to strategize what my overriding problem might be, what effects it might be having on my firm, and what benefits could accrue from your efforts.
- You *listed* that information (which I've displayed in Figure 3.14).
- You briefly discussed that information during a phone call with me to arrange a meeting so that we could discuss the "lead" further.

As in most proactive leads, *you* are the triggering event, in this case making me conscious that I might have an overriding problem and that a Planning and Implementation Project might be needed.

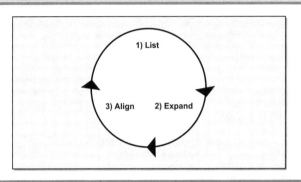

Overriding Problem: An Ineffective Organizational Structure		
Problem's Effects (cell 2)	*Planning Benefits (cell 6)*	*Implementation Benefits (cell 6)*
Low morale	By using cross-functional teams during the planning phase, better communication across functions	Increased operational effectiveness

FIGURE 3.14   The "list" step of aligning effects and benefits

Step 2: Expand

After listing the effects and benefits above, you can use the power of the baseline logic to increase your depth of understanding of my probable situation by expanding the listed items. To do so, you keep asking yourself, "What is the effect of this effect?" "What is the effect of that new effect?" "What is the effect of this benefit?" "What does or might it lead to?" As you examine column 1, you decide that lowered morale could lead to higher turnover, which could lead to increased costs related to hiring and training. As you examine column 2, you decide that a plan using cross-functional teams could lead to increased teamwork across the organization. As you examine column 3, you decide that increased operational effectiveness and customer responsiveness could lead to lowered costs. Your expanded list looks like Figure 3.15.

Step 3: Align

Typically, the "expand" step takes you down the columns, as you continually ask, "What is the effect of this effect?" and "What benefit would accrue from this

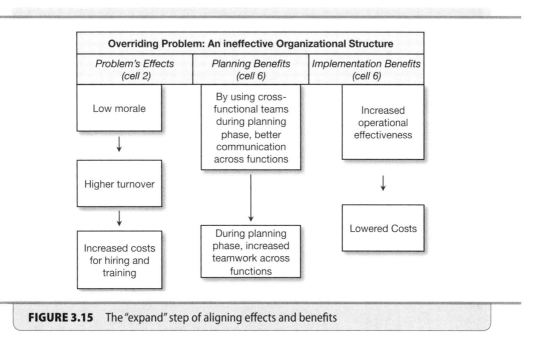

FIGURE 3.15   The "expand" step of aligning effects and benefits

benefit?" For the "align" step, you move across the columns, in both directions. In moving left to right: For every effect in column 1, you want to include a related benefit in column 2 and/or column 3. In moving right to left: For every benefit in column 2 or 3, you want to include an effect in column 1.

Let's move left to right, first by aligning effects with benefits and then by aligning planning benefits with implementation benefits. If your project involves implementation, many of your potential implementation benefits are the converse of the overriding problem's effects. If an overriding problem's effect is decreasing market share, once the overriding problem is solved, as it would be in an Implementation Project, a likely implementation benefit would be maintained or increased market share (or at least the deceleration of share loss). At the top of Figure 3.16, note the two (horizontal) alignments between effects and implementation benefits as well as the two alignments between planning benefits and implementation benefits.

Now let's move right to left, identifying planning and/or implementation benefits that are not aligned with effects. If subsequent to implementation, my firm has increased teamwork across functions, it's *possible* that my current situation is characterized by less teamwork. If subsequent to implementation, my firm has more shared knowledge because of fewer functional silos, it's *possible* that my current situation is characterized by less shared knowledge because of larger or more numerous functional silos. On the bottom of Figure 3.16, note these two alignments (dashed arrows), between implementation benefits and effects.

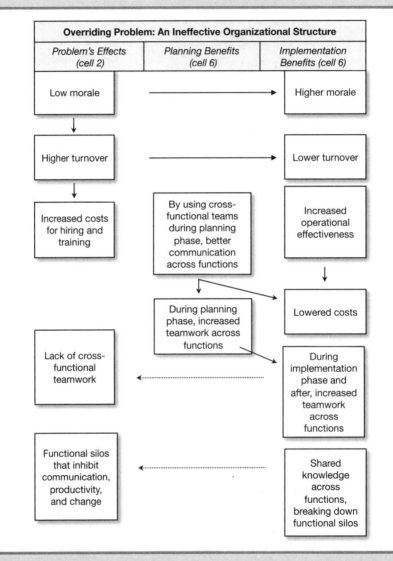

FIGURE 3.16 The "align" step of aligning effects and benefits

When aligning right to left, from benefits to effects, you usually do not generate new effects of the overriding problem. You generate what I call "lack of benefits." They are not the primary reason why I'm thinking about engaging you, but they might be important aspects of my current situation, which involves more than just a problem and its effects. It also includes a lack of benefits. That is, I want to reach S_2 because being there is inherently better, *and* I do not want to be at S_1 because certain aspects of that situation are not beneficial. The current situation is undesirable not only because it includes an unaddressed or unsolved problem and its effects but also because it lacks benefits (such as, in the ABC case, consensus among the management team).

By checking the alignment of the overriding problem's effects and the benefits, you can generate a good deal of additional content to be used in your situation and benefits slots. You can use the alignment as a powerful discovery process to deepen your understanding of my problem or opportunity and the benefits that would accrue from your helping me solve or realize it. Just as important, the benefits you decide to include in your proposal will look all the more beneficial if they are compared to my current lack of benefits, as demonstrated in Figure 3.17.

My guess is that you could have generated Figure 3.16's information in about five minutes. In 15 minutes, you probably could fill several pages of effects and benefits, identifying them through the process of alignment. Nevertheless, nearly every one of those effects and benefits would need to be red flagged. In the phone call to arrange our meeting, you mentioned four items that I appeared to ratify. Everything else is your conjecture, and even those four items might be as well. My focus during our phone conversation was on scheduling the meeting. I might have been "nodding my head" at everything else. In a brief phone call, I certainly could not have thought deeply about your four items. They might just have been interesting enough for me to accept a meeting.

So everything should be red flagged, and that's a good thing. Now you have talking points for our meeting. You have points for discussion, items to be confirmed or rejected. During our meeting, you will have caused me to define more precisely my current situation and the potential benefits from improving it. You will have added value, a "richness" of logical thinking, in the business-development process, even though before the meeting I had no idea that you had already begun to "write" your proposal.

One last point about alignment: Once you've aligned effects and benefits, you are not finished with all the alignments we have discussed. Unless you wish to throw logic to the wind, there is no end to the iterative alignment process, on the Logics Worksheet and in your head, until your final proposal has been submitted. Every element of the Logics Worksheet is logically related with every other element. Therefore, when you change one element, that change cascades through the entire system (like altering a cell in a spreadsheet), potentially affecting every other element and providing you (and potentially me) new points of view through informed discussion. That discussion adds value, building our relationship and demonstrating your qualifications long before the proposal might be due.

You should be realigning constantly, after every discussion with me and my team and after every discussion between you and your team—whenever new information must be added to the Logics Worksheet. As a result of this iterative process, you may well differentiate yourself from your competition because it shows me you really are thinking about me and my organization's situation and needs.

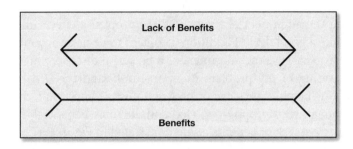

FIGURE 3.17   When compared to the lack of benefits, benefits will look even more beneficial.

The Baseline Logic and Your Value Proposition

In using the baseline logic, you are identifying and aligning key elements of your value proposition. As you probably know, your value proposition is a concise statement of your offering. As such, it contains at least five elements:

1. Where I am now: S_1, my current situation
2. Where I want to be: my desired result(s), S_2, as expressed by your project's objective(s)
3. When I will get there (the duration of your project)
4. How much it will cost (your fees and expenses)
5. The benefits (B) of achieving my desired result(s)

The first, second, and fifth of these elements are part of the baseline logic, which you can readily see within the partial value proposition developed for a major airline (Figure 3.18). Clearly, your value proposition is vitally important as you are discussing with me major elements of your proposed project. It is the executive summary of the executive summary of your offering. As such, you can use the elements of the baseline logic in a follow-up email or conversation that can help you confirm that you and I agree on the foundational elements of your potential offering.

The Relationship Among the Generic Structure Slots, the Baseline Logic, and Your Proposed Project

Figure 3.19 provides a high-level summary of what I have been discussing in this and the previous chapter. The foundation of Figure 3.19 is the baseline logic, on top of which are mapped the six generic structure slots, and those slots are sequenced based upon what your project proposes to do:

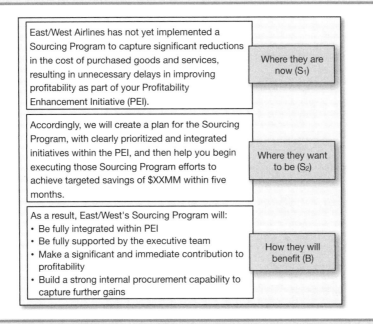

East/West Airlines has not yet implemented a Sourcing Program to capture significant reductions in the cost of purchased goods and services, resulting in unnecessary delays in improving profitability as part of your Profitability Enhancement Initiative (PEI).

Where they are now (S₁)

Accordingly, we will create a plan for the Sourcing Program, with clearly prioritized and integrated initiatives within the PEI, and then help you begin executing those Sourcing Program efforts to achieve targeted savings of $XXMM within five months.

Where they want to be (S₂)

As a result, East/West's Sourcing Program will:
• Be fully integrated within PEI
• Be fully supported by the executive team
• Make a significant and immediate contribution to profitability
• Build a strong internal procurement capability to capture further gains

How they will benefit (B)

FIGURE 3.18   The baseline logic and your value proposition

- Your project begins by addressing my current situation, S_1, which you discuss in your proposal's situation slot.
- To move me and my organization to something better, you will employ two inputs—the methodology you will use supported by your qualifications for conducting it. You discuss your methodology in the methods slot, and your qualifications in the qualifications slot.
- As a result of those inputs, you will provide me with two major outputs, or outcomes—the achievement of my desired result(s) and the benefits of my having made the transition from one situation to another. You discuss the desired result(s) in the objectives slot. You discuss the benefits in the benefits slot.
- Because the transition takes time and because time costs money, I will pay you for the value you deliver. Your fees are discussed in the costs slot.

Chapter 5 will discuss how to construct a logical methodology that will convince me that you can move me from S_1 to S_2. Before we can turn to methodologies, however, I need to discuss in the next chapter other matters related to objectives. But first, I want to commend you, dear reader, for your perseverance in almost finishing the most difficult chapter in this book. I can assure you that mastering the baseline logic gets far easier with practice and is well worth the effort. You'll see the

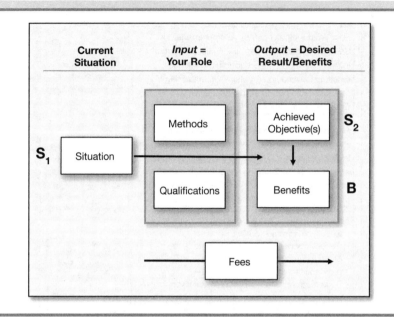

FIGURE 3.19 The relationship among generic structure slots, baseline logic, and the project

"richness" created in aligning the ABC situation in the upcoming work session, where you'll be able to watch "yourself" fill out a Logics Worksheet for the proposal to the ABC Company.

Hang in there: nothing ahead is as difficult as what is now behind you.

CHAPTER 3 REVIEW

Aligning the Baseline Logic

To test the alignment of the elements within the baseline logic:

- Be certain that the project objective(s) are aligned with S_2.

    If $S_1 \rightarrow S_2$ = one step, the project will have one objective.

    If $S_1 \rightarrow S_2$ = two steps, the project will have two objectives.

    If $S_1 \rightarrow S_2$ = three steps, the project will have three objectives.

- Be certain that the potential client's strategic direction, triggering event, overriding problem, and effects are aligned.

- As shown in Figure 3.1, be certain to align the following:

    1. The strategic direction and the triggering event
    2. The triggering event and the overriding problem
    3. The strategic direction and the overriding problem

4. The overriding problem and its effects/lack of benefits
5. The overriding problem and the overriding question(s)
6. The overriding question(s) and the objective(s)
7. The overriding question(s) and the desired result(s)
8. The objective(s) and the desired result(s)
9. The desired result(s) and the deliverables
10. The desired result(s) and the benefits
11. The deliverables and the benefits
12. The benefits and the effects/lack of benefits

⦿ The baseline logic contains three important elements of your value proposition, explaining, in the highest-level summary of your offering, where I am (S_1), where I want to be (S_2), and how I will benefit by getting and being there (B).

WORK SESSION 2: Aligning the Baseline Logic for the Situation at ABC

You approach the subject of your proposal's baseline logic with a good deal of care because you know that it provides the foundation for your entire proposal and because you also know that you can use its alignment to help you think more strategically about ABC's current situation, desired result, and potential benefits. Everything else in your proposal will build on this foundation, and mistakes in thinking and understanding at this point will have dire consequences later. Similarly, good strategy and analytical thinking at this point will pay great dividends later on (for example, making the writing process more efficient and extending even to the project's execution after you win). To ensure that you construct a solid baseline logic, you use the cells in the Logics Worksheet, shown in Appendix B, or the complete worksheet itself, which can be downloaded from http://web.me.com/rfreed/Writing_Winning_Business_Proposals/Home.html.

The Logics Worksheet: Cell 1 (See Figure 3.20.)

Most of the information for the "Prospect Profile" you can gather from Gilmore's notes (see Appendix A for the people involved), but some crucial information is lacking. Although you know that ABC is profitable, you don't know its last year's revenue or the trends related to profitability and revenue. These you decide to red flag, using that symbol to mark an uncertainty, vulnerability, gap in information, or anything that you just plain don't like. In addition, you find nothing in Gilmore's notes about ABC's strategic direction. You feel comfortable that the proposed project is very much in line with ABC's strategic direction, but, it seems to you, the proposal will be stronger if it has some discussion about this topic.

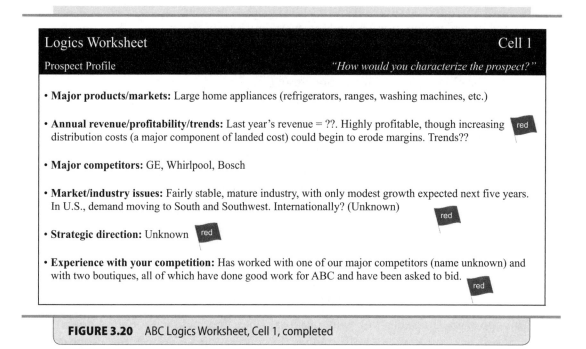

FIGURE 3.20   ABC Logics Worksheet, Cell 1, completed

Finally, you yourself are unaware of who among your competitors ABC has used before, and nothing in Gilmore's notes helps you complete this part of Cell 1.

The Logics Worksheet: Cell 2 (See Figure 3.21.)

You know that this cell asks you to define several elements of the "problem bundle"— the overriding problem your project will address or solve, the triggering event or events that brought that problem to the prospect's consciousness, and the effects of the problem itself. Clearly, the triggering event is ABC's market forecast, and its overriding problem, at least from ABC's point of view, is a looming lack of capacity. However, you don't necessarily see the overriding problem as they do (for the same reasons related to the discussion in Figure 3.22). So you red flag this item, as well as the effects of the problem. Many of these effects (and lack of benefits) were generated by your aligning them with benefits. And while they seem to fit ABC's situation, many of them are not addressed in Gilmore's notes. Those that aren't, you believe, will lead to fruitful follow-up discussions with Ray Armstrong, the president, and his team.

The Logics Worksheets: Cell 3 and Cell 4 (See Figures 3.22 and 3.23.)

The first of these cells asks you to identify the kind of project; the second, ABC's overriding question(s).

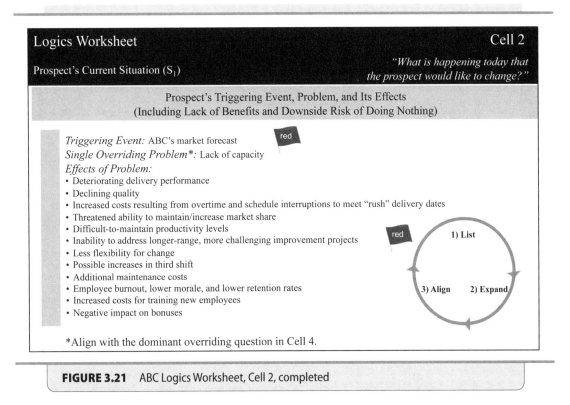

Logics Worksheet   Cell 2

Prospect's Current Situation (S₁)

"What is happening today that the prospect would like to change?"

Prospect's Triggering Event, Problem, and Its Effects
(Including Lack of Benefits and Downside Risk of Doing Nothing)

Triggering Event: ABC's market forecast [red]
Single Overriding Problem*: Lack of capacity
Effects of Problem:
• Deteriorating delivery performance
• Declining quality
• Increased costs resulting from overtime and schedule interruptions to meet "rush" delivery dates
• Threatened ability to maintain/increase market share
• Difficult-to-maintain productivity levels
• Inability to address longer-range, more challenging improvement projects [red]
• Less flexibility for change
• Possible increases in third shift
• Additional maintenance costs
• Employee burnout, lower morale, and lower retention rates
• Increased costs for training new employees
• Negative impact on bonuses

1) List
2) Expand
3) Align

*Align with the dominant overriding question in Cell 4.

FIGURE 3.21   ABC Logics Worksheet, Cell 2, completed

ABC, you believe, has insight about its current situation—they know they have a production capacity problem, and they desire a plan to address that problem. On the face of it, then, it would appear that you will be proposing a planning study. However, you're not certain that ABC has the right insight. For example, although they do have a sales forecast—and one in which Marcia Collins, the vice president of marketing, has considerable confidence—you believe that any forecast must be validated, since it provides the basis for all further analysis.

A validated forecast might reveal that ABC doesn't need quite as much capacity as they now believe or that the timing for implementing additional capacity will be sooner or later than is now anticipated. Furthermore, although Gilmore's inspection of the main manufacturing facility revealed good workflow and housekeeping and excellent equipment utilization, your experience tells you that various marginal improvements at that facility (and perhaps at the satellite facilities) could provide some additional capacity, perhaps without ABC's having to invest in bricks and mortar so soon.

Finally, there's the issue of outsourcing. At present, ABC appears to manufacture most of its components rather than relying on outside suppliers to provide them. Various make-versus-buy scenarios could provide capacity that ABC does

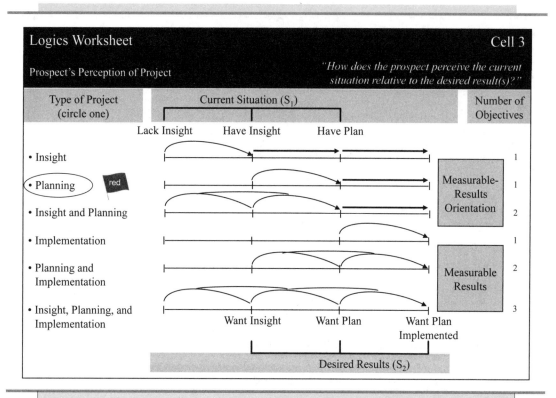

Logics Worksheet   Cell 3

Prospect's Perception of Project   *"How does the prospect perceive the current situation relative to the desired result(s)?"*

Type of Project (circle one)	Current Situation (S₁)	Number of Objectives

Lack Insight   Have Insight   Have Plan

- Insight   1
- Planning   red   Measurable-Results Orientation   1
- Insight and Planning   2
- Implementation   1
- Planning and Implementation   Measurable Results   2
- Insight, Planning, and Implementation   3

Want Insight   Want Plan   Want Plan Implemented

Desired Results (S₂)

FIGURE 3.22 ABC Logics Worksheet, Cell 3, completed

Logics Worksheet   Cell 4

Prospect's Overriding Questions   *"Given the number of objectives (noted in Cell 3), what overriding question(s) does the prospect want answered to improve the current situation?" (List one overriding question per objective.)*

Prospect's Single Overriding Insight *Question**	Prospect's Single Overriding Planning *Question**	Prospect's Single Overriding Implementation *Objective*†
■ _____ _____ _____ _____ ?	■ How best should ABC increase capacity to meet the sales forecast? red	■ _____ _____ _____ _____

*To state the project objective, rephrase the overriding question using an active verb.

†Implementation projects have no overriding question.

FIGURE 3.23 ABC Logics Worksheet, Cell 4, completed

not currently enjoy and thus eliminate or certainly delay the need for additional capacity.

In short, this might be a classic insight and planning study. Like many such combination studies, this one could involve phasing, a possible "go/no go" decision point at the end of the insight piece. That is, the first phase of the study might supply ABC with the insight it needs to determine whether it indeed requires additional capacity as soon as it believes it does (and, if so, how much by when).

On the other hand, you don't believe that you could sell an insight and planning study to ABC or that ABC senses a decision point. All the buyers seem to believe that additional capacity is necessary, although the amount and timing are uncertain. More specifically, Collins would certainly object to an insight study and, depending on her influence, so might others. So you decide to characterize this opportunity as a planning study. It will certainly have an insight element, in the form of a deliverable validating Collins's forecast, but it will have only one objective: to develop a plan. Therefore, because there will be no decision point after validating the forecast, you decide to call the project what in your mind ABC believes it to be: a study to develop a plan for increasing production capacity. You do, however, assign a red flag indicating a potential disagreement between how you and ABC view the kind of study this should be. Because of this uncertainty, you also need to red flag Cell 4 (Figure 3.23), since in your mind, the study could very well have both an insight and a planning question.

Because you have now circled "Planning" in Cell 3, you know that you will use the Planning column in Cells 4, 5, and 6. That is, you are continuing to complete the cells from ABC's point of view, red flagging whenever your point of view differs. From ABC's point of view, this is a planning study. Consequently, you will use the Planning (rather than the Insight or Implementation) column to enter information related to the overriding question, desired result, deliverables, and benefits.

The Logics Worksheet: Cell 5 (See Figure 3.24.)

This cell asks you to specify the desired result or results to be produced by your project and the deliverables that, taken together, will produce them. The desired result, you know, should be a simple rephrasing of the overriding question, and it should express your project's objective, which, in this case, would be to develop a plan to increase capacity to meet the market forecast. Because the overriding question is flagged, the desired result also must be flagged.

You know that the deliverables are outcomes produced during the project. They are the key outputs that will move ABC from its current situation to its desired result. Although you are comfortable with most of the deliverables you have identified, you are concerned about two matters. First, all the deliverables should be, by definition, red flagged since the desired result also is flagged. If the

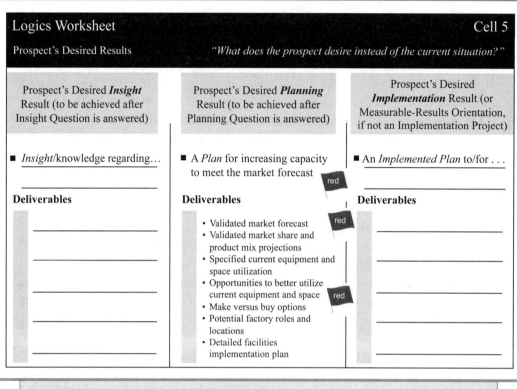

FIGURE 3.24   ABC Logics Worksheet, Cell 5, completed

overriding question and desired result changed, the deliverables would change as well. Second, two of the deliverables are particularly worrisome. The first, the "validated market forecast," could anger Collins, who developed the forecast and appears to be confident of its validity and reliability. The phrasing, you realize, reflects your point of view rather than Collins's.

You believe, of course, it's essential to validate the forecast; the whole study could depend on it. Perhaps what you really want to say is "updated market forecast to reflect current market conditions." The fifth deliverable, "make versus buy options," is also troublesome because it's not really aligned with ABC's understanding of capacity, which tends to focus on bricks and mortar and on additional equipment.

The Logics Worksheet: Cell 6 (See Figure 3.25.)

You know that this cell allows you to align many elements of the baseline logic and, while doing so, to identify additional benefits and effects that could very well deepen your understanding of ABC's current situation and the advantages of changing it. After considering the "list/expand/align" procedure in Cells 2 and 6 (and the material in the next chapter), you know the following:

- You should complete the benefits in the Planning column.
- To indicate to ABC the likely benefits of implementing the plan you will develop, you should indicate the likely benefits that will accrue subsequent to implementation. This "measurable-results orientation" strategy not only will provide ABC a good sense of the "end game," it also could position you well to be chosen to conduct the Implementation Project.
- Benefits flow from the achievement of the desired result and from the deliverables produced along the way. Therefore, you should attempt to identify one or more benefits from the stated desired result as well as from each deliverables in Cell 5.
- For each benefit you list, you should then expand by asking yourself, "What likely benefits will accrue if this listed benefit occurs."
- You should align each expanded benefit by asking the following questions:
  - Is there at least one deliverable that will generate this benefit? If not, you should add one and consider whether this new deliverable is aligned with the desired result.
  - Is there an effect (or a lack of benefits) aligned with this benefit? If not, you should add at least one in Cell 2.
- After completing the alignment process, you should red flag any newly generated benefit, deliverable, effect, or lack of benefit that has not been discussed with ABC and/or that appears "out of scope."

When you are finished, your efforts look like those in Figure 3.25, with most of the implementation benefits red flagged and two of the planning benefits green flagged, a symbol you are using to indicate a particular strength. These green-flagged items, you believe, will be particularly persuasive to ABC, given the situation described to you by Gilmore. You realize that you could go on ad infinitum generating additional effects and benefits. However, you decide for now that you have enough to show to Gilmore, who can confirm what you have or seek additional confirmation from the major players at ABC. Just as important, you feel confident that the foundation to your proposal is indeed sound and logical—and much more extensive than you had realized. You have used the alignment process to develop ideas that could help ABC better understand their own situation as well as differentiate you from your competitors.

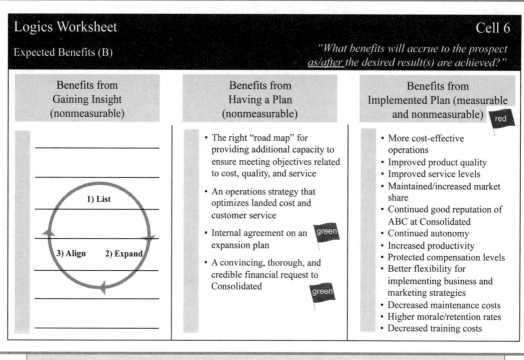

FIGURE 3.25 ABC Logics Worksheet, Cell 6, completed

Your Value Proposition

After all this hard work, you find that your value proposition practically writes itself. Taking information from the worksheets related to the current situation, the desired results, and the benefits, you write the following in less than five minutes, which also includes the overriding problem's effects:

> ABC's market forecast indicates that you will exceed manufacturing capacity in as little as two years, potentially leading to declining quality, deteriorating delivery performance, and threatened market share. Accordingly, Paramount Consulting will develop a thorough and comprehensive plan to increase capacity, providing a solid "road map" ensuring that you meet your objectives related to cost, quality, and service. Subsequent to implementation, we expect that your operations will be more cost-effective and that your product quality and service levels will improve, significantly helping you maintain your standing as Consolidated Industries' premier division.

This paragraph, you realize, will make a solid contribution to the proposal's introduction. Given what you know of Gilmore's business-development process, you expect that he will e-mail the value proposition to each of ABC's buyers, well before the proposal is due, with the aim of validating the triggering event, over-riding problem, effects, objective, and benefits.

CHAPTER 4

Using a Measurable-Results Orientation

et's assume for a moment that you're writing a proposal to a foundation. More than likely, the foundation's RFP (request for proposal) will ask you to state quantifiable, measurable objectives. Because your objectives are the expression of your project's intended results, the funding agency probably will also ask you to include a plan for evaluating (i.e., measuring) the project's outcome and your performance. This is standard operating procedure for foundations as well as for U.S. local and federal government agencies because, quite simply, they want some measure of assurance that their money will be well spent and will generate a return on their investment. For multiyear projects, they want to be able to measure the results of one year's effort before funding the efforts of another year. If you're like me, you find these agencies' desires reasonable and unobjectionable.

In many ways I, as a potential client, have the same desires, and you shouldn't object to them. For most of the work you do for me, I want change and I'm willing to pay you to help me get it. So I might request some evidence, after your project is completed, that change has occurred, and I might request some plan, included in your proposal, for how you will determine whether change has, in fact, occurred. Of course, I might not be or need to be so rigorous. I might be satisfied if the evidence is anecdotal—that is, if some people in my organization tell me that they believe change has taken place. Or I might be satisfied if the evidence is personal—that is, if I myself believe that change has occurred because things look and feel different than they did before your involvement. But sometimes this "good feeling" is not enough. I might only be satisfied with hard evidence, the numbers, objective rather than subjective proof of improved processes, saved money, better-served customers, and the like.

Even if I don't request such information, your providing it in your proposal could differentiate you from your competitors and thus be very persuasive. There is, however, a major obstacle: You can't achieve measurable results unless your project involves implementation. Only after, and sometimes during, implementation can I expect processes to be improved, money to be saved, customers to be better served, or market share to increase. Only Implementation Projects can provide measurable results, which I define as tangible, quantifiable, demonstrable improvements in my organization. So only in Implementation Projects can you promise such concrete results. But in Insight Projects and Planning Projects, you can provide what I call a "measurable-results orientation."

Measurable-Results Orientation: The Insight Project

Let's recall the three kinds of projects discussed in Chapter 2, remembering that a combination of them is not only possible but common.

In an Insight Project, I don't know if I should change because either I'm not certain that I have a problem or I sense that a problem exists but I'm unsure of its nature, scope, or severity. Therefore, I need insight to determine if I should change or if I should maintain the status quo. I might, for example, have some questions about my manufacturing processes. They might be suitable or they might not; I don't know. Perhaps they are terribly inefficient, or perhaps they are adequate but improvable. I don't know, but I might be willing to engage you to conduct an audit or a competitive assessment to provide me with that insight. You might benchmark my processes with someone else's to determine whose are better. That insight is not a measurable result; it is not by itself a change in any of my business processes. Therefore, you can't express measurable results by the project's insight objective. But note how you still might be able to provide a measurable-results orientation (see Figure 4.1).

In an Insight Project, I am paying you for insight. That insight is beneficial to me and is what I expect you to deliver. But you can go beyond my expectations by looking farther ahead, by including content in your objectives slot that indicates the measurable value to me and my organization if we act on that insight and move ahead with subsequent planning and implementation. Your methods slot could provide a general discussion of tasks related to evaluating potential savings of subsequently closing the gaps, and the benefits slot could discuss the potential value of closing them. Note the key word *subsequently*.

Insight Project	Project Objective
The project objective expresses non-measurable results. However, note the measurable-results orientation expressed in the last sentence.	Our project will focus on three representative product lines: Graybeard, Bluebird, and Redbeak. The objective of our project is to compare manufacturing processes that produce these lines to those of your competitors and to the "best of the best" in other industries using these processes. If gaps exist, we will evaluate the potential savings and other benefits of closing them.

FIGURE 4.1   An Insight Project's objective that expresses a measurable-results orientation

Measurable-Results Orientation: The Planning Project

In a Planning Project, I know that I need to change but don't know how, and so I desire a plan for changing. But you can exceed my expectations by looking farther ahead, by including content in your objectives slot that indicates the measurable value to me and my organization if we were to implement that plan. Once again, you will not be providing me with a measurable result (a realized improvement) during your project; I've only asked you for a plan. Therefore, measurable results can't be expressed by the objective itself, but within the objectives slot you might be able to demonstrate a measurable-results orientation (see Figure 4.2).

The benefits slot could indicate possible savings if the plan were implemented, discuss the benefits of the measurable results for my organization as well as for

Planning Project	Project Objective
The project objective expresses non-measurable results. However, measurable results, as far as they can be expressed at this point, are included. Achieving these results could likely be the objective of a subsequent implementation project.	Our project will focus on three representative product lines: Graybeard, Bluebird, and Redbeak. The objective of our project is to develop for Graybeard the most appropriate manufacturing plan to reduce scrap and rework and increase productivity. We believe that for the Graybeard line alone, a fully implemented plan could reasonably be expected to: • decrease rework from 30% to 5% • reduce scrap rate from 20% to 5% • decrease cycle time from 30 days to 10 days

FIGURE 4.2   A Planning Project's objective that expresses a measurable-results orientation

me, and stress the possible realization of measurable results (and the benefits that might accrue) even before implementation.

Given that you haven't yet completed the plan, you might ask how it is possible to include potential measurable results. Isn't including measurable results like those in Figure 4.2 just bad business, leaving you open to criticism (or, worse, a lawsuit) if later you can't deliver them or if I can't implement your plan successfully?

These are valid questions, so let me address them. First of all, I'm not saying that you should include measurable results in all proposals, not even in Implementation Projects. Second, I'm not suggesting that you can exactly quantify the expected results (e.g., reduce cycle time from 30 days to 10 days); you might be able to quantify within some range (e.g., a reduction of 10 to 20 days). Third, note that the quantification in the preceding planning example is qualified: After careful consideration, you *believe* these are the results that *could* be expected after the new process has been implemented. In summary, then, while you cannot promise measurable results in all projects, you can communicate an orientation toward such results.

Additionally, to the extent that you can identify and even implement short-term, typically minor improvements during your projects, I will be pleased. These are measurable insight or planning results, but not the primary ones or the significant ones that will accrue when the entire plan is implemented. This "low-hanging fruit" or "pay-as-you-go" orientation is good. Although it doesn't address implementing my primary result, I still consider it a measurable-results orientation.

Your orientation toward results, your focus on trying to achieve recognizable and quantifiable change for me and my organization, tells me something about you. It tells me you are interested in my eventually receiving measurable results rather than just another report that will sit on my shelf.

By the way, if you, in fact, have all that experience listed in your boilerplated qualifications section (e.g., you have performed 40 similar studies in my industry over the last two years), you should be able to provide me some estimate of my potential measurable results. By including a measurable-results orientation that considers my potential risks and rewards, you indicate your true qualifications to support me—far better than do most qualifications descriptions or discussions I've had to read or sit through. So consider generating some reasonable estimates, if only to provide you and your team some targets.

Measurable-Results Orientation: The Implementation Project

In an Implementation Project, I want to change—I know what to do, but I need additional resources or expertise to implement the change. That change will alter my organization, and that result can be measured. Therefore, you should propose achieving an objective that will increase or decrease certain factors by definable parameters. In an Implementation Project, then, measurable results can be expressed by the objective itself (see Figure 4.3). The benefits slot can focus on the benefits of achieving measurable results not only to my organization but to me.

In Figures 4.1–4.3, your project's objectives are the expression of S_2, of my organization's desired results, whether those results are new insight, a well-developed plan, and/or implemented actions. The achievement of these objectives will produce the results I am paying you for, and these results will be beneficial to me and my organization.

Implementation Project	Project Objective
The project objective itself expresses measurable results.	The objective of our project is to implement for Graybeard an optimum manufacturing process that will: • decrease rework from 30% to 5% • reduce scrap rate from 20% to 5% • decrease cycle time from 30 days to 10 days

FIGURE 4.3   An Implementation Project's objective that expresses measurable results

─CHAPTER 4 REVIEW─

Using a Measurable-Results Orientation

- Measurable results are tangible, quantifiable improvements in my business processes.
- Measurable results can occur only in projects that involve implementation.
- Therefore, Insight and Planning Projects cannot provide measurable results, but the objectives slot in insight and planning proposals can express a measurable-results orientation (i.e., a range of what might be likely to result after a plan eventually is implemented).

WORK SESSION 3: Applying a Measurable-Results Orientation for ABC

To apply a measurable-results orientation, you know that you must try to quantify those items in Cell 6 of the Logics Worksheets (see Figure 3.25) that fall under the category "Benefits from Implemented Plan." Some of those items, such as "continued autonomy" vis-à-vis Consolidated, aren't necessary or even possible to quantify. Others, such as "higher morale," are probably too difficult to quantify. Many of the items, however, are subject to quantification or estimation, assuming that you have relevant data from ABC or from previous projects whose results have been tracked.

Therefore, you decide to get relevant data from follow-up questionnaires that were sent to clients at various times after projects were completed. These data track implemented actions, measurable improvements, that could be attributed to projects completed by you or your firm. The question you want to answer is something like this: In projects similar to the one you hope to conduct at ABC, what measurable results have accrued in terms of overall cost-effectiveness of operations, improved product quality and service levels, maintained or increased market share, and so on? Assuming those data are available and that you are confident that the situations have enough similarities, you plan to incorporate a range of such increases, decreases, and improvements within the proposal itself to indicate to ABC that you, in fact, have significant experience and expertise to achieve the company's project's objective.

Using Logic Trees to Construct Your Methodology

As was discussed in Chapter 2, the objectives[1] in your proposal express the steps your project will take me. These steps can result in my having insight, a plan, and/or an implemented plan. The objectives are an important set of outcomes of your project, and your methodology describes how you will achieve them. It consists of a logically sequenced group of actions that will achieve the objectives.

Unfortunately, many of the methodologies you present in your proposals don't persuade me that you will effectively achieve the project's objectives. Sometimes, those methodologies contain vague generalities such as "interview management," "gather data," "analyze data," and "report results." These generalities provide me with very little or no insight about how, precisely, you will achieve the objectives. Other times, the methodologies contain more specific tasks, but the logical relationship among the tasks and the objectives is unclear, as is the relationship of the tasks to each other. From my perspective, it often appears that you cut and paste from previous proposals to describe what you will do in *this* project. That's not good enough to prepare winning proposals, especially if a thoughtful, tailored methodology is one of my hot buttons or one of the selection committee's evaluation criteria.

You might believe that a compulsively logical methodology is not an important factor in my decision-making process—and sometimes that's the case. But more often than not, I suspect you use this belief to rationalize your lack of effort in developing logical methodologies (and effective project workplans after you have been awarded the assignment).

Likewise, you may believe that the more detailed the methodology, the greater the chance that I will take it and apply it myself, using my own resources. Yes, I'm certain that such things happen, but nowhere near as frequently as you believe. Listen, I want as good a relationship with a dependable, results-oriented problem solver as you want with me. If we can develop an acceptable level of trust, I believe that the risk to you is minimal. Moreover, if I believe that the methodology is critical, you won't win without a logical, well-thought-out one.

I also suspect that you may not have a structured and rigorous way of constructing a clear and logical methodology. I do. Let me share it with you. It involves the following four steps:

1. Clearly identify the project's objective(s), based on my overriding question(s).
2. Place each objective at the top of a logic tree, and order the actions necessary to achieve it.
3. Sequence the actions.
4. Identify and integrate the activities necessary for planning and communicating your proposed actions.

I'll discuss each of these steps in this chapter. But first, because the key to completing them is a logic tree, I need to tell you what that is and how to construct one.

Using Logic Trees

According to Barbara Minto in *The Minto Pyramid Principle*,[2] a logic tree (Minto calls it a pyramid) is a framework for organizing ideas, a framework for logical thinking. It structures a group of actions and their consequences that, taken together, produce a desired result. A logic tree is based on the assumption that sequences of actions are performed to achieve a specific result. That is, actions are not random; they are undertaken deliberately. A logic tree expresses these actions and the reason they are performed. For example, let's say you decide to perform the following two actions in Figure 5.1. Why would you do so?

The answer might be to make a butter sandwich (Figure 5.2), which is not necessarily a great sandwich or a culinary challenge but is a good illustration for my purposes at this point.

Here we have a logic tree. It contains a single box at the top. That box implies a result, the ends, in this case a butter sandwich. The boxes below it are the actions,

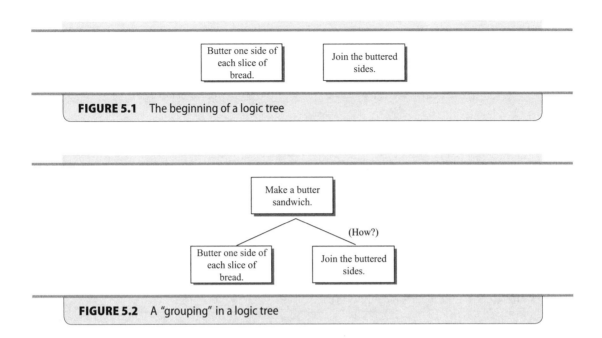

FIGURE 5.1   The beginning of a logic tree

FIGURE 5.2   A "grouping" in a logic tree

the means, necessary to produce that result. If you told me, in the methodology of your proposal, that one of your tasks would be to make a butter sandwich, I might ask, "How?" You would answer by naming the two steps on the lower row.

Note two things. First, the boxes are related through a logic that goes both bottom-up and top-down; second, whether you read bottom-up or top-down, the boxes always exist in a question-answer relationship. From the bottom, the lower boxes are the actions necessary to achieve the result implied by the top box to which they are joined. So, if you were building your logic tree from the bottom up, you would ask yourself, "What result would be produced from these two actions?" That answer would generate the top-level box, a butter sandwich. From the top down, the higher-level box also generates a question: "How would you achieve the result implied by this action?" That answer would give you the two boxes (the actions) at the lower level.

As Figure 5.3 illustrates, a well-constructed logic tree has four characteristics. The fourth characteristic, MECE, in Figure 5.3 means this:

- A grouping refers to any number of actions on one level that achieve the result implied by the action above.
- The actions in that grouping appear nowhere else in the logic tree (i.e., they are *M*utually *E*xclusive).
- No other actions within the grouping are required to achieve the result implied by the action above (i.e., they are *C*ollectively *E*xhaustive).

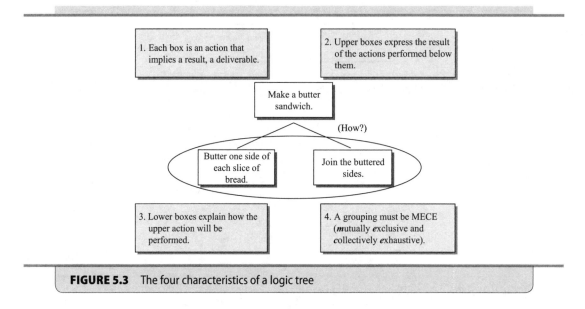

FIGURE 5.3　The four characteristics of a logic tree

Now let's assume that you want more to eat than a butter sandwich, though given the limited amount of food in your refrigerator, the butter sandwich will have to serve as the main course. So instead of the box "make a butter sandwich," we substitute the box "prepare main course," and we include two other boxes on the same level, as shown in Figure 5.4.

What will be the result of those three top boxes? Prepared food, as shown in Figure 5.5. The top box, then, will again be an action that expresses that result: Each box needs to be an action that expresses a result because depending on your perspective, each box is either an action or a result.

Figure 5.6 builds the logic tree further, illustrating that each box on a higher level must be connected to a grouping below it comprising at least two boxes.

Now, if I wanted to try your patience even more, I could continue building the logic tree ever upward. I also could continue to build it downward, since further actions could be required to explain how you butter one side of each slice of bread and join them together. What determines where you start and how far down you go? I can explain the "down" part in one sentence: As far down as you need to go so that your reader or listener no longer asks "How?" That's easier said than done, considering that your methodology will rarely be presented to just one person. Someone like Ray Armstrong, ABC's president, for example, may not want to see a methodology built as low as would someone like Paul Morrison, the chief industrial engineer.

Explaining where the logic tree begins will take two more paragraphs. Assume you have a potential client to whom you've been trying to sell for some time. You have had several meetings with her and have developed a fairly sound business relationship, but so far you've been unable to make the sale. It so happens that she and your best friend

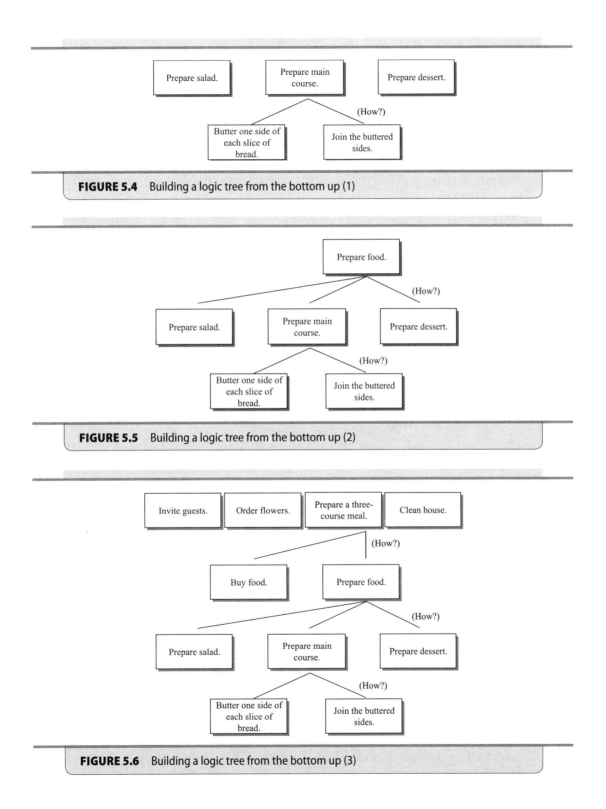

FIGURE 5.4   Building a logic tree from the bottom up (1)

FIGURE 5.5   Building a logic tree from the bottom up (2)

FIGURE 5.6   Building a logic tree from the bottom up (3)

went to school together and haven't seen each other for over 20 years. She would like to see your friend, and your friend would like to see her (and you, of course, would like to make the sale). Next week, this potential client will be in town for two days. Your over-riding question is: "How can I further my relationship with her to increase the likelihood of a sale?" Your answer is to give a dinner party that she and your friend will attend (and during which, we'll assume, you won't serve butter sandwiches as a main course).

Note that three things have generated the logic tree in Figure 5.7 and therefore deter-mined where it begins. First, a problem: in this case, your not having yet made a sale. In your proposal, the problem is discussed in the situation slot. Second, an overriding question related to the problem: in this case, "How can I further my relationship with my potential client to increase the likelihood of a sale?" Third, an objective, which is the answer to the overriding question: in this case, "Give a dinner party." The objective is stated in your proposal's objectives slot. It also becomes the top box in your logic tree, as shown in Figure 5.7, which provides the logically related actions necessary to achieve that objective.

In the rest of this chapter, I'll show you how all those actions under the objective form part of your proposed project's methodology. I'll also take you through the revi-sion of a methodology of an internal proposal written to the XYZ Company, a provider of information systems.

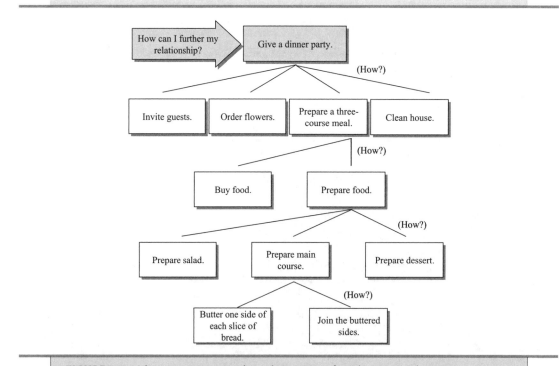

FIGURE 5.7   A logic tree structures the tasks necessary for achieving an objective.

Some years ago, XYZ's marketing group wanted to explore the idea of offering its services to a new market, the motor freight sector, possibly in partnership with a motor carrier. Figure 5.8 lists the objectives and the tasks as they first appeared in the proposal. After you've read Figure 5.8, I'll take you through the four-step process of constructing (in this case, revising) the methodology. Because constructing a logic tree seems complicated the first few times you try to build one, I'll repeat much of what I said when building the logic tree for giving a dinner party. In the work session at the end of this chapter, you'll have yet another opportunity to see a logic tree constructed. After that, you should be able to start building your own.

Step 1: Clearly Identify the Objective(s), Based on the Overriding Question(s)

Because the methodology contains the tasks you will use to achieve your project's objectives, the starting place for building your methodology has to be the objectives themselves. It makes little sense to plan a trip if you don't know where you're going, and it makes equally little sense to tell me how you're going to go about achieving what you're uncertain about accomplishing. Fortunately, I've given you some important tools for thinking about your objectives. As we've seen, they can be of only three kinds: Insight, Plan, or Implementation. If yours is an Insight

---

Objectives
- Develop market and competitive information to assist XYZ in determining if there is a demand for the proposed service offering and how it could be tailored to better meet customers' needs.
- Determine how the product should be marketed given customers' needs, the marketplace, and the activities of competitors.
- Identify potential actions for XYZ to be successful in this marketplace.

Tasks
- Conduct kickoff meeting.
- Identify market participants and develop questionnaires.
- Evaluate motor carriers' requirements.
- Evaluate competitors' capabilities.
- Evaluate shippers' needs.
- Review progress with top management.
- Assess overall market potential.
- Define market opportunities.
- Assess strategic alternatives.

FIGURE 5.8   The original objectives and tasks for the XYZ proposal

Project, you will have only one objective, related to insight. A Planning Project will have only one objective, related to developing a plan. An Implementation Project also will have only one objective, related to implementing a plan. Understandably, a project intended to develop a plan and implement it will have two objectives. So will one that combines insight with a plan.

Two overriding questions existed in the XYZ situation, one related to insight and one related to a plan. XYZ wanted to know whether entering the market was desirable, and, if it was, the company wanted to know how best to do so. But you'd be hard pressed to glean that information from the objectives shown in Figure 5.8. In fact, the objectives as originally stated don't even suggest that the study might only involve one phase—the market assessment. After all, if the market were not worth entering, XYZ wouldn't need or even want a plan for entering it. Therefore, the consultants should have revised their objectives so that the first related to insight and the second related to a plan:

- Determine if XYZ should enter the information-service market for motor carriers.
- If entering the market is feasible, develop a plan for doing so.

These objectives much more clearly capture the desired results and also indicate the phased nature of the project.

Step 2: After Placing Each Objective at the Top of the Logic Tree, Order the Actions Necessary to Achieve It

In building a logic tree, you need to keep two principles in mind:

- Each box in the logic tree is a single action that expresses a result.
- The actions must be as specific as possible.

Because all the actions in the logic tree work together to produce the objective, all are logically integrated. The integration occurs because each action on each level is part of a group of actions that produces a result at a higher level. Figure 5.9 depicts this condition. On the lowest level are three groups of actions. Since the logical reason for performing any group of actions is to achieve some result, each group on the lower level produces an implied result at the next higher level:

Actions 1, 2, and 3 are performed in some logical manner to achieve Result 1. Actions 4, 5, and 6 produce Result 2. And so forth.

As you construct your methodology, you must phrase these three results as actions because they are undertaken to produce a higher-level result or group of results. At the very top of the structure, regardless of how many levels it contains,

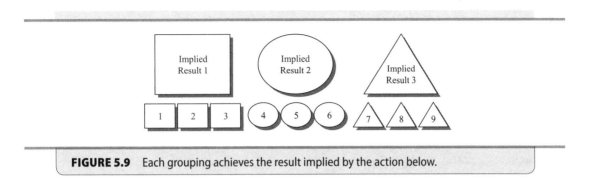

FIGURE 5.9   Each grouping achieves the result implied by the action below.

is always the final result: the project's objective. In a well-structured logic tree, as Figure 5.10 illustrates, every box—no matter how far down the tree it might reside—contributes to achieving the objective.

If your project has more than one objective (if, for example, it's a combined Insight and Planning Project, as in the proposal to XYZ), you will need to build a logic tree for each objective, as shown in Figure 5.11.

In constructing your logic tree, you must try to phrase the actions as specifically as possible because I might want to know precisely and specifically what you will accomplish. An effective technique is to test your action by rephrasing it in your mind as an actual result.

Consider these poor examples: The result of the action "gather information" would be "gathered information." The result of "interview top management" would

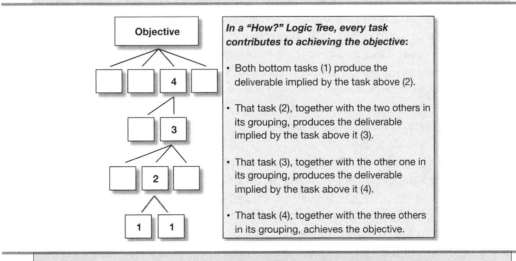

FIGURE 5.10   Every action at every level contributes to achieving the objective.

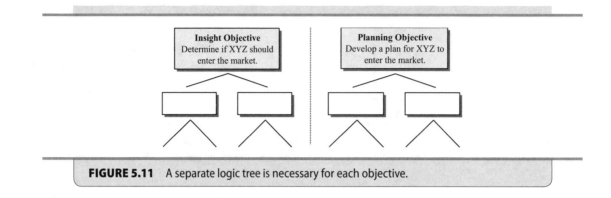

FIGURE 5.11   A separate logic tree is necessary for each objective.

be "interviewed top management." These results, I think you see, aren't very specific. They don't express a result. After you've gathered information, all you have is a bunch of information. After you've interviewed top management, all you have is a bunch of interviewed managers. Compare these nonspecific actions to "identify resources and timing required" or "specify capabilities required." These actions express specific results, which, as we'll discuss later in this chapter, are deliverables: "identified resources" and "specified capabilities." These are things I can see; I can visualize a list of resources or capabilities.

Now, let's examine part of the logic trees that could have been developed by XYZ's internal consultants. In Figure 5.12, I've included all of the first two levels and part of the third.

This and any well-constructed logic tree develops your ideas by way of a series of arguments. In Figure 5.12, several arguments exist that are mutually exclusive and collectively exhaustive. First, whether XYZ should enter the market can be determined by three major tasks: identifying market opportunities, specifying the capabilities and resources required to capitalize on those opportunities, and comparing XYZ's capabilities and resources to the market requirements. Second, the market opportunities can be determined by identifying the motor carriers' needs for the proposed information system, the needs of the motor carriers' customers, and the capabilities of XYZ's competitors. Finally, to develop a plan for actually entering the market, XYZ needs to know (1) which actions are necessary for closing the gap between what the market demands and what XYZ can do and (2) what resources and timing are necessary to carry out those actions.

In checking the logic of your logic tree, use the several requirements I've discussed:

● Each box must be an action that expresses a result. Therefore, each box must be phrased as specifically as possible.
● Each group of boxes on one level must produce a result, a deliverable, on the next level. That group and its result form an argument that goes something

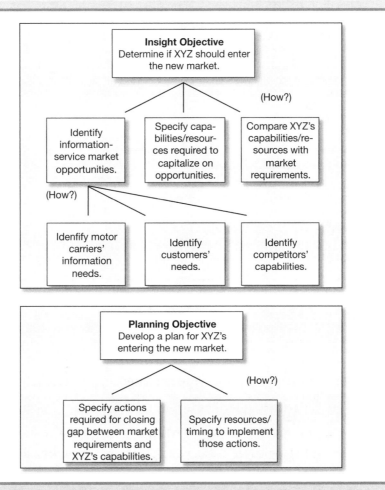

FIGURE 5.12   A partial logic tree for the XYZ proposal

like this: "To achieve result A, action X, action Y, and action Z, and only those actions, must be performed."

◉ All arguments are mutually exclusive and collectively exhaustive (MECE).

Applying this logic tree technique will help you indicate logical relationships and identify the gaps in your logic, letting you know where you have left something out.

Step 3: Sequence the Actions

In this straightforward step, you can sequence the actions by using a typical outline or bullet form, as I've done in Figure 5.13. Once again, I've taken the steps

Phase I Determine If XYZ should enter the market	Phase II Develop a plan for XYZ's entering the market
• Identify information-service market opportunities. • Identify motor carriers' information needs. • Identify customers' needs. • Identify competitors' capabilities. • Specify capabilities and resources required to capitalize on market opportunities. • Compare XYZ's capabilities and resources with market requirements.	• Specify actions required for closing the gap between market requirements and XYZ's capabilities. • Specify resources and timing to implement actions.

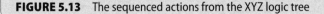

FIGURE 5.13   The sequenced actions from the XYZ logic tree

completely down to two levels and only partially, for illustrative purposes, to a third. Note now how the project is phased, with the project's objectives used, in this case, as the titles of the phases.

Because the outline form does not readily reveal logical relationships or logical inconsistencies (as the logic tree does), you should use the outline form only after you have constructed your logic tree.

Step 4: Identify and Integrate the Activities Necessary for Planning and Communicating Your Proposed Actions

In building your logic tree, you must distinguish between actions and activities. When you take your car in for repairs, you want your mechanic to perform two very different kinds of tasks. First are those *actions* directly related to achieving your objective of fixing or maintaining your car. These are the hands-on procedures to diagnose and solve the problem. Second are the kinds of tasks related to planning and communicating. These *activities* might involve the mechanic calling you when the car is fixed or calling you if the problem will cost more than was originally estimated. Then you could decide whether to have the car repaired, trade it in, or live with the problem. Both kinds of tasks—those *actions* necessary for achieving the

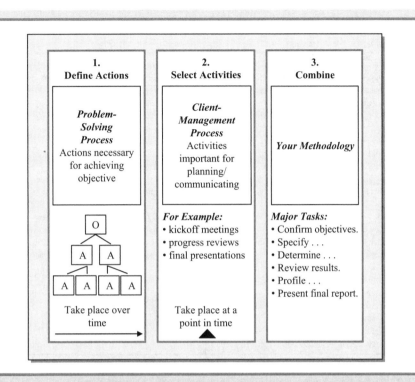

FIGURE 5.14 Your methodology combines the actions for achieving the objective and the activities for planning and communicating.

objective and those *activities* necessary for planning and communicating—are part of the mechanic's methodology, and they're also part of yours. (See Figure 5.14.)

Although an activity such as presenting a planning study's final report might be extremely important to the success of your efforts, it is crucial only in presenting the plan you constructed. It is not an action necessary for actually achieving the project's objective of developing the plan. The same holds true for other typical activities, such as presenting interim reports and conducting kickoff meetings. Even those activities, however, should be phrased as specifically as possible. Therefore, instead of "conduct kickoff meeting," you might phrase the activity as "confirm project objectives in a kickoff meeting." After identifying the activities, you can sequence them in your outline, as I've done in the right-hand column of Figure 5.15, which compares the original methodology with part of the one we've been building by using a logic tree.

As you compare the original and the revision, I'm certain you'll agree that the latter much more clearly defines the desired results and how you will achieve them. The original methodology is typical of those I see in proposal after proposal—boilerplate lifted from past proposals. The relationship of

Original	Revised
Objectives • Develop market and competitive information to assist XYZ in determining if there is a demand for the proposed service offering and how it could be tailored to better meet customer demands. • Determine how the product should be marketed given customers' needs, the marketplace, and the activities of customers. • Identify potential actions for XYZ to be successful in this market.	**1. Determine if XYZ Should Enter the Market** • Confirm Phase 1 objectives in a kickoff meeting. • Identify information-service market opportunities. • Specify capabilities and resources required to capitalize on market opportunities. • Compare XYZ's capabilities and resources with market requirements. • Report Phase 1 results and, if appropriate, confirm Phase 2 objectives.
Tasks • Conduct kickoff meeting. • Identify market participants and develop questionnaires. • Evaluate motor carriers' requirements. • Evaluate competitors' capabilities. • Evaluate shippers' needs. • Review progress with top management. • Assess overall market potential. • Define market opportunities. • Assess strategic alternatives.	**2. Develop Plan for Entering the Market** • Specify actions required to close gap between market requirements and XYZ's capabilities. • Specify resources and timing to implement actions. • Report Phase 2 results.

FIGURE 5.15   Comparison of the original and revised XYZ objectives and tasks

the tasks to the objectives is unclear, as is the relationship of the tasks to each other. The revised methodology, in contrast, is much more specific to our situation and clearly reveals the project's objectives and how they will be achieved. If a logical methodology were important to me, I would surely reward you for that clarity. In my evaluation of your proposal, I would most certainly give you some of the two to five extra points you need to win. And even if a logical methodology were not important to me, it would provide you with the basis for a logical workplan that will help you more effectively execute the project after you've won.

The Logic Tree, Deliverables, and the Logics Worksheet

In Chapter 3, I discussed deliverables, one of four kinds of outputs suggested by the baseline logic, the other three being desired results, achieved objectives, and benefits (see Figure 5.16).

Desired Results: The outputs of the project or its phases: insight, a plan, and/or an implemented plan. *Example from ABC: a plan for increasing capacity (a non-measurable result).*
Objectives (achieved): The expression of S_2, the desired results. *Example: develop a plan for increasing capacity.*
Deliverables: The outputs produced during the transition from S_1 to S_2. *Example: specifications of current equipment and space utilization.*
Benefits: The good things that accrue to the prospect as/after its desired result is achieved. *Example: a thorough justification of the chosen option that provides the basis for requesting funding from Consolidated.*

FIGURE 5.16   The four outputs of the baseline logic

In this chapter, we have also been discussing deliverables. Because the boxes in your logic tree are actions that imply a result, each result should be a deliverable produced by your methodology. Accordingly, as Figure 5.17 shows, you can use your deliverables from the Logic Worksheet's Cell 5 (see Figure 3.24) as a first step in building your methodology. Once you have constructed your logic tree, you will undoubtedly discover additional deliverables that you should add to that cell and red flag if necessary, making certain that they are aligned with the desired results and benefits.

◉ ◉ ◉

Before you read this chapter's work session, I want to say something about workplans, which, as I've hinted before, can be formed in part from your logic tree. As Figure 5.18 illustrates, a workplan is nothing more than your methodology sequenced over time, with the actions indicated by horizontal lines and the activities by triangles. In proposals, the workplan is often presented in the form of a Gantt chart that includes the actions and activities on one axis and the timing of those tasks on the other. This kind of chart is most helpful in letting me see when you expect each task to begin and end. A Gantt chart also indicates which tasks will be performed concurrently and which tasks will overlap. Before you can develop your workplan, however, you need to construct a logical methodology. You'll get some practice in the following work session, which develops a logic tree for the proposal to ABC.

Logics Worksheet

Type of Project	Overriding Question
Prospect Profile	Deliverables
Current Situation	Benefits

- Validation of ABC's market forecast
- Validation of ABC's market share and product-mix projections
- Specification of current equipment and space utilization
- Determination of opportunities to better utilize current equipment and space

Methods

Specifically, our methodology includes the following four tasks:

- Task 1: Validate ABC's market forecast
- Task 2: Validate ABC's market share and product-mix projections
- Task 3: Specify current equipment and space utilization
- Task 4: Determine opportunities to better utilize current equipment and space

FIGURE 5.17   The major deliverables on the Logics Worksheet could become your methodology's major tasks.

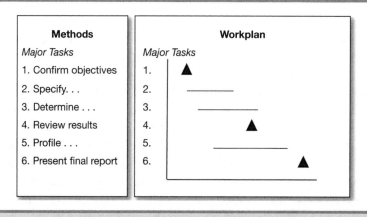

Methods

Major Tasks

1. Confirm objectives
2. Specify. . .
3. Determine . . .
4. Review results
5. Profile . . .
6. Present final report

Workplan

Major Tasks

1.
2.
3.
4.
5.
6.

FIGURE 5.18   The workplan shows the methodology's actions and activities plotted over time.

─CHAPTER 5 REVIEW─

Constructing a Logical Methodology

1. The proposal's methodology consists of two kinds of tasks: actions and activities.

- **Actions** are tasks necessary for achieving the project's objectives. Usually occurring over a period of time, actions are necessary in the problem-solving process—that is, for achieving the project's objectives. Each action should express a result.
- **Activities** are tasks important for planning and communicating. Usually occurring at a point in time, activities are important in the client-management process. Examples include: confirming the project's objectives, reporting interim results, and delivering a final report. As much as possible, these tasks also should be phrased to express results.

2. Constructing the proposal's methodology requires four steps:

- **Clearly identify the objective(s), based on the overriding question(s).** An Insight Project has only one objective—providing insight. A Planning Project has only one objective—developing a plan. An Implementation Project has only one objective—implementing a plan. A combined Insight and Planning Project has two objectives. A combined Planning and Implementation Project has two objectives.
- **After placing each objective at the top of the logic tree, order the actions necessary to achieve it.** Develop one logic tree for each objective. Every box in the logic tree expresses an action implying a result. Every box on one row is connected to at least two boxes on the next lower row. These lower-row boxes are the set of actions necessary to achieve the result implied on the row above. These lower-row actions, however, also imply results in the boxes connected to them on even lower rows. Each box in every row implies a result produced by the related actions on the row below. Therefore, each box is an action implying a single result. The actions should be expressed as specifically as possible.
- **Once the logic tree is constructed, list the actions in sequence.** Use indentations or standard outline form to indicate the hierarchical relationships. You have now logically organized the actions.
- **Identify and integrate the activities necessary for planning and communicating your proposed actions.** You have now constructed the methodology.

3. Once the logic tree is completed, identify deliverables that do not exist on the Logics Worksheet, add them to the Logics Worksheet, and align as necessary.

WORK SESSION 4: Developing the Logic Tree for ABC

Confident that your baseline logic is complete and well aligned, you turn your attention to the final element that provides a proposal with its logical foundation: the methodology. The methodology indicates how you plan to close the gap between the current situation, S_1, and the desired result, S_2; it effects the transition from S_1 to S_2.

A comprehensive and logical methodology will play a significant role in convincing ABC's management that Paramount can best help it develop a plan to address its capacity problem. That you know. Because you also know that manufacturing strategy isn't one of your own strengths, you suggest to Gilmore that he assign some of the firm's functional specialists to work with you to develop the methodology. Gilmore quickly acts on your suggestion and joins the group himself.

Validating the Overriding Question and Objective

Because the methodology is the means to achieve the project's ends (its objectives), the group's first task is to define ABC's overriding question. As you expected, the group members differ about what the overriding question should be. Some believe it should be phrased like this: "How can ABC best provide product to meet forecasted demand?" Proponents of this question suggest that internal resources and capital investment can be conserved by having more operations, especially low-value-added ones, performed by outside suppliers.

Others believe the question should focus not on product supply but on capacity: "How should ABC increase capacity to meet the sales forecast?" Both you and Gilmore argue for this question. Gilmore explains to the group that Armstrong gave him the clear impression that ABC preferred to have closer control of its manufacturing processes by performing most of its major operations within its own facilities. As a result of Gilmore's counsel, the group agrees that the project's objective should be this: "Develop a manufacturing facility strategy that will provide the capacity necessary to meet forecasted demand." Of course, this objective should be tested and revised, if appropriate, with ABC's management. This testing and discussion is a key element is building a stronger relationship during the business-development process.

Building the Logic Tree

After about two hours, the group completes a first draft and a second draft (Figures 5.19 and Figure 5.20) of the logic tree for ABC. As you look over the x'd-out and italicized boxes in the second draft, you see clearly why various changes were made and still need to be made. For example, various x'd-out boxes didn't survive the second draft because they didn't express a result, a deliverable. Cases in point include "review and discuss existing forecast" and "examine current space

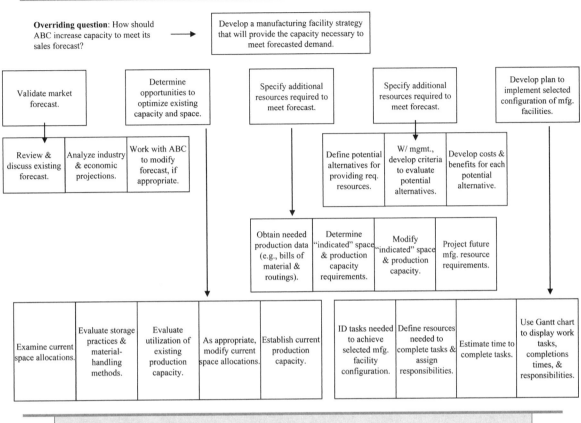

FIGURE 5.19   The ABC logic tree, first draft

allocations." The results implied by these tasks are a review and an examination. These, you recognize are processes, not end products like deliverables. What, you must always ask yourself, is the end product of that review or that discussion?

The same is true of tasks you've seen in many proposals, tasks such as "to analyze [something]" and "to evaluate [something]." An evaluation and an analysis are processes, not end products. You are beginning to understand that an "expansion analysis" just isn't as specific as "a detailed list of expansion alternatives." A "detailed list of alternatives" describes what the prospect will receive, rather than the process, the analysis, that will produce the deliverable.

Other boxes in the second draft are problematic in another way: They aren't necessary for achieving the result implied in the box above them. The task "modify forecast" is a case in point: It expresses the same result as the box above it. These "mistakes" confirm to you the power of the logic tree in constructing a

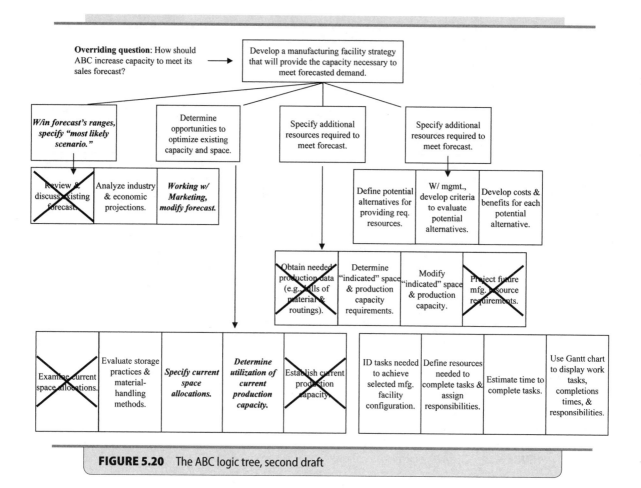

FIGURE 5.20   The ABC logic tree, second draft

logical argument for your methodology: The logic tree clearly displays gaps and errors in logic and helps you, more quickly and effectively than you could otherwise, generate a third draft, as shown in Figure 5.21. Even this draft, you recognize the next day, has some problems, but you are satisfied that it is good enough for now. It will provide you with the guts of your methodology and the building blocks for your methods section. It also generates some additional deliverables that you record on your Logics Worksheet.

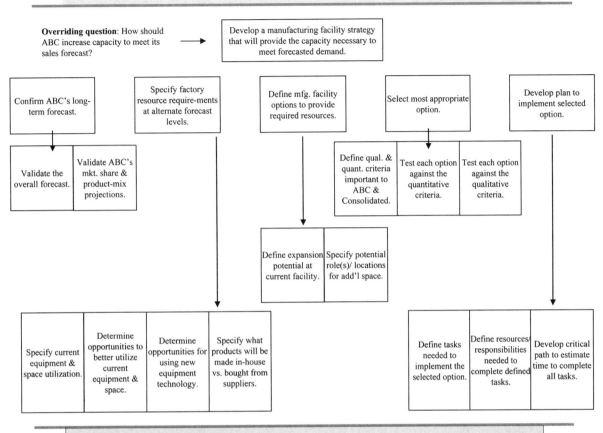

Overriding question: How should ABC increase capacity to meet its sales forecast? → Develop a manufacturing facility strategy that will provide the capacity necessary to meet forecasted demand.

Confirm ABC's long-term forecast.

Specify factory resource require-ments at alternate forecast levels.

Define mfg. facility options to provide required resources.

Select most appropriate option.

Develop plan to implement selected option.

Validate the overall forecast.

Validate ABC's mkt. share & product-mix projections.

Define qual. & quant. criteria important to ABC & Consolidated.

Test each option against the quantitative criteria.

Test each option against the qualitative criteria.

Define expansion potential at current facility.

Specify potential role(s)/ locations for add'l space.

Specify current equipment & space utilization.

Determine opportunities to better utilize current equipment & space.

Determine opportunities for using new equipment technology.

Specify what products will be made in-house vs. bought from suppliers.

Define tasks needed to implement the selected option.

Define resources/ responsibilities needed to complete defined tasks.

Develop critical path to estimate time to complete all tasks.

FIGURE 5.21   The ABC logic tree, final draft

Proposal Psychologics

Now that you've completed Part 1 on proposal logics, you may believe that your more logical presentations and proposals will win far more often, and they might. But logics provide you only the base—the necessary but not the sufficient—because I buy for psychological as well as for logical reasons. I want to feel comfortable with you, to trust you, and to sense with confidence that you understand my situation, my risks, and, perhaps most important of all, my potential rewards—the benefits I will receive from the project you propose.

So your task now is to combine the logical with the psychological, the head with the heart, and to combine your analysis of my situation and what you will do to support me with how I feel about you. I want to be confident about your ability to deliver on your promises to meet my objectives. I want a relationship based on trust and founded on rapport.

In Part 2, therefore, I assume that your logics are in place and that relationships or "psychologics" are now critical to your success. Accordingly, I show you how to align yourself with me and the other members of the buying committee and how to position yourself favorably against the competition. Finally, I show you how to use that alignment and positioning to develop themes—important messages that you will weave throughout your document or presentation to make me say, "Yes, these people have listened to and understand us, they appreciate our risks, and they have articulated our rewards."

CHAPTER 6

Analyzing the Buyers

Generic structure, as we discussed in Chapter 1, primarily relates to the logic of proposals. Unless you're selling equations to a logician or theories to a scientist, however, logic is rarely enough. That's why you'll have to use more than logic. You'll have to give me, your potential client, more than technical expertise or a logically constructed methodology, more than elegant-sounding résumés or qualifications statements that I know look pretty much the same in every proposal you prepare. You'll have to convince me that I want to work with you.

Think about what you offer to me: you often don't know what you're going to make (i.e., what you'll deliver to me) until you make it. You operate more like a medical doctor than a civil engineer. An engineer designs a bridge to span a river, while a doctor creates, tests, and re-creates hypotheses to discover something unknown, something hidden, and perhaps something not agreed to. Accordingly, to choose you as my "doctor" I need to develop trust that you, your team, and your firm can address my uncertainty, my often ill-defined, even illogical current situation. In such cases, attitude or "bedside manner" is just as important as or even more important than expertise.

You see, although you may think we know each other well, we don't—certainly not during our initial meetings. I don't know or probably trust you completely or appreciate your complex personality. And you, certainly, don't know me completely or know how I will respond in a given situation. In some situations, I become extremely analytical, seeking a lot of evidence, asking a lot of questions, and behaving methodically and systematically. This orientation toward information and reasoned, rational analysis may be based on the risk or magnitude of a potential decision I must make. In this situation, I might desire a detailed methodology (perhaps even your sharing of your logic tree).

In a different situation, I become more concerned about people and their relationships within my organization. This more supportive orientation is one I often take during implementation projects in which I must convince others in my organization to change. In this situation, therefore, I may desire your sensitivity, your care for the personal and developmental concerns of me and others.

At yet other times, especially when I'm dealing with a future issue, one that is often ill defined, I become more concerned with ideas and hypotheses and creativity. This orientation leads me to rely more heavily on intuition and feelings. Therefore, I may desire from you a more conceptual and open-ended orientation.

Finally, in yet other situations, I become more assertive, more oriented to action, more desirous of control. I may adopt this directing or controlling orientation when I sense urgency and the need for rapid change or a forceful response. I become more task-oriented, more insistent on getting something accomplished quickly. Therefore, I may desire from you a certain assertiveness, a far more proactive orientation.

So even if you think you know me because you've seen me operate in one kind of situation, you may be surprised at my response in another situation. Your task is to make reasonable and educated guesses about the nature of my likely response so that you, in turn, can respond to my situation and convince me that you understand my organization's problems or opportunities and that we can work together successfully.

Additionally, if I'm not the only one making the buying decision (which is almost always the case), you also need to know my colleagues on the evaluation committee, how they perceive the situation, and what they like and don't like about the scope and range of potential solutions, as well as their relationship to me, and mine to them. Would you be surprised to hear that we may see the situation differently, have different selection criteria, and even have different biases? Well, more often than not, we do. So you and your team need to deal with me and each of my colleagues. This can be a very complex interchange.

Miller and Heiman's Four Buying Roles

Let me recommend a book to you that isn't at all about writing but is about selling (and that's what your proposal process needs to do: sell). The book, *The New Strategic Selling*,[1] contains a powerful method for analyzing the members on a buying team. Each of these individuals, in what Miller and Heiman call a "complex sale" (i.e., one with multiple decision influencers), plays one or more roles: economic buyer, user buyer, technical buyer, or coach.

The economic buyer (only one exists in most selling opportunities) has direct access to and control of the budget, discretionary use of those funds, and veto power over the sale. This buyer's focus is primarily on the bottom line and on the impact the project will have on the organization. Figure 6.1, briefly summarized and adapted, is Miller and Heiman's description of the economic buyer.

I have played the role of economic buyer, and I have also been a user buyer (see Figure 6.2), focusing primarily on the project's potential day-to-day effect on my

The Economic Buyer's Role: To give final approval to buy	
Focus	Concerned with bottom line and overall impact on the organization. For example: • Strategic position • Profitability • Competitiveness • Productivity • Market growth • Budget fit • Cash flow • Meeting broader business goals
Number	Only one per sale (but may be one set of people, such as a board or a committee; if so, try to determine "the first among equals")
Characteristics	• Has discretionary use of funds • Can release those monies • Has veto power
Primary Question	"What will be the overall performance improvement and return on this investment?"

FIGURE 6.1   The economic buyer

The User Buyer's Role: To judge the impact of operational performance	
Focus	• Objectives and adequacy of proposed approach • Potential effects on the buyers' organizational unit
Number	Often several
Characteristics	• Will be directly affected by the project • Will often have a subjective response to the proposal • Is very important for implementation and for continuing relationships
Primary Question	"How will the project affect my job and those I manage?"

FIGURE 6.2   The user buyer

own area of responsibility or organization. If I am a user buyer, you'd better not ignore me if you want a long-term relationship. If, by chance, you sell an initial project that circumvents me, I may sabotage subsequent projects or even hinder acceptance and implementation during the initial one. That is the case because your project will have a direct impact on my job performance and on those I manage. If I'm a user buyer, you'd better convince me that the winds of change are pleasant or, if they're not, that the hurricane will at least clear out a lot of unwanted dust and debris, leaving me as one of the survivors.

I also might be a technical buyer (Figure 6.3), who primarily judges the measurable and quantifiable aspects of your proposal. If so, I'm a gatekeeper, making recommendations to the other groups of buyers. As a technical buyer, I don't usually have the authority to accept your proposal, but I can play a decisive role in eliminating you from further consideration.

The fourth buying role is the coach (Figure 6.4), an individual (or individuals) whom you hope to find and develop to help you make the sale. It's highly desirable to have a coach or coaches on the buying team. It's ideal, of course, if one of your coaches is the economic buyer.

Why do you need a coach? Well, sometimes you don't. But often you do, probably more often than you realize. You see, sometimes I don't fully trust you. I don't know you well enough for you to have earned my trust. In fact, if you're a consultant, as I stated earlier, I often would prefer not having you or other consultants around, asking me a lot of time-consuming questions and prying into my affairs. You are an outsider, and I would prefer that you stay that way. I wish that I didn't need you and that I could resolve my own organization's issues. But

The Technical Buyer's Role: To screen out	
Focus	Concerned with measurable, quantifiable aspects related to this situation. For example: • ROI • Match of specifications • Price • Adequacy of technical solution
Number	Often several
Characteristics	• Judges proposal by measurable, quantifiable aspects • Acts as gatekeeper • Makes recommendations • Can't say "yes"; can say "no"
Primary Question	"Do the proposed approach and qualifications meet our specifications?"

FIGURE 6.3   The technical buyer

The Coach's Role: To act as a guide for this opportunity	
Focus	Your success with this selling opportunity
Number	Develop at least one
Can be found	Inside the prospect's firm or, sometimes, outside (e.g., on the Board of Directors)
Characteristics	Wants you to win and therefore provides/interprets information about the potential client's environment. For example: • Current situation • Competition • Other buyers • Benefits, individual and • Hot buttons collective • Evaluation criteria • Pricing considerations
Primary Question	"How can we pull this off together?"

FIGURE 6.4   The coach

even though I might need you (you still have to convince me), I'm not likely to reveal everything. I might not believe that what you need to know from me is actually worth your knowing. Even those things I'm reluctant to tell, you might forget to ask, and you might not have another opportunity to do so. Or you may never even have the opportunity to meet me at all, because I'm too busy to see you or I judge you too unimportant to see.

This is where your coach (or coaches) comes in. The coach may be able to arrange introductions with me or with other buyers on my team; identify buyers you have overlooked or normally would not be able to identify; elaborate on our evaluation criteria; provide advice and counsel about selling strategies and maybe even the competition; and, in general, act as a guide and confidant during the selling process. Although coaches often can help you indirectly by arranging introductions and providing intelligence, sometimes (as an experienced consultant and friend of mine explains), they can actually help you sell. As my friend tells the story:

> A young fellow who is an internal consultant for a company I was trying to sell invited us in a competitive situation to talk about inventory. We had a long meeting with him and then a long second meeting, and then we had to write a proposal to go with him to his boss. I hate that kind of situation. We never met his boss; all we knew was that his boss is a hard-charging, young, very creative guy who, like all the other top people at XYZ, shot up in the organization. And I said, "Does he like

presentations, or does he like written documents?" The internal consultant said, "He gets annoyed at too many words and things; he likes creative presentations."

So I put together a presentation with about 25 pages, a little flip-chart thing that I would put on the boss's desk, so I was totally in control. It was mostly cartoons and all kinds of wild stuff, a lot of meaning and very few words. The last cartoon showed a boat with the captain leaning over the bow. On the captain were the words "XYZ Management." In front of the boat were a bunch of icebergs. On the tops of the icebergs, I wrote things like "reduce inventory" or "cut inventory costs," and on the bottoms, I wrote phrases like "destroy customer confidence." At the very top of the cartoon, I wrote, "Our objective is to steer you through these icebergs, avoid some of them, go right through others because they are so small that they don't make any difference, and show you where to set dynamite charges to get rid of the really bad ones."

Now the internal consultant asked me for a copy of all this in advance, so I sent him a letter, giving him the philosophy of what we were trying to do. Word by word, I explained that whole last cartoon. At the meeting, I flipped through the charts and when I came to the last one, I said, "It's sort of like icebergs," and then paused. Suddenly, the internal consultant said, "Yes, as a matter of fact . . . ," and he just took over, independently quoting right from my little personal letter to him, which really was the proposal. Now, he looked smart. His boss liked it, and we got the job. If he wouldn't have said anything, I would have kept talking. But we made him part of the creative team without soliciting it. He could be part of our team, which he wanted to be; he could be smart in front of his boss, and be selling to his boss.[2]

Coaches (at least in their coaching role) are interested in the strokes or recognition or visibility they will get from helping you make a successful sale and thus initiating a project that proves valuable. They will gain recognition or visibility, get strokes, or be seen as problem solvers if they have played a part in your selection and were therefore instrumental in helping to choose the right firm that eliminated pain or capitalized on opportunity and therefore allowed results to be delivered and benefits to accrue.

A Fifth Buying Role

Would you believe that I might not select you even if your firm scored the highest number of points on our evaluation scale? Even though you would "beat" the second-place finisher by two to five points, you (and not they) would place second; they (and not you) would win. In many of those situations, you will lose because a fifth buying role—the ratifier—strongly prefers someone else.

A ratifier doesn't exist in all selling situations, and when one does, the ratifier isn't an official member of the selection committee. The ratifier is, however, consulted by the economic buyer to approve or bless the selection committee's decision. In the ABC situation, for example, there might be a ratifier at Consolidated, an individual from whom Ray Armstrong normally would seek approval before selecting a consulting firm. Even if Paramount Consulting were ranked highest by ABC, Armstrong might want to have that choice blessed by the ratifier. And the ratifier could say no—because she has a poor opinion of Paramount, because she has a better opinion of one of the other competitors, or simply because she wants to play it safe by going with a higher-profile or better-known firm. If the ratifier refuses to bless ABC's decision, the selection committee very well may have to continue its deliberations.

In the role of blessing the recommendation of the economic buyer, the ratifier wants to be certain that the proposed project (and the proposers themselves) meets the ratifier's broader political and/or personal objectives and desires. As such, the ratifier is most concerned about the potential cultural or environmental conflicts within the organization. He or she wants to know, as Figure 6.5 shows, whether the project or proposers will cause conflicts with colleagues, with the organization's culture and constituencies, or with other projects then being or soon to be undertaken.

The Ratifier's Role: To bless the recommendation of the economic buyer		
Focus	Concerned with available resources and their allocation as well as potential broader cultural/environmental conflicts within the organization. For example, conflicts with: • Colleagues • Corporate culture • Constituencies • Other programs/initiatives	
Number	If exists, usually only one in corporate organizations; sometimes several in governmental organizations.	
Can be found	Higher up in the organization	
Characteristics	• Ratifies the recommendation • Acts as gatekeeper	• Often at the highest levels of the organization • Has veto power
Primary Question	"Will this project and these bidders meet my broader political and/or cultural objectives?"	

FIGURE 6.5 The ratifier

Beyond $S_1 \rightarrow S_2 \rightarrow B$

Note that in using the various categories of buyers, Miller and Heiman aren't talking about individual people but about roles people on the selection committee play during the selling situation. An economic buyer, regardless of whom he is personally, individually, is always concerned about your proposed project's bottom-line impact on the organization; therefore, he focuses on return on investment (ROI) or good budget fit or increased productivity. A user buyer, regardless of title, is always concerned about your service's day-to-day impact on her department's operation; therefore, she may focus on the ease and effectiveness of implementation or on improved efficiency.

The real significance of these different orientations is that individuals playing each of the roles will expect different kinds of benefits than will others playing a different role. Allow me to emphasize this last point. Because you, I, and everyone else buys because of benefits, you must recognize that we have different expectations about how we will each benefit from your proposed approach and results. We aren't really buying your product or service; we are buying what that product or service delivers—benefits. *Therefore, the major reason that you want to identify buyers' roles is this*: You will better be able to identify how they, as opposed to their organization, will benefit from your engagement. That's why the first cell of the Psychologics Worksheet,[3] which will be discussed in this chapter's work session, focuses on:

- the individual buyers and the role(s) they play
- the perception of benefits the buyers, based on those roles, believe will accrue to them

When we discussed the baseline logic in Chapter 2 and Chapter 3, we did so from the perspective of my organization, my firm. But organizations don't buy your services; I and my colleagues do. And I and my colleagues have different perceptions of S_1 and S_2 based upon the role(s) we are playing in *this* selling situation. As a result, the simplified baseline logic that I used in Chapter 3 needs to be revised when you are considering the psychologics rather than the logics, when you are considering the people rather than their firm. Chapter 3's simplified baseline logic would be adequate only if you were selling to a one-person buying team with that single individual playing all the buying roles. Because this situation almost never occurs, the formula must be expanded, as depicted in Figure 6.6.

This second formulation is much more realistic (and strategic) for three reasons:

1. **The perception of S_1, the current situation, and of S_2, the desired result, varies by buyer and is conditioned by buying role.** Never assume a groupwide

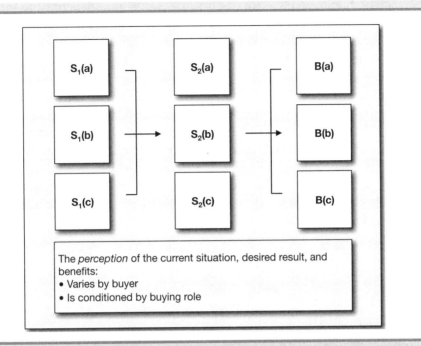

The *perception* of the current situation, desired result, and benefits:
- Varies by buyer
- Is conditioned by buying role

FIGURE 6.6 Different buyers, playing different roles, will have different perceptions of the current situation and the benefits they, individually, expect to receive.

or firmwide perception of the current situation. S_1 refers to individual pain, uncertainty, or opportunity. The difference between one person's perception of S_1 and S_2 is the distance *she* must go to eliminate *her* pain or realize *her* opportunity. The distance her fellow buying committee members must travel is likely different, because they start from different points, have different orientations, and travel a different terrain. Individual perceptions of S_1 might be different because, obviously, people are different, with different needs, desires, responsibilities, and perspectives. What to one person might be a problem in customer service might be a problem in sales effectiveness to another. What to one person might be perceived as increased inefficiency might be seen as eroding profits by another.

2. **Regardless of individual perceptions of the current situation, definable agreed-upon results, S_2, will eliminate everyone's perception of S_1.** Therefore, the importance of getting right the overriding question and objective. If all parties agree on the project's objective, they will be able to visualize a future situation in which their current pain or their existing opportunity is addressed.

3. **The perceived benefits accruing from buyers' perceptions of S_2 will vary by buyer and by buying role.** If S_1 is an ineffective information system and S_2 is the

implementation of an effective one, the user buyer may benefit from increased versatility and efficiency; the economic buyer, from increased efficiency, yes, but primarily as it affects profitability; the technical buyer, from obtaining more sophisticated state-of-the-art capability and functionality.

In Chapter 7, I'll begin to show you how to convince me and each of the other buyers that you and your firm are better, more convincing, and more responsive than anyone else. This persuasion will take you a giant step toward gaining the two to five points that make the difference between winning and losing. Before that, you need to read the following work session, which identifies the buying roles played by individuals on ABC's selection committee and the benefits that will accrue to each once the plan is developed and after it's implemented.

CHAPTER 6 REVIEW

Analyzing the Buyers

To begin to analyze the buyers:

1. Classify the members of the buying team according to the role or roles each will play in making the decision. Each single buyer can play one or more of four possible buying roles: economic, user, technical, coach. A buyer also can play the role of ratifier. A ratifier can play only one additional role: coach.
2. Identify each buyer's perception of S_1, the current situation, remembering that that perception will be conditioned by buying role, position in the organization, and personality.
3. Identify for each buyer the individual benefits that will accrue from achieving S_2, remembering that those benefits will be conditioned by the buyer's role, position in the organization, and personality.
4. If at all possible, develop at least one coach.

WORK SESSION 5: Identifying Buying Roles and Generating Benefits for ABC

In your previous work sessions, you focused on the "logics" of the selling situation: the logical relationship among the current situation (S_1), the desired result (S_2), and the benefits (B) that will accrue, as well as on the logical methodology that will ensure ABC's transition from its current situation to its desired result.

The logics necessarily focus on the ABC organization collectively. You're not selling, however, to an organization but to people within it, people who will evaluate your proposal through the lenses of their own perceptions, desires, and needs. Now, therefore, you must begin to focus on the individuals on the consultant-selection committee.

These are some of your thoughts as you review your notes from the initial meeting with ABC's consultant-selection committee and carefully study Gilmore's interview notes from his follow-up visit. You consult your Logics Worksheet to review the current situation and desired result (from a collective, corporate point of view). Then you complete Cell 1 of the downloadable Psychologics Worksheet, on which you identify the various buyers, their buying roles, and the benefits each will enjoy from having a plan for increasing capacity, as well as from having that plan implemented in a subsequent engagement.

Ray Armstrong, President

You believe that Ray Armstrong is currently the economic buyer because he will give final approval for the study. You realize, however, that if Armstrong has a budget threshold beyond which he will have to gain approval from Consolidated, then someone at Consolidated will be the economic buyer if your or your competitors' proposed fees exceed that limit. Not recalling any discussion of this matter and not finding such a discussion in your colleague's notes, you decide to bring up this issue with Gilmore.

Armstrong appears pleased with ABC's past and present performance. Success has been heavily dependent on the ability of manufacturing to produce at low cost, with high quality and with a high degree of responsiveness to the needs of ABC's customers. However, Armstrong's warning bells are now ringing because the division's performance probably will deteriorate dramatically within the next few years, when, as marketing's forecasts show, product demand will significantly exceed current manufacturing capacity. Armstrong has two other concerns, you believe. One is that ABC must decide quickly on the amount and type of capacity needed because lead times for additional building and/or manufacturing equipment are quite long, perhaps six to twelve or more months. A second concern is that however ABC decides to provide additional capacity, its plan must be thoroughly documented and justified. The plan must be understandable, logical, and convincing to Consolidated, which will have to evaluate the ROI and provide capital funding for the expansion.

Armstrong desires that the consultant's study quickly shows ABC how to provide the capacity it needs by defining the amount and type of capacity required, identifying and evaluating various alternatives for providing that capacity, and documenting the results of its analysis in a report and possible presentation that will convince Consolidated of the need for and the viability of the additional capacity.

When S_2 is reached, Armstrong believes he will have a road map that will show ABC how to get where it wants to be and a report that will help persuade Consolidated to release the necessary funds. To date, Armstrong has a good reputation with the parent company, and he would like to keep that reputation, you believe, for at least two reasons: first, to increase his chances of getting future requests approved, and second, possibly, to increase the likelihood of his own career advancement. You have no hard evidence in this regard, but your research about his employment history indicates that Armstrong's ambitions could take him higher than the presidency of the ABC Division. For these reasons, the outcomes of your potential study will be critically important to Armstrong. Your analysis of Armstrong's buying role and benefits is shown in the first row of Figure 6.7.

Psychologics Worksheet — Cell 1

Individual Buyers' Titles, Roles, and Benefits

"What benefits will accrue to each buyer as/after the desired result(s) are achieved?"

Based upon their respective roles, each buyer's . . .

	Buyer/Title	E	U	T	C	R	Benefits from *Insight* or *Plan*	Benefits from *Implementation*
1	Ray Armstrong, President	✓			red	red	• Road map for ABC • Better-trained internal team • Improved ability to compete for capital funding	• More cost-effective operations • Success for division and employees • Continued good reputation at Consolidated • Perhaps increased opportunities for advancement
2	Anil Gupta, VP Operations		✓				• Through a solid road map, better chance of meeting objectives related to cost, quality, and service performance	• Through successful implementation, protected compensation levels and continued autonomy from Consolidated
3	Marcia Collins, VP Marketing		✓	✓			• A road map for ensuring the maintenance of or improvement in service levels	• Adequate capacity in the right place to ensure current or increased levels of service
4	Paul Morrison, Industrial Engineer		✓	✓			• Opportunity to show analytical ability using his model • Resolution of troubling number of alternatives	• Right amount and type of added capacity in right location to support business and marketing strategies to satisfy demand • Perhaps added prestige of leading teams during implementation
5	Ralph Metzger, Plant Manager		✓	✓			• Assuming a plan to increase capacity at the current site, increased reputation among his staff	• Assuming increased capacity at current site, ability to promote well-deserving supervisors and maintain control

FIGURE 6.7   The Psychologics Worksheet, Cell 1, completed

Anil Gupta, Vice President of Operations

You clearly see Anil Gupta as a user buyer because he has overall responsibility for manufacturing operations and because the study will recommend the best alternative for increasing capacity. Your notes indicate that Gupta has concerns about adding that capacity at the current site because the available space may not be adequate for expansion. Furthermore, even if sufficient space were available, Gupta believes ABC would be vulnerable by having the majority of manufacturing resources centralized at one location. Gupta also suggested the possibility of adding capacity at the satellite sites, although he expressed some doubt that all of ABC's expansion needs could be provided there. Recognizing the wide range of possible expansion alternatives and the capital-intensive nature of the proposed project, Gupta knows that they need a thorough and convincing study.

As vice president of operations, Gupta has the responsibility for producing quality products at competitive costs and for meeting customer delivery requirements in a timely manner. With inadequate capacity, delivery performance will deteriorate, quality could suffer, and costs could rise because of overtime and schedule interruptions to meet rush delivery dates. Gupta's expectations from the study are rather straightforward: He wants the consultants' analysis to produce a well-documented, convincing plan for providing additional capacity. For him, achieving S_2 means that he and his manufacturing team will have a comprehensive plan for providing the additional capacity in the most advantageous manner. Your analysis of Gupta's buying role and benefits is shown in the second row of Figure 6.7.

Marcia Collins, Vice President of Marketing

You conclude that Marcia Collins is a technical buyer because she wants to make certain that the study's methodology uses customer-service levels as a criterion for selecting and evaluating the expansion alternatives. By doing so, Collins believes that customer service must be maintained or improved after additional capacity is implemented. She undoubtedly will also play the role of user buyer because the results of the study will most certainly affect her marketing function and her desire to gain market share. At present, Collins is anxious to see that additional manufacturing capacity is provided to remedy the shortfall that her forecasts predict in just a few years. Without that additional capacity, service levels will deteriorate. She also believes that capacity should not be added at the present site for two reasons: first, because of the shift in product demand away from ABC's current location in the U.S. Midwest; second (and, in this, she agrees with Gupta), because with most of the manufacturing resources in one location, ABC could risk its hard-won reputation for excellent customer service if there is a catastrophe or labor stoppage that disrupts production at that location.

Therefore, Collins not only wants the selected consulting team to develop and evaluate various alternatives for adding manufacturing capacity, she would prefer that the team's recommendation enhance (or, at minimum, not diminish) current service levels. If service levels are used as an evaluation criterion, Collins is confident that the recommended alternative will enable ABC to serve its customers better and contribute to the division's financial and market performance and, consequently, to her own compensation and career advancement. Your analysis of Collins's buying roles and benefits is shown in row three of Figure 6.7.

Paul Morrison, Chief Industrial Engineer

Paul Morrison, you conclude, will also play two buying roles. He's a technical buyer because he will be concerned with the thoroughness and rigor of the proposed methodology. Morrison believes that these qualities will be necessary to address the complex issues involved in selecting the best alternative. Given that he developed the in-house distribution model, he probably will focus on the parts of the methodology that focus on logistics, landed cost, and service levels. He's also a user buyer because he undoubtedly will lead the ABC project team that will use the study's results to plan for and implement the new capacity plan. If your study resulted in ABC's building a new factory, Morrison could become plant manager at that site.

Morrison has expressed several concerns about the current situation. First, although everyone seems to agree that additional capacity is needed, no one has attempted to quantify the amount or its timing. Second, some individuals, he believes, may be pushing their own agendas, advocating expansion alternatives that could be better for themselves than for ABC. Finally, and related to the previous point, he doesn't believe that the current site will support the additional manufacturing capacity needed (though adding at the current site would be advantageous to others, particularly Metzger). Morrison expects the study to produce specific results: to define the amount of capacity necessary to meet the forecast, to evaluate thoroughly the alternatives both quantitatively and qualitatively, and to produce a recommendation that will enable ABC to provide capacity effectively and expeditiously. Your analysis of Morrison's buying roles and benefits is shown in row four of Figure 6.7.

Frank Metzger, Plant Manager

You conclude that Frank Metzger is also both a user and a technical buyer. As plant manager with intimate knowledge of ABC's manufacturing operation, he certainly will be part of the project team that uses the results of the consultant's study to plan and implement the additional capacity. In his technical buyer role, he probably will examine the methodology closely to determine whether it gives adequate consideration to adding capacity at the current facility.

Metzger is concerned that his operations are already approaching capacity and that as demand continues to grow, he will be forced to operate uneconomically (e.g., with excessive overtime, reduced time to maintain equipment, and higher freight costs). Like others, he agrees that ABC badly needs additional manufacturing capacity.

Metzger is looking forward to reviewing the consulting team's quantification of ABC's need for capacity. He is hopeful, however, that the amount of capacity indicated is such that most, if not all, can be accommodated at the existing site, particularly if newer manufacturing technology is utilized. As a result, his managerial responsibilities would increase and he would be able to promote some of his supervisors who have supported him and performed well in the past. Your analysis of Metzger's buying roles and benefits is shown in row five of Figure 6.7.

Examining Your Notes: What's Missing?

In examining your detailed notes on each buyer, you now know what you know and, just as important, what you don't know. For example, none of the buyers, according to your determination, can be considered a coach. This makes you uneasy, given that the situation is competitive and that at least two of your competitors have done previous (and, apparently, good) work for ABC. Those firms could very well have special access to people and intelligence at ABC that you do not and perhaps will not have. According to Anil Gupta, Paramount had been recommended to ABC. That's what he told Gilmore. But as far as you know, Gilmore didn't find out who the recommender was. That person could very well be (or be turned into) a coach. You decide to discuss this matter also with Gilmore, and you red flag the Coach column on Cell 1 of the Psychologics Worksheet (as shown Figure 6.7). Just as troubling, none of the five buyers meets the criteria for a ratifier, who could very well exist at Consolidated and who could strongly influence Armstrong's opinion about whom to select. If you had a coach, you might be able to work with that person to identify the ratifier.

You know that your firm's win rate is considerably lower when you don't have a coach (and, chances are, a competitor does), and you also know that even a strong relationship with an economic buyer means very little when an unidentified ratifier refuses to bless the economic buyer's decision. Accordingly, you also place a red flag in the Ratifier column of the worksheet.

CHAPTER 7

Identifying, Selecting, and Developing Themes

Determining What to Weave in Your Web of Persuasion

n Chapter 6, I indicated that if you're going to write a fully responsive proposal to me, your potential client, you need to do more than meet my buying team's requirements related to the analytical and technical aspects—the logics—of your proposed support. You also need to respond to the psychologics of our situation, to us, to our individual and group concerns, desires, and needs. I'm not devaluing expertise here. I want it. But you're not the only expert around. Your expertise is necessary, but it alone is usually not sufficient. So what else do I want?

In addition to expertise, I want a relationship, built on trust, founded on chemistry and rapport, characterized by understanding and assurance. Although I want to be confident about your technical abilities, I also want to be confident about your willingness to serve me, to put me first, to be there when I need you, to answer questions neither of us anticipated during the business-development process. That's a tall order, but I'm willing to reward you now and perhaps in the future for supporting me in that role.

Let me give you a good example of what I mean. I was once a vice president at RST, one of the world's largest industrial companies. We were introducing a new organizational concept in all our domestic and foreign factories, an effort that would be extraordinarily complex, involve massive change in the organization, and require a high level of rapport between us and the consultants. We were looking for outside support to work together with us in an ill-defined situation to detect problems, resolve issues, and implement solutions that neither of us could anticipate. The risk was potentially high, and the rewards potentially higher. Nobody had tried this sort of thing before, and, obviously, no consultant had ever tried to help someone do it.

None of this, of course, was lost on the consultant who wrote the winning proposal. Here's the first major section of his proposal letter. Study it carefully, and you'll see what I mean.

Our Understanding of Your Situation

During the past few weeks, we appreciated being included in the evolution of your thinking on this difficult project and our potential involvement to help implement your XYZ Cost Concept. This letter concisely describes how we can help you successfully accelerate the worldwide integration.

Over the years, RST has managed its manufacturing on a plant-by-plant basis. As a result, similar and related products were produced using different methods and technology in different locations. For this reason, costs and quality often varied. To reduce variability and costs, you are in the process of establishing integration centers to be responsible for products or related component groups wherever they are manufactured. In other words, each center will be responsible for developing products at the lowest cost and at high quality in order to optimize results.

Each center will be responsible for total worldwide volume for its selected products and for developing a common manufacturing process to improve technology utilization and reduce overhead. In this way, each center will balance design, manufacturing, use of automation, and scheduling. Each will become involved early in the product design effort to set design ground rules to ensure optimum production. Furthermore, each will consolidate worldwide throughput, yields, defect control, costs, inventory, turnaround time, etc., for its product or component responsibility.

Implementation of this concept will be extremely complex. This complexity was emphasized when we reviewed the matrix of centers and locations. Indeed, changes in coordination, measurement and evaluation systems, training, motivation, organizational structure, communications, and control will be significant.

Yet the breadth of these changes is only the first complicating factor. Next is the exceptional magnitude of the change in terms of the number of plants involved, the varieties of locations, countries, and cultures, and the depth of change in your traditional manufacturing style.

In addition, the speed with which the integration will be implemented leaves little opportunity for error. Furthermore, the introduction of the XYZ Cost Concept provides an additional complication of significantly higher product volumes to your company, which is traditionally accustomed to low-volume production.

Finally, no precedent exists for such a complex change except perhaps that which occurred in your own marketing organization.

What this passage has that so many proposals lack is the theme of this chapter, which is *themes*:

The
Highlighted
Essential
Messages that
Express the character of my
Story

What Themes Are

Themes are the *highlighted messages* of your proposal because they are repeated and gain force and emphasis through their repetition. They are *essential messages* because they come from three essential elements of the selling process: my and the other buyers' hot buttons, our evaluation criteria, and your counters to your competition. As one of the best consultants I know once said to me: "To sell consulting services, your client needs to feel as if the two of you grew up in the same house together"—i.e., that you shared the same history, the same story, and that your proposal *expresses the character of that story*.

The writer of the RST proposal knew (and knew that I knew) that the effort would be extraordinarily complex, would involve massive change in my organization, and would require a high level of rapport between the consultants and my people as we all worked together to detect problems, resolve issues, and recommend solutions in a situation that was ill defined, to put it mildly. Recognizing that these three ideas (complexity, change, and working together) were key issues to be addressed during the proposed project, he used them (and others) as themes throughout the document.

In the first sentence, he subtly suggests three of the themes we will discuss here:

> we appreciated being included in the evolution [i.e., "change"] of your think-ing on this difficult project ["complexity"] and our potential involvement ["working together"].

After narrating the past, present, and future of the improved operating concept in the next two paragraphs, he concentrates on two of the themes, beginning with "Yet the breadth of these changes." From there on, he uses *complex*, *change*, and related words 10 times and heightens the effect through parallelism[1] ("breadth of these changes," "exceptional magnitude of the change," "depth of the change"). He also uses many "additive" transitions (*Indeed, Yet, Next, In addition*, and *Finally*) to create a crescendo effect. The flourish comes in the last sentence, which is signaled by "Finally," underscored in importance by "no precedent exists," and concluded by a phrase—"complex change"—that uses both themes together.

The writer doesn't pretend that the task is less than arduous or that he has performed numerous studies similar to this one. Instead, he recognizes my con-cerns (my story) and makes them his own. He knows that I'm anxious and that my colleagues are anxious, and he even intentionally writes the section to make me anxious, to make me recall my anxiety and the high risk involved. But at pre-cisely the right point, in that last sentence, he compliments my organization by suggesting that if any firm can weather the coming storm, it is RST. Well, maybe RST. "Perhaps" RST. Despite the compliment, he implies that we cannot do it alone; despite our considerable resources and expertise, additional support and abilities are crucial. That support is underscored by the document's next heading (which I haven't included). "How We Can Work Together" begins the methods slot, and it continues the proposal's third theme, "working together."

By selecting and playing the right themes, then, the writer demonstrates to me that he understands far more than just the logics of my situation. By the time I finish reading the first section of his proposal, he has reinforced the qualities I saw in him during our several hours of preproposal discussions: his sensitivity to the complexity of human organizations (including mine) and the cultural shocks resulting from change and his ability to work with me and my people construc-tively and competently to implement change. As a result, he increases his and his organization's credibility. He makes me an accepting rather than an objecting or rejecting reader, one much more inclined to agree with his proposal's later discussions of objectives, methods, qualifications, costs, and benefits. And those discussions, like this one, are certainly not boilerplate, nor were they written by a junior "just-happened-to-be-available" consultant who never met me. Clearly, the writer developed his themes specifically for my situation.

Where Themes Come From

You're selling not in a vacuum but in response to my specific situation. That situation is conditioned by what the buyers, individually and collectively, on the one hand, and your competitors, on the other, bring to it. Therefore, you must (1) address the individual needs and desires of me and each of the other buyers, (2) respond to our collective needs and desires, and (3) counter your competition. These three actions provide you with the three sources of themes: hot buttons, evaluation criteria, and counters to the competition, which I'll discuss in turn (Figure 7.1.)

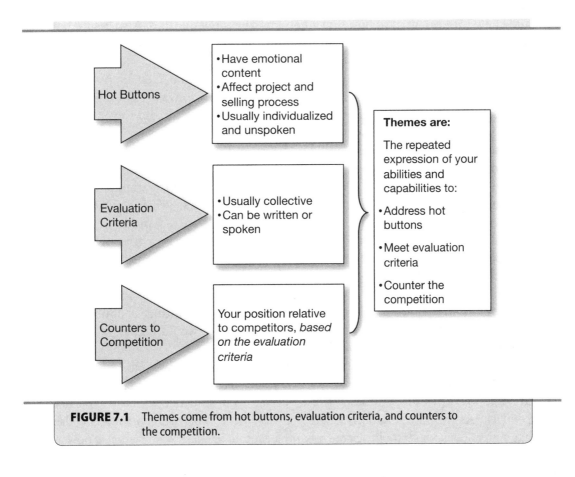

FIGURE 7.1   Themes come from hot buttons, evaluation criteria, and counters to the competition.

Hot Buttons

Hot buttons (Psychologics Worksheet, Cell 2; see Figure 7.2) are needs and desires of individual buyers that can be addressed during your face-to-face meeting with me and other buyers, by altering your project's methodology, and/or by changing your project's team. Hot buttons are almost always psychologically oriented and process oriented. For example, in the RST excerpt, complexity happened to be one of my hot buttons. I was concerned about the complex nature of the project, about all the possible pitfalls, including those I could see and those that I couldn't see at the time but knew would present themselves. Complexity, then, wasn't a result of the study, but it was an issue from my point of view that had to be addressed strategically during the study. Therefore, the writer built into his proposal's methodology specific tasks for managing the study's complexity. And he conditioned my response to that methodology by convincing me, in his proposal's opening section, that he understood the complex nature of our undertaking.

Addressing hot buttons is extremely important in selling your services because your recognizing and acting on my hot buttons significantly helps build the trust and chemistry essential to building a good business relationship. Also, using hot buttons offers you a further advantage: They help you generate additional benefits for your proposal. The following little stories suggest how.

Several years ago, my spouse and I had our house remodeled by people we would never hire again. Their expertise or craftsmanship wasn't at issue—they did a fine job at what we hired them to do. The way they did it, however, caused us unnecessary time, frustration, and anger. In a word, they were slobs. They tracked mud inside, failed to control the dirt and dust, and even left cigarette butts on the floor. As a consequence, my spouse and I returned from work every evening with more work to do: mopping, vacuuming, and, most strenuous of all, controlling our tempers. The problem wasn't with the "what" (their expertise) but with the "how" (the application of that expertise). If we were to remodel our house again, the contractors bidding on the job would be confronted with our unmistakable hot button—call it neatness or cleanliness or just plain consideration.

Note that two effects would occur if the contractors would have addressed that hot button, neither of which involves their technical approach to addressing our problem. First, they would alter how they work for us (assuming, of course, that they weren't already paragons of neatness). Second, we would benefit from that alteration: We would be saved both time and aggravation.

Here's another, but similar, situation. You know how to drive your car, and you know a bit about how your car works, but you don't know very much about how to fix it. So when your car doesn't work, you take it to someone with the expertise you lack. As in some situations where you have little expertise and someone else has a great deal, you have little control and feel quite helpless. Knowledge is power,

Psychologics Worksheet					Cell 2
Hot Buttons					*"What desires or concerns of each buyer must be addressed?"*
Buyer's Hot Buttons*	How Addressed	SA	M	PO	Benefits to Each Buyer from Addressing His/Her Hot Buttons
1					
2					
3					
4					
5					

*Hot button: Process-related desire or concern of a buyer that will affect your sales approach (SA), project's methodology (M), and/or project organization (PO); often personal, having emotional rather than technical content. Use single words or short phrases such as:

- Thorough, integrated, balanced, or flexible approach
- Urgency (e.g., to get quick results)
- Creativity
- Control
- Fear or change

- Project complexity
- Objectivity
- Sensitivity to . . .
- Involvement
- Teaching/training

FIGURE 7.2   Psychologics Worksheet, Cell 2: Hot buttons

and, in this case, you have very little of either. When you pay the bill and the expert tells you the problem wasn't the relatively inexpensive fan belt but the much more expensive starter or alternator, you have no way of evaluating that claim, no way of knowing for certain whether you're being "taken." Worse, even if you're not being taken, you have no way of knowing that you're not. So when you take your car to a mechanic, you have a hot button—call it trust or honesty or clear communication.

Again, note that if your hot button had been addressed, two effects would have occurred, neither of which involves the mechanic's technical expertise for addressing your problem. First, the mechanic would have to change how he works with you (for example, by calling you for approval if the solution turned out to be different from or more expensive than what you anticipated, or by returning to you the damaged part, or by clearly showing you how or why the part was damaged). Second, you would benefit from that change. You would feel better. You'd be less anxious or apprehensive and more certain, not that the car got fixed but that what was wrong got fixed.

I can think of three principles these two stories share:

1. **Those without expertise who have to work with those who have it are frequently cautious, uncertain, and distrustful.** If I'm thinking about having you do a project for me, I'm doing so because you probably have knowledge, skills, or experience that I lack. Because what you tell me will be based on the knowledge that I lack and that you have, I don't have the proper framework to evaluate the veracity of your claims.
2. **If I have a hot button and you choose to address it, you will have to work with me in a certain way.** Quite likely, this means you will work with me in a different way than you would work with another potential client on a similar project. Addressing hot buttons usually affects how you conduct your project.
3. **If you do indeed address my hot button, I will benefit.** Because my hot button reflects one of my needs, desires, or concerns, I will have that need, desire, or concern satisfied or addressed if you respond to that hot button.

Consequently, for every hot button you identify on Cell 2 of the Psychologics Worksheet (Figure 7.2), you should generate at least one benefit that accrues from your addressing it. Take, for example, one of Ray Armstrong's possible hot buttons discussed in the work session of this chapter: teaching/training. A solid teaching/training component in the project could be beneficial to him. It could help produce for Armstrong the beginnings of a more competent internal team, one that better appreciates different functional disciplines and has a broader, multidisciplined view rather than a parochial orientation toward company operations.

Evaluation Criteria

Hot buttons as well as evaluation criteria (Psychologics Worksheet, Cell 4; see Figure 7.3) are used by me and others to evaluate your proposal (and in the case of hot buttons, often subconsciously so). Whereas hot buttons are always individual considerations, evaluation criteria are collective considerations—that is, shared and agreed upon. While most hot buttons have emotional content (involving individual needs and desires), evaluation criteria generally have technical content (involving requirements, specifications, and the like).

That said, it's important to note that one category of hot buttons does have technical content: the hot buttons of technical buyers. Marcia Collins has a hot button (conditioned by her technical buyer role) related to "maintaining or improving service levels." In preparing your proposal to ABC, you certainly would want to include the impact on service levels as a hot button. But unless the focus on service levels is shared by all the members of the buying committee, it isn't likely to be one of the group's evaluation criteria.

Psychologics Worksheet		Cell 4
Evaluation Process/Criteria	*"What process/criteria will the buying committee use, collectively?"*	
"What is the prospect's budget for this project?"		
"How will the selection decision be made?"		

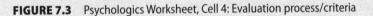

	"What collective evaluation criteria will be used?"	Knockout	Relative Weighting
1			
2			
3			
4			
5			
			100%

FIGURE 7.3　Psychologics Worksheet, Cell 4: Evaluation process/criteria

Though evaluation criteria are collective and may be written in a request for proposal (RFP), they are not always specified in a section of the RFP that lists and sometimes weights the criteria to be used in evaluating the proposal (see Appendix G on reading and responding to RFPs). The following three criteria were essential to consider in a recent proposal to manage a U.S. hazardous waste program, even though the criteria did not appear in a lengthy RFP:

- **National consistency:** To demonstrate our commitment to accomplishing national goals, consistency in approaches used to set priorities is essential in a decentralized program. The strategic management framework identifies key areas where national consistency is needed to ensure that we are achieving progress in meeting national goals.
- **Flexibility:** Flexibility in setting program priorities is key to the regions and states closest to environmental needs. The strategic management framework must preserve regional and state flexibility while assuring progress toward national goals.
- **Trade-offs:** We cannot implement the entire agenda at once. Strategic management planning recognizes the need for trade-offs. We all must articulate

these trade-offs and ensure that we make informed and defensible decisions about the resulting environmental and programmatic impacts.

The previous list wasn't called evaluation criteria at all, but "Principles governing strategic management of the program." However, these principles were used in evaluating the proposal, and the proposers certainly could have used themes such as consistency and flexibility to increase the persuasiveness of their document.

Two final notes about evaluation criteria. First, as Figure 7.3 indicates, you should try to weight the evaluation criteria even if they haven't been weighted in an RFP. As we'll see below, you will be better able to select your themes if you indicate the evaluation criterion's degree of importance. Second, you should designate which criteria are "knockout." Sometimes called threshold criteria, knockout criteria are those that you must meet or you will be eliminated from the competition. One example of a knockout criterion could be "Must have an office in Kuala Lumpur." If you do, you're in the running. If you don't, you're knocked out of the competition.

Counters to the Competition

Included in Cell 5 of the Psychologics Worksheet (Figure 7.4) are counters to the competition, the selling points that allow you to differentiate yourself from the known or likely competition's approaches or expertise. If you are a small engineering consulting firm bidding against a larger, more diverse competitor (for example, a broad-line management consulting firm), you might try to claim that your narrower focus and your size are strengths. That is, the project, you might argue, involves an IT problem requiring a rather narrow IT solution, especially by a consultancy whose relatively small client base allows for better, more client-oriented service. Of course, the larger firm would argue quite differently. Similarly, if you headed a team of in-house professionals proposing a particular study and if management was thinking of soliciting outside bids for the same study, you would probably need to argue that your team's greater familiarity with your own organization and its situation was highly advantageous and beneficial.

In identifying your competition, you should always consider potential in-house competitors as well as the prospect's other initiatives. The latter and your proposed initiative are always competing for the allocation of the prospect's scarce resources. In generating counters to the competition, however, you must consider this as well: Counters to the competition need to relate to the evaluation criteria. Assume that yours is an international firm with 25 offices around the world and that the competitor is a "single-shingle" outfit—one consultant, perhaps a university professor, operating out of a home office. Your large firm with strategically placed offices offers you little or no competitive advantage unless your size and location are meaningful for the proposed project—that is, unless the evaluation criteria make them meaningful.

Psychologics Worksheet			Cell 5
Competition		"*Based upon the evaluation criteria, how does the prospect compare you with competitors?*"	
Competitors	Considering the Prospect's Evaluation Criteria for *This Opportunity* . . .		
	Competitors' Strengths		Competitors' Weaknesses
• In-House/Other Initiatives			
•			
•			
	Your Strengths		Your Weaknesses
• You			
"How might you counter competitors' strengths or exploit their weaknesses?"		"How might competitors counter your strengths, exploit your weaknesses, or redefine the overriding question?"	
•		•	
•		•	
•		•	

FIGURE 7.4   Psychologics Worksheet, Cell 5: Competition

Selecting the Themes

Themes, as we've seen, come from three potential sources—hot buttons, evaluation criteria, and counters to the competition. If you have downloaded the complete Psychologics Worksheet, you will notice that arrows from each of these sources point to the Themes cell (Cell 6). However, not all hot buttons, evaluation criteria, and counters to the competition should become themes. Themes are your *highlighted* essential messages, and they can be highlighted, like the italicized word in this sentence, only if other things are not. Therefore, you want to use themes sparingly, choosing perhaps three to five in an average-length proposal. Given that your Psychologics Worksheet might have as many as 20 hot buttons, evaluation criteria, and counters to the competition, which three to five should become themes? These are my suggestions:

1. **Concerning hot buttons**, choose the desires and concerns of medium- and high-power-base buyers. As the Psychologics Worksheet, Cell 3 (see Figure 7.5) suggests, you should indicate each buyer's power base and receptivity. *Power base* refers to a buyer's relative influence in *this* buying opportunity, not to the buyer's general level of influence within the organization. *Receptivity* refers to a buyer's relative reception to your selling efforts to date, from "++" (a strong

ally) to "−−" (an outright enemy). Note the lack of a neutral rating. Eventually, everyone will have to say "Yea" or "Nay."

2. **Concerning evaluation criteria**, select those on which you believe you rate highly or that the buyers weight highly.
3. **Concerning counters to the competition**, choose those that provide an opportunity to significantly counter competitors' arguments or moves, remembering that your competitors also can include in-house players or another of the potential client's initiatives competing for the same resources.

Selecting your themes is a dynamic and creative process because the themes you end up with will not necessarily be phrased the same way or even be the same as one or more of the hot buttons, evaluation criteria, or counters to the competition. Some of your themes will be combinations or transmutations of these.

One likely combination exists in the ABC situation. "Service levels" is a hot button with obvious importance for Collins. Paul Morrison's hot button, "well-defined and agreed-upon evaluation criteria," is similarly important to him. To leverage both hot buttons, you could combine them. When you discuss Morrison's desire for well-defined and agreed-upon evaluation criteria, you can use service levels as an example of the kind of criteria the study will employ.

The hazardous waste example discussed previously offers an example of a possible transmutation. "National consistency" and "flexibility" were two of the principles established to govern the program, and those two principles would

Psychologics Worksheet							Cell 3
Buyer Receptivity							*"How receptive is each buyer to your efforts to date?"*
	Power Base			Receptivity			
	L	M	H	−−	−	+	++	Rationale for Your Ratings
1								
2								
3								
4								
5								

FIGURE 7.5   Psychologics Worksheet, Cell 3: Buyer receptivity

seem incompatible and perhaps even contradictory. But a new theme could emerge from them—call it "balance." That is, a salable quality of the proposers could be the ability to understand the national need for consistency but to remain flexible by balancing that need in light of the states' and regions' local circumstances. This theme of balance also leverages the third principle listed: "trade-offs."

Developing the Themes

The downloadable Themes Development Worksheet is shown in Figure 7.6, although you won't be able to see it very well in this book. That's because it needs to be printed out in 11″ × 17″ or in A4. As several chapters in Part 3: Proposal Preparation illustrate, the worksheet allows you to develop much of the persuasive content you will employ both during the proposal process and in the proposal itself.

Using this worksheet, you can create a web of persuasion throughout your communication. The worksheet uses some of the generic-structure slots you're already familiar with:

> Given my organization's SITUATION, these are the METHODS, out of a universe of possible methods, that you will use to solve our problem or realize our opportunity. Given those methods, these are your QUALIFICATIONS for conducting them. Given those methods and qualifications, these are the BENEFITS we will receive from your solving our problem or realizing our opportunity.

This logic can be applied to each of your proposal's themes, and in a completely filled-out worksheet the argument gets developed both horizontally and vertically. From left to right, the worksheet spins a web of persuasion related to your theme. Assuming, for example, that your theme derives from a hot button, you will be demonstrating your responsiveness to that hot button in four different ways: first, that you understand its existence and my desire to address it; second, that your approach is designed to consider it; third, that you are qualified to act on it; and fourth, that I will benefit by your acting on it. The bottom of the Themes Development Worksheet contains an example of a theme, "urgency," developed horizontally.

When the worksheet is expanded to contain several themes, an argument will begin to be developed vertically for several of the proposal's major slots. For example, a completed worksheet would supply you with several good reasons for why you have designed your methodology as you have and for why you believe you are best qualified to conduct the project.

Themes Development Worksheet

Prospect: _____ Date: __ / __ / __

1) Selected Theme		2) Situation	3) Methodology	4) Qualifications	5) Benefits
"What repeated messages will increase your probability of winning?"		*"Given the current situation, what do the buyers need related to this theme?"*	*"Given this need, how have you designed your methodology or project organization to meet it?"*	*"Given those methods, how are you qualified to perform them, related to that need?"*	*"Given those methods and qualifications, how will the buyers benefit by your meeting that need?"*
		State as prospect's needs… (Focus on the Prospect)	…which will be met by you (Focus on You)	State as good reasons (Focus on You)	State as good reasons (Focus on the Prospect)
Theme	Source* HB EC CC				
1		Because . . . , you need . . .	Therefore, we will . . .		
2		Because . . . , you need . . .	Therefore, we will . . .		
3		Because . . . , you need . . .	Therefore, we will . . .		

* **HB = hot buttons; EC = evaluation criteria; CC = counters to competition**

Example: Urgency	Because forecasted demand will soon outstrip capacity and because building new capacity will require long lead times, you need a study that produces a decision quickly.	Therefore, we will involve management in preparing the final report, which will be the proposal to Consolidated, thereby eliminating one step in your decision-making process.	We will immediately commit a project team with the practical experience to develop and execute a work plan that will minimize the study's elapsed time.	By our conducting this study expeditiously, you will have time for detailed planning and implementation, which will allow maintained customer service during the transition.

FIGURE 7.6 Themes Development Worksheet

In the following work session, you'll see clearly how these techniques can be applied when you fill out a Themes Development Worksheet relevant to the opportunity at ABC. This worksheet is *very important*: It supplies a substantial amount of the persuasive content that will help you when you prepare your proposal. You also will be filling out Psychologics Worksheet cells related to hot buttons, evaluation criteria, and counters to the competition. I should note that you probably will find that filling out these cells is time-consuming. However, over time, as you gain experience, I guarantee that you will write the proposal itself much more quickly and persuasively. Additionally, on those occasions when others help you prepare your proposal, the worksheets provide an excellent method for communicating a consistent message to your team and, therefore, help you avoid the characteristics of so many of the proposals I've read that sound like they have been written by different people and then cobbled together.

Identifying, Selecting, and Developing Themes

1. **Identifying themes.** Themes are the repeated expression of your abilities and capabilities to address hot buttons, meet evaluation criteria, and counter the competition:
   - **Hot buttons** are needs and desires of individual buyers that can be addressed during your face-to-face meetings with me and other buyers, by altering your project's methodology, and/or by altering your project staffing. Hot buttons almost always have emotional content.
   - **Evaluation criteria** are collective needs and desires of the buyers. They often are written, especially in an RFP. Evaluation criteria typically have technical content.
   - **Counters to the competition** are your strengths relative to the competition vis-à-vis the specific evaluation criteria for this proposal opportunity.

2. **Selecting themes.** Themes should be selected from:
   - **Hot buttons** of medium- and high-power-base buyers whose receptivity you want to maintain or increase. *Power base* refers to a buyer's relative influence in this buying opportunity, not to the buyer's general level of influence within his or her firm. *Receptivity* refers to a buyer's relative receptivity to your selling efforts to date.
   - **Evaluation criteria** on which you believe you rate highly or that the buyers weight highly
   - **Counters to the competition** that provide you with an opportunity to significantly counter competitors' arguments or moves, remembering that your competition can also include in-house (do-it-themselves) options or other initiatives competing for the same resources

3. **Developing themes.** Themes spin a web of persuasion throughout the proposal. They can be developed by using the Themes Development Worksheet, which uses four proposal slots:
   - **SITUATION:** Given the problem or opportunity, what is needed by the potential client, related to this theme?
   - **METHODS:** Given that need, how will the project be configured, related to this theme?
   - **QUALIFICATIONS:** Given those methods, how are you qualified to perform them, related to this theme?
   - **BENEFITS:** Given those methods and qualifications, what benefits will accrue, related to this theme?

WORK SESSION 6: Identifying Hot Buttons and Evaluation Criteria, Countering the Competition, and Developing the Themes for ABC

You understand that before you can develop your themes, you must identify the buyers' hot buttons and evaluation criteria as well as determine how you will counter your competition.

Identifying Hot Buttons

You know that hot buttons involve the buying team members' desires or concerns about the project and therefore have to be addressed by the way you and your team propose to conduct the project. You also know, because consultant Gilmore has told you and because you've seen it over and again in discussions with Gilmore and in his notes, that one of the hot buttons is thoroughness. Armstrong said the study needs to be "thorough and convincing." Anil Gupta said the same. Morrison hinted at the same. Given these repetitions—hardly coincidental, you believe—it's quite likely that Armstrong first sang the tune and that the others joined in the harmony.

That tune probably sounds good to the others, but for different reasons based on their buying roles and even their personalities. For Armstrong, thoroughness is a means by which he can achieve his goal of remaining competitive and persuading Consolidated to provide the capital funding. So thoroughness to him has an economic-buyer, bottom-line meaning. For Morrison, however, because he's a technical buyer and because of his background and temperament, thoroughness may mean something quite different: perhaps the logical rigor required in a project of some complexity, a project whose alternatives are being advocated, he believes, without a comprehensive analytical basis. Those alternatives, according to Morrison, need to be examined thoroughly and convincingly, ideally by using his distribution model.

So as you develop your hot buttons, you try to remember that the roles individuals play on the selection committee influence their expectations and thus the hot buttons themselves and how they are construed. You also realize that detecting hot buttons is something of an art because you're not necessarily dealing with hard data but with feelings, desires, perceptions, and hidden agendas. You have to try to get below the obvious and into the personalities, the "inside the buyers' heads" issues, and the psychologics, because hot buttons almost always have emotional content.

For example, Armstrong said something to Morrison, who remarked about it—almost as an afterthought—to Gilmore. You missed it when the two of you discussed his meetings as well as the first two times you went through Gilmore's notes, but this time it struck you as possibly important. Armstrong had encouraged Morrison and his project team to develop the in-house distribution model because he had been convinced that doing the project in house was both feasible and cost-effective. Armstrong also believed "that the project would provide a beneficial learning experience, so he gave his approval to proceed."

Armstrong, it appears, not only desires professional development but actively supports it. And, it strikes you, he has a good many managers who need it. Collins, for example, appears to know little about the operations outside of marketing. She certainly knows little about manufacturing, a point she readily admitted to Gilmore. Most likely, manufacturing and marketing don't talk very much to each other, even though what the one produces the other must sell and even though the selling itself and the customer service that goes along with it must rely on accurate production schedules, quality production, and the like. Frank Metzger, it appears, is in a similar position, knowing much about manufacturing but far less about marketing.

So if Armstrong is into teaching/training (that's how you decide to phrase this potential hot button, although "professional development" and "staff development" are other options), maybe you can find a way to build teaching, training, and team building into your methodology.

You're particularly sensitive to this hot button because of the recent experience of one of your colleagues. He had bid on but lost a proposal to a competitor. Following up, he called the company to try to determine why the project had been given to another firm. The winning firm, he was told, had included a significant training component in its methodology. In response, your colleague remarked that no one he interviewed had said anything about a training component. Every bidder, came the reply, was told the same thing. Perhaps every bidder was. Perhaps your colleague had missed a hot button that his competitor had detected and capitalized on. Perhaps the competitor was more adept at reading between the lines and getting below the surface.

As you turn to the hot buttons cell (Cell 2; see Figure 7.7), you try to keep four things in mind:

- First, hot buttons aren't always explicitly stated. In searching for them, you should examine not only what was said but also what was left unsaid, or said between the lines, or said just below the surface. You're looking for the psychological, the emotional, not just the logical.
- Second, hot buttons can be conditioned by the buyer's role. For example, cost-related matters are likely to be hot buttons of an economic buyer or of a chief financial officer playing a technical buyer.
- Third, to make it easier to convert them into themes, you should try to designate hot buttons by key words or short phrases, such as thoroughness or complexity or involvement/respect.

- Fourth, for every hot button you detect, you should generate a benefit that will accrue from your addressing that hot button during the project. The likelihood of these benefits accruing often sways a buyer toward one competitor versus another.

Your completed Cell 2 looks like Figure 7.7. The red flags indicate your current uncertainty about exactly how the hot buttons should be addressed. Those specific tactics you decide to bring up with Gilmore.

Identifying Evaluation Criteria

Here, you are troubled. As far as you can tell, Gilmore identified no evaluation criteria during his discussions with ABC. True, the technical buyers have hot buttons that they, singly, will use to evaluate the proposal. But no shared evaluation criteria exist—at least none that you know of. And Gilmore, as far as you know, didn't ask

Psychologics Worksheet						Cell 2
Hot Buttons		*"What desires or concerns of each buyer must be addressed?"*				
Buyer's Hot Buttons	How Addressed	SA	M	PO	Benefits to Each Buyer from Addressing His/Her Hot Buttons	
1 **Armstrong**: • Comprehensiveness • Thoroughness • ROI/Bottom Line • Teaching/Training	red	✓			• Because report will be thorough, comprehensive, well documented, and directed to Consolidated, improved ability to receive capital funding and expedited process for getting it • Beginnings of a sound internal team	
2 **Gupta:** • Thoroughness	red		✓		• Credibility from leading development of a plan accepted by Consolidated	
3 **Collins**: • Service Levels • Risk	red		✓	✓	• Maintained, if not increased, service levels	
4 **Morrison**: • Thoroughness/Logical Rigor/Complexity • Involvement/Respect	red		✓	✓	• Perhaps added prestige/responsibility of leading teams to implement selected plan at new sites	
5 **Metzger:** • Consideration of Metzger's preferred option	red		✓	✓	• If capacity is increased at the current site, Metzger will have the ability to promote well-deserving supervisors and to maintain control	

* Address hot buttons through your sales approach (SA) and/or by altering your proposed methodology (M) and project organization (PO).

FIGURE 7.7   The hot buttons, analyzed

about them. This fact has two ramifications. First, you cannot fill out Cell 4 for the evaluation criteria; second, because your counters to the competition (as well as your analysis of your and the competitors' teams) need to be articulated in relation to those criteria, you must consider suspect everything you list on Cell 5 for the competition. Because you haven't identified the evaluation criteria, you could be at a significant competitive disadvantage, especially since ABC has had good experience with one or more of your competitors.

It occurs to you that if a consultant-selection committee hasn't identified evaluation criteria, a consultant has the opportunity to "help" the buyers identify those criteria. This is a win-win situation. The buyers win because they will have evaluation criteria that they can apply during their evaluation of the proposals. You win because you can influence the buyers so that the criteria are favorable to you—or at least not unfavorable.

Your completed (uncompleted, really) Cell 4 is shown in Figure 7.8. It contains a global red flag for the lack of evaluation criteria, as well as additional red flags for other information about which you haven't a clue: ABC's budget for this study and the process in which it will engage to select a consultant. Both these items, you believe, are crucial. ABC might very well have a budget for this study, and if you bid beyond it, you could trigger another economic buyer, probably at Consolidated,

Psychologics Worksheet		Cell 4
Evaluation Process/Criteria	*"What process/criteria will the buying committee use, collectively?"*	
"What is the prospect's budget for this project?"	Unknown red	
"How will the selection decision be made?"	Unknown red	

"What collective evaluation criteria will be used?"	Knockout	Relative Weighting
1		
2		
3 red		
4		
5		
		100%

FIGURE 7.8 The evaluation criteria, analyzed

thereby introducing another buyer into the equation, of whom you would be completely unaware. That process could be one part of ABC's decision-making efforts to select a consultant, another crucial element about which you're uncertain. You know very well that a coach could help you with both of these key elements of the proposal-development process. You're becoming increasingly aware that having a coach (or, ideally, coaches) is much more important than you had anticipated.

Analyzing the Competition

At the end of your initial meeting with ABC, Gilmore asked which other consulting firms were likely to bid on the project. Anil Gupta named three competitors. One is a firm similar to your own, with similar capabilities, against whom Paramount has competed numerous times. The other two are local companies specializing in facilities planning, plant layout, materials handling, and productivity improvement. In fact, ABC used one of those consultants several years earlier to help solve a materials-handling problem.

Your task is threefold: first, to understand these competitors' strengths and weaknesses relative to those of Paramount; second, to determine Paramount's strengths and weaknesses relative to the competition's; and third, to determine how you can leverage your own strengths and exploit each competitor's weaknesses. Of course, you also want to put yourself in your competitors' shoes and think about how they might exploit your weaknesses. To help you complete this task, you turn to Cell 5 to analyze the competition (Figure 7.9), and following are some of your thoughts as you do so.

Gilmore knows the capabilities of your major competitor all too well. Paramount has competed against it with lackluster results. Once Paramount won, three times it lost, and, on one occasion, Paramount and the competitor both lost to a third firm. Because this competitor's capabilities are every bit as diverse and strong as Paramount's, you believe it's important to have much more intelligence about it. On the project Paramount won, for example, did the client make available this competitor's proposal? If so, what did the proposal contain, and what can you learn from it? On the studies Paramount lost, was Gilmore able to find out not only why Paramount lost but also why this competitor won? In all these situations, did the proposal-evaluation committees use evaluation sheets or circulate memos or otherwise keep records of their deliberations, and if so, did Gilmore request access to those documents? If he did not get insight at the time, can he get it now? Have there been other instances when your firm (but not Gilmore specifically) bid against this competitor on similar kinds of studies, and if so, what lessons were learned?

At this point, you wonder if your firm even has a "lessons learned" process, an established procedure for answering questions such as the preceding and a database containing the answers. You decide to discuss this issue with Gilmore.

Psychologics Worksheet		Cell 5
Competition		*"Based upon the evaluation criteria, how does the prospect compare you with competitors?"*
Competitors	Considering the Prospect's Evaluation Criteria for *This Opportunity* . . .	
	Competitors' Strengths	Competitors' Weaknesses [red]
• A major competitor	• strong, diversified consulting skills • capabilities equal to our own	need to discuss with Gilmore
• Local "A" and Local "B"	• specialized capabilities in some relevant functional areas • have performed satisfactory work for ABC (Local "B")	• may not be sufficiently experienced or creative to identify full range of expansion alternatives • probably lack marketing abilities needed to assess forecasts • probably don't have adequate logistics analysis capabilities • may lack financial analysis abilities to evaluate alternatives convincingly • may not have sufficient staff to initiate and complete study quickly • may not be sufficiently knowledgeable to evaluate qualitative factors
	Your Strengths [red]	Your Weaknesses [red]
• You	need to discuss with Gilmore	need to discuss with Gilmore
	"How might you counter competitors' strengths or exploit their weaknesses?"	"How might competitors counter your strengths, exploit your weaknesses, or redefine the overriding question?"
	• Emphasize project's comprehensiveness, requiring wide range of functional skills • Counter Local "B's" previous experience by discussing successful projects for similar companies • Find a way to use Morrison's model • Bring Consolidated into the loop to compress time needed for top-level approvals	Need to discuss with Gilmore [red]

FIGURE 7.9   The competition, analyzed

This competitor's weaknesses? Perhaps because of its success rate against Paramount and because of its excellent reputation, your competitor may be somewhat complacent in addressing ABC's needs. Or perhaps the ABC project may not be important enough for it to mount a major proposal effort. But all this, you realize, is pure speculation, and dangerous speculation at that. You're wooing *yourself* into complacency (and making yourself feel less anxious) by surmising that this fierce competitor, this firm that has beaten Paramount all too often, will suddenly become complacent (and just at the right time, too—when you are preparing this proposal). Nevertheless, you record these supposed weaknesses in the designated place on Cell 5, making a mental note that you're not very satisfied with your analysis.

You have just as much difficulty assessing the two local competitors, but for different reasons: You're not familiar with them, and you haven't found any details listed in your research on consulting firms. However, you suspect that they have strong capabilities in specific functional areas to be addressed during the proposed study. And you know, of course, that one of those companies has a major strength: It has already worked successfully with ABC. An equally important strength will be their cost. Since their proposed fees could be tens of thousands of dollars less than yours, how will you be able to communicate value for your higher-cost service? Since they aren't full-service firms, these competitors have definite weaknesses, you believe, because they don't have expertise in all the functional areas to be addressed during the project, including (among others) customer service and supply chain analysis, nor do they have sufficient experience and knowledge to properly evaluate the critical qualitative factors. In addition, their staffs may be too small to enable them to initiate and complete the study quickly, which is a major concern (a hot button, you hope) to key ABC management.

Your proposal strategy will have to stress the comprehensive nature of the project, which will demand a wide range of business skills that probably are beyond the more functional capabilities of these two firms. But you also must stress your considerable strength in the specialized skills of these smaller firms while convincing ABC that it needs more than such skills. You can counter the one firm's successful experience with ABC by stressing Paramount's successful completion of similar studies for comparable companies. Above all, you will have to stress the added value provided by your full-service firm and perhaps the risks to ABC of choosing a consulting firm whose more narrow focus could result in a study that is less comprehensive and thorough.

In these situations, there are always two other potential competitors: in-house competition and other initiatives competing for the same resources that would have to be used for your project.

- **Concerning in-house competition:** Morrison admitted to Gilmore that he had volunteered to do the study in-house. For all you know, Morrison may be working behind the scenes even now to sell this approach. Or, during the selection process, he could take one or another of the consultant's methodologies and try to convince Armstrong that Morrison's team could use it. You consider these possibilities unlikely, however. Besides, you undoubtedly will have good themes to counter this in-house competition. Because you decide that in-house competition is unlikely, you don't complete that portion on Cell 5.
- **Concerning other initiatives:** It would be helpful if you knew ABC's strategic direction, but you note a red flag next to that item on Cell 1 of your Logics Worksheet. By understanding ABC's strategic direction, you could anchor your proposal's argument by clearly linking the proposed initiative with that direction. Nevertheless, you are confident that this initiative is absolutely vital not only for ABC's health but also for its survival. You decide, therefore, not to include that analysis in Cell 5, which, in modified form, looks like the one shown in Figure 7.9.

Selecting and Developing the Themes

In selecting your themes, you pay close attention to the analysis of power base and receptivity in Cell 3 (Figure 7.10).

This information helps you determine which hot buttons you want to emphasize. For example, although Metzger has a hot button ("Consideration of his preferred option)," Metzger is a low-power-base buyer, and your time will be better spent trying to persuade the more influential buyers. Metzger, moreover, also has a "−" receptivity rating, probably preferring one of the competitors (and likely a coach for it). Little you do will persuade him to support you. The themes you select, which are displayed in Figure 7.11, will be developed on your Themes Development Worksheet (Figure 7.12a and 7.12b), which will supply your proposal and presentation with the majority of its persuasion. The entire Themes Development Worksheet can be downloaded from http://web.me.com/rfreed/ Writing_Winning_Business_Proposals/Home.html.

Psychologics Worksheet							Cell 3
Buyers' Power Base and Receptivity							*"How receptive is each buyer to your efforts to date?"*
	Power Base			Receptivity			Reason for Your Ratings
	L	M	H	−−	−	+	++	
1			✓			✓		*(Armstrong)* red
2		✓				✓		*(Gupta)* red
3		✓			✓			*(Collins)* red
4		✓			✓			*(Morrison)* red
5	✓				✓			*(Metzger)* Metzger undoubtedly prefers one of the boutiques

FIGURE 7.10 Power base and receptivity, analyzed

Psychologics Worksheet	Cell 6
Themes	*"What repeated messages best characterize the Prospect's story and/or differentiate you?"*

Themes Come from Hot Buttons, Evaluation Criteria, and Counters to the Competition
1 Urgency
2 Comprehensiveness/Thoroughness/Complexity
3 Teaching/Training
4 Well-defined and agreed-upon evaluation criteria
5 Broad business perspective/extensive functional skills

FIGURE 7.11 The identified themes

Themes Development Worksheet

Prospect: _____ Date: ___ / ___ / ___

1) Selected Theme		2) Situation	3) Methodology
"What repeated messages will increase your probability of winning?"		*"Given the current situation, what do the buyers need related to this theme?"*	*"Given this need, how have you designed your methodo-logy or project organization to meet it?"*
Theme	Source* HB EC CC	State as prospect's needs . . . (Focus on the Prospect)	. . . which will be met by you (Focus on You)
1 Well-defined and agreed-upon evaluation criteria	✓	Because of the many and varied proposed expansion alternatives, you need well-defined and agreed-upon criteria for evaluating them.	Therefore, we will conduct strategy sessions with all relevant ABC managers to gain consensus on and establish the proper criteria.
2 Teaching/Training	✓	Because this will be a cross-functional study, ABC has the opportunity to train its management to analyze and plan for future manufacturing capacity.	Therefore, we will form a joint ABC/Paramount study team, with ABC's managers playing an integral role.
3 Urgency	✓ ✓	Because forecasted demand will soon outstrip capacity and because building new capacity will require long lead times, you need a study that produces a decision quickly.	Therefore, we will involve mgmt. in preparing the final report (the proposal to Consolidated) to eliminate one step in your decision-making process.

FIGURE 7.12a The Themes Development Worksheet's developed themes (columns 1–3)

Themes Development Worksheet

Theme	Source* HB EC CC	4) Qualifications "Given those methods, how are you qualified to perform them, related to that need?" State as good reasons (Focus on You)	5) Benefits "Given those methods and qualifications, how will the buyers benefit by your meeting that need?" State as good reasons (Focus on the Prospect)
1) Selected Theme "What repeated messages will increase your probability of winning?"			
1 Well-defined and agreed-upon evaluation criteria	✓	Our team understands the range of potential criteria and is adept at leading strategy sessions to secure consensus.	Because the final decision will be based on agreed-to criteria, the selected alternative will be "owned" by your management team.
2 Teaching/Training	✓	Our people are experts in transferring knowledge, building teams, and managing and implementing change.	ABC management will have the ability to update the study and assess capacity needs as business conditions change in the future.
3 Urgency	✓ ✓	We can immediately commit a project team with the practical experience to develop and execute a work plan that will minimize the study's elapsed time.	By our conducting this study expeditiously, you will have more time to manage customer service and other important issues during the transition.

FIGURE 7.12b The Themes Development Worksheet's developed themes (columns 1, 4, and 5)

In the first column of each row, you record a theme; for example:

> Well-defined and agreed-upon evaluation criteria

In the second column (Situation; Figure 7.12a), you state ABC's needs related to that theme, follow the worksheet's prompts, and therefore use the sentence structure "Because . . . you need. . . ." In this column, the focus (and therefore the subject of the sentence) is the prospect, what the prospect needs given the current situation:

> Because of the many and varied proposed expansion alternatives, you need well-defined and agreed-upon criteria for evaluating them.

In the third column (Methodology; Figure 7.12a), you explain how your study will address that need. In this column, the focus is on you, on what you will do to move the prospect away from the current situation and toward the desired result:

> Therefore, we will conduct strategy sessions with all relevant ABC managers to gain consensus on and establish the proper criteria.

In the fourth column (Qualifications; Figure 7.12b), you explain your qualifications for addressing the need. In this column, the focus is again on you, on how you are qualified to do what you claim you will do:

> Our team understands the range of potential criteria and is adept at leading strategy sessions to secure consensus.

In the last column (Benefits; Figure 7.12b), you state the benefits of meeting the need. In this column, the focus returns to the prospect, on the benefits the prospect will receive related to this theme:

> Because the final decision will be based on agreed-to criteria, the selected alternative will be "owned" by your management team.

As you complete subsequent rows for your additional themes, you try to stay alert to the interrelationships among the themes, the lines of force that connect them. For example, you consider two selected themes that aren't yet developed in Figure 7.12a and Figure 7.12b: Your broad business perspective is a counter to some of the competitors and will help ensure the study's comprehensiveness, a hot button. So in writing or rewriting the row for one theme, you try to include language that intersects with another.

With the Themes Development Worksheet completed, you now have your web of persuasion, spun out among the proposal's various slots: SITUATION, METHODS, QUALIFICATIONS, and BENEFITS. In subsequent work sessions, you will place that persuasion strategically throughout your written proposal and throughout your discussions with ABC as well as in your proposal presentation. For example, the Situation and Methods columns will provide you the persuasion necessary to answer this question: "Why, out of a universe of possible approaches, have you chosen this one, for this situation?" That question's answer (though the buyers might not consciously recognize why the answer is so powerful) is this: "We have designed our approach as we have because it addresses your hot buttons, meets your evaluation criteria, and counters our competition." Done right, that kind of rationale for your methods section is extraordinarily persuasive.

CHAPTER 8

Green Team Reviews

Collaborating to Improve Your Odds of Winning

"How do you always seem to create outstanding, creative proposals?" I asked a partner in a consulting firm that has won many assignments from and completed great work for us.

"Can you keep a secret?" the partner replied.

"Probably not," I said, "especially if my organization could use that secret to make our own proposals to our potential customers more effective."

"Well, I'll tell you anyway," she said. "It's not really a secret, but we have found a wonderfully effective process that uses our firm's collective knowledge to great advantage, especially when we are faced with extremely complex issues. Harnessing our collective strength, our collective wisdom, multiplies our ability to 'work smarter.' And this 'secret' can also work to improve your own selling opportunities. Our process is based on four key assumptions.

"*First, proposal inquiries are an opportunity to build a long-lasting relationship, an opportunity to learn, to educate, to persuade, to sell—from the moment you, our potential client, first meet us until you make a final consultant-selection decision.* This context drives us to look for opportunities to share our perspectives, capabilities, experiences, and qualifications throughout the business-development process. We view every interaction with you and your colleagues as an opportunity to offer value—sometimes implicitly, sometimes explicitly—that could benefit you and your organization now and in the longer term.

"Think about all the logical and psychological factors you discuss in your book, including the anecdotes about selecting a car mechanic or a remodeling contractor. Well, we apply similar concepts to selling professional services to both existing and potential clients. We view every step, each interaction, in the selling process as an opportunity to build a relationship that will make you feel better about us and the value we can provide.

"*Second, there is significant competition for your work because you are considering other well-qualified consultants, either individuals or firms, and each desires your business.* We assume that our competitors will work as hard as we will to win. We like solving challenging problems and helping clients implement measurable change in their organizations, but we know that others may be as capable as, or even more capable than, we are for any particular issue. We know that you have many good choices among consultants and that many of them can do high-quality work.

"*Third, a business-development opportunity must be viewed holistically, as a series of interrelated events and behaviors, any one of which could be the difference between the few evaluation points separating winning and losing.* We do all we can to meet our commitments, whether it's arriving on time, listening empathetically in discussions, asking insightful questions, sending information you request, or meeting promised deadlines during the business-development process. We come as prepared as possible and try to put ourselves in your shoes.

"Therefore, our proposal team debriefs frequently as we speculate about why certain responses were made to our questions and why you asked the questions you did. We also extensively research your issue, your organization, your markets, and your competitors. We work hard to demonstrate how much we care about you both collectively and individually. If we didn't care, we couldn't do our best to identify how we might be able to help.

"*Finally, we look for any opportunity to provide benefits to you during the business-development process.* These benefits are almost always insight related as we share our knowledge about and experience with your current situation. During this time, we are particularly sensitive to our manner: how we do and say things, how we relate to you and your team, how we share our perspectives to answer your questions.

"We keep reminding ourselves that there are no right and wrong approaches or answers in business development. No ready-made prescriptions to apply. No rules about how to play the game. Everything is situational, dependent on your specific issue, history, people, timing, and priorities. This dependency is one of the reasons why our work is so fascinating. Nothing is black or white, only varying shades of gray.

"In a word, our secret is collaboration. We put collaboration into practice for your benefit, and, of course, our own. We have developed a process, a technique, for working jointly to get many of our best minds (even those not directly involved in the proposal effort for your organization) involved to help us review and improve our selling efforts to you."

During the rest of our conversation, I learned that the partner's firm does considerable business with the U.S. government, including the U.S. Army, which uses a technique called a Red Team Review when it considers whether to invest in new matériel/weapons systems.

The premise of a Red Team Review is this:

> Before submitting a proposal, you increase your odds of winning if you determine your strengths and weaknesses and then identify and implement actions to leverage the former and eliminate the latter.

The consultant's firm borrowed and modified the red team concept and applied it to its own business-development efforts, but it changed the color to green to accord with one of Edward deBono's colored hats.[1]

According to deBono, developer of numerous creative-thinking methods, different colored hats can be used to signify different styles of thinking. By focusing on one aspect of thinking at a time, you reduce confusion in your mind among multiple objectives. In his book *Six Thinking Hats* (Back Bay Books, 1992), deBono suggests that you and your team choose one of the six colored hats to wear at a particular moment. You figuratively put on a different hat, a different framework for thinking, and then everyone plays the role defined by that hat. In this way, individual egos are protected because everyone is wearing the same color hat. The hats allow you to think and say things that you might not otherwise think and say. They are a liberating device.

In deBono's model, the green hat represents new ideas, new concepts, new perceptions. It encourages the deliberate creation of new ideas, alternatives, and more alternatives. In essence, it seeks to identify new approaches to a situation. Green is deBono's color for this hat because "green is the color of fertility and growth and plants that grow from tiny seeds." Green is the symbolic color for the thinking hat specifically concerned with creativity, new ideas, and new ways of looking at things, escaping from the old ideas in order to find better ones. DeBono suggests why green-hat thinking is so difficult, for me as a client as well as for you:

> For most people . . . creative thinking is difficult because it is contrary to the natural habits of recognition, judgment and criticism. . . . The brain is designed to set up patterns, to use them and to condemn anything that does not "fit" these patterns. Most thinkers like to be secure. They like to be right.
>
> Creativity involves provocation, exploration and risk taking. . . . You cannot order yourself (or others) to have a new idea, but you can order yourself (and others) to spend time trying to have a new idea. The green hat provides a formal way of doing this.

So the consultant's firm structured a Green Team Review process, a technique to analyze its selling strategy and proposal-development efforts before submitting final proposals. In so doing, it purposefully takes off another of the six colored hats, the black hat. The black hat is specifically concerned with negative assessment, with criticism, with what is incorrect and will not work, with risks and dangers. This hat is the one that most consultants are paid to wear when they conduct projects for clients, when they identify problems and solve them. While black-hat thinking plays an important and often crucial role in problem solving and decision making, this negative orientation is not appropriate all the time.

Therefore, before a proposal is submitted, while there is still time to modify the offering (or improve personal relationships with the potential client), green-hat thinking can offer new information, new possibilities, constructive ideas to build on. Subsequently, all the logical, legitimate, critically important negative aspects of a situation can be considered with black-hat thinking.

Many consultancies have adopted the Red Team Review technique, which traditionally occurs after the document has been assembled. Those who have written the proposal, as well as many who have not been involved in the business-development process, gather to examine the document, often ripping it apart and suggesting dozens if not hundreds of changes. Imagine that you had managed the proposal-development effort and were involved in the Red Team Review, listening for four hours or sometimes longer than a day as hundreds of revisions were being recommended. After hours of such discussion, you would feel that each new recommended revision was unbearable, knowing that the proposal would have to be almost entirely rewritten (and submitted in less than a few days).

In the rest of this chapter, I will show you a different process, one that can occur at any time during the business-development process, even (in a proactive lead) before you have had your first meeting with me. Instead of taking hours, this process takes minutes (40 minutes to be exact).

The Strategic Premise of Green Team Collaboration

The Green Team process is specifically designed to change participants' behaviors from black-hat thinking to green-hat thinking, from "what won't work" to "what may be possible." In facilitating this change, the process attempts to expand the proposal team's knowledge, moving beyond what it currently knows so that it also learns what it doesn't know and discovers what its firm knows, and beyond. (See Figure 8.1.)

Figure 8.1 displays these four levels of knowledge. Most people write proposals based only on what they know, and many times they are successful. They work from a base of knowledge represented by the smallest circle in the Figure 8.1. They have interacted with me and others in my organization, have tried to work smart, and "know what they know." Based on what they know, they prepare the best proposal they can.

Unfortunately, they sometimes lose because of what they don't know, because of the many red flags used in the work sessions of this book that represent a lack of information, risks, and vulnerabilities. They don't try to determine what their proposal team doesn't know. Quite often a proposal team, like a sports team, is

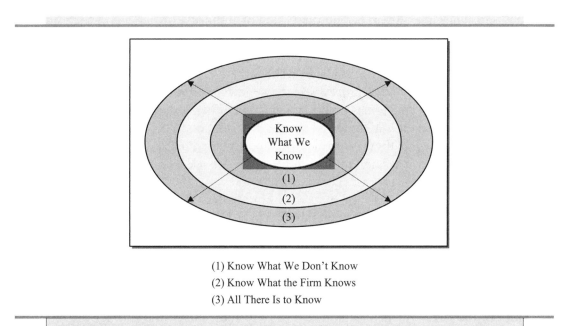

(1) Know What We Don't Know

(2) Know What the Firm Knows

(3) All There Is to Know

FIGURE 8.1   The strategic premise of the Green Team Review: expanding your team's base of knowledge

optimistic, feeling good about its competitive position and chances of winning. This optimism may blind the team to potential biases, hidden problems, and risks.

Worse, they fail to determine what their firm knows, other broader perspectives of which the proposal team is unaware. This collective wisdom is the combined knowledge, the sum of intellectual capital, capability, and experience of others in the firm not directly involved with the proposal team.

Beyond this level of knowledge, of course, is "all there is to know." There will always be more information, more intelligence, than any individual, team, or firm will ever know. Your goal during business development should be to expand your base of knowledge, going beyond what you know to what you don't know and to what your firm knows. You can do that by using a 40-minute Green Team Review.

The Green Team Review: What It Is

The 40-minute Green Team Review is a focused, high-impact process through which a proposal team can expand its knowledge and improve its selling strategy by learning what it doesn't know and what the firm knows. With this increased knowledge, the team can be made aware of and choose to execute strategic actions that leverage its strengths and/or offset its weaknesses relative to its competition. The Green Team has no direct line of authority; ownership of the lead and decisions regarding changes to the selling strategy continue to reside with the proposal team. The Green Team provides the proposal team with constructive, creative suggestions for its consideration.

The Green Team Review process seeks to supply important missing, unverified, and uncertain information as well as information or perspectives about which the proposal team might not completely agree. Information, most likely the lack of information, in any of these categories could pose vulnerabilities or red flags to the proposal team's firm as I and my colleagues make our selection decision. Red flags are not created by the process. They already exist even if they are not identified or acknowledged, even if they are hidden within my firm. The Green Team Review process allows these potential vulnerabilities to be identified, prioritized (given the time remaining before the proposal is submitted), and systematically addressed.

The Green Team: Who It Is

Ideally, the Green Team includes six to twelve individuals who are not directly involved in the selling opportunity and who can provide a range of different perspectives, attitudes, and points of view. They might bring to the Green Team Review different functional perspectives (e.g., marketing, information technology, manufacturing, logistics, finance) as well as different leadership styles (e.g., the Myers-Briggs descriptors—Intuitive, Sensing, Thinking, and Feeling—or more simplified matrices that use categories such as Controller, Analyzer, Promoter, and Supporter).

By including individuals with different industry and geographic experiences, as well as different styles of thinking, you can configure a Green Team with perspectives well beyond those of your proposal team. In brief, you're asking the members of the Green Team to use their range of experience and expertise to imagine my mind-set and to view the proposal team's thinking as if they themselves were I and my colleagues. This orientation allows the Green Team to consider the proposal team's thinking from divergent perspectives.

How do you persuade your busy colleagues to participate and to collaborate on selling opportunities about which they haven't even been involved and about which they know little or nothing? You design the review process to be quick and to the point, but not judgmental and not open-ended. Even the busiest people can spare 40 minutes to help their colleagues improve their chances of winning important opportunities—if you honor their time commitments. You can with a properly structured Green Team Review.

The Green Team Review: How It Works

As Figure 8.2 illustrates, the 40-minute Green Team Review includes five distinct steps, each with a specific task, that together are aimed at identifying creative potential actions to improve your probability of winning.

Step 1: Listen

During Step 1, the proposal team presents, without interruption, the most important elements from the Logic and Psychologics Worksheets (which should be poster-size and taped to the wall),[2] the logical and psychological elements of its thinking about the proposed problem or opportunity to date. The Green Team listens silently and takes notes. This fast-paced, to-the-point presentation must, by design, focus only on the big picture and identified red flags, not on less critical details of the selling situation. A timekeeper (who must not be a member of the proposal team) alerts the proposal team's presenter(s) at several checkpoints to ensure that this high-level overview is completed within 15 minutes.

Step 2: Ask

In this step, members of the Green Team ask questions of the proposal team to understand the lead better and to determine weaknesses or red flags that have not yet been identified. As the proposal team responds, the Green Team "fills in the blanks" of its understanding of the lead's current status. Since only 10 minutes is

Step	Who	Task	Timing (min.)
1	Proposal Team	Present overview of logical and psychological aspects of proposal thinking to date	15
2	Green Team	Ask questions; identify red flags	10
3	Both Teams	Summarize strengths and red flags	5
4	Both Teams	Brainstorm potential actions to improve positioning	10
5	Both Teams	Debrief	----

FIGURE 8.2   Timing for the 40-minute Green Team Review

permitted for this step, questions and answers must be direct and without editorial comment. Questions should be stated constructively ("Were you able to discuss X with the VP of marketing?"), not judgmentally ("Why didn't you discuss X with the VP of marketing?"). Obviously, you want to avoid questions that cast aspersions, implying that the proposal team has been less than diligent in its efforts.

Step 3: Flag

During this step, the Green Team and the proposal team spend five minutes summarizing the proposal team's strengths (green flags) and weaknesses (red flags), given the information from steps 1 and 2. One or two recorders or scribes (again, not members of the proposal team) display the responses with a data projector or, preferably, write them on flipcharts. The responses should be divided into the two categories, strengths and weaknesses. During this rapid-fire listing, the scribes record what is stated as quickly as possible. No discussion, clarification, or evaluation takes place during this listing. Because strengths and red flags may be called out in any order, it is helpful for the respondents to voice their comments as follows:

- A strength is . . . our relationship with the economic buyer.
- A red flag is . . . we haven't quantified benefits.
- A red flag is . . . we have no coach.

- A strength is . . . well-defined deliverables.
- A strength is . . . good project work we've done in another division of the potential client's organization.

Step 4: Strategize

Using the lists of strengths and red flags that are now taped to the wall and were created as a starting point for green-hat thinking, the proposal team and the Green Team call out, in a 10-minute brainstorming session, as many potential improvement actions as possible. Beginning their suggestions with an active verb, participants randomly suggest widely varying ideas such as the following:

- Call Neil Nakadate in our Tokyo office to learn about his experience with [this client] last year.
- Talk to Bjorn Ryns about the benefits we actually achieved for Company X on a similar study.
- Add Brian Brown to the proposed project team to utilize his experience with [the potential client's industry].
- Propose an initial scoping phase to better quantify the measurable benefits from [some action].
- Drop the lead if we are unable to meet the economic buyer.
- Check to see if we have any relationships with members of the Board of Directors who could influence buying committee members.
- Invite the VP of marketing to our international seminar on [whatever] next week.
- Ask our research department to find out the background of [a member of the buying committee we know little about].
- Apply Neuro-Linguistic Programming techniques to mirror the behavior of [a difficult user buyer].
- Change our project leader because of potential personality differences [with client personnel].
- Structure a pay-as-you-go fee arrangement based on the potential client's actual accrual of benefits.
- Invite the VP of manufacturing to visit [a past satisfied client] to discuss how we worked in a challenging union environment.
- Emphasize the theme of urgency to reflect our ability to generate measurable results quickly.

My consultant friend, the one I was talking to at the beginning of this chapter, told me that some of her Green Team Reviews have generated as many as 40–50 potential actions, all called out and transcribed without any comment, discussion, or evaluation (either good or bad) from Green Team participants, all during the 10-minute brainstorming session. Subsequently, the proposal team uses black-hat thinking to evaluate the potential actions, but only after the Green Team has disbanded. During the brainstorming, there are, by definition, no bad ideas. In fact, off-the-wall ideas are encouraged: They can lead someone else to identify what later is judged as another good idea.

Step 5. Debrief

After the first four phases of 40 minutes of elapsed time, the Green Team Review is officially over, and some members of the Green Team may have to leave. They should be excused and thanked. Others should be invited to stay for a quick 10-minute debriefing, since their initial feedback could be helpful. All Green Team members should be encouraged to continue thinking about the lead so that they can suggest other improvement actions that come to mind over time.

The Green Team Review: What Happens Afterward

The Green Team is encouraged to be creative, to stretch its thinking to identify linkages to other people, projects, and experiences that, if implemented, might help the proposal team improve its offering. The key word is "might": The process identifies actions that the proposal team will subsequently consider and potentially execute as it sees fit. There is no measurement system that evaluates the value of specific ideas or suggestions. In fact, there is no requirement that the proposal team use any of the Green Team's suggestions.

After the Green Team Review, the proposal team's assessment of the potential actions might be something like this: Out of these 40 potential actions, these 10 we've already thought of (though they've now been reinforced), these 10 we don't have time to implement (though we might have, if we had held the Green Team Review earlier), these 10 are the silliest ideas we've ever heard (though some of them led to other, incredible ideas), and these 10, if we implement them, could significantly improve our probability of winning.

In short, the proposal team retains accountability for the lead; it determines how best to proceed, how best to win. But this determination is accomplished with a much higher degree of confidence, with the knowledge that a wide variety of colleagues with differing perspectives and points of view have reviewed the logical and psychological aspects of the selling efforts to date.

Green Team Reviews: Some Final Thoughts

Proposal team leaders and members typically find themselves working against the clock, unable to do all the things they want to do to prepare an outstanding proposal. There is no shortage of actions the team would like to execute, but time is almost always limited. So getting ready for a Green Team Review with colleagues, some of whom may be in senior positions, could be perceived as threatening or time-consuming: "The Green Team will highlight what we don't know, what we haven't done. They'll identify actions we should have taken. They'll see that we don't have our act together."

But consider this: Many, if not all, proposal teams lack complete information and have a long list of potential actions they could have taken and haven't, at least not yet. Many don't have their act together—yet. All this isn't really surprising to anyone who has seen how you work. There is never enough time; there are seldom enough resources. Remember: As your potential client, I don't ask you to help me answer easy questions. This is the essential nature of the business.

The value of Green Team Reviews, if they are done early enough in the process, is that broader, more experienced minds will help identify improvement actions (and potential additional resources) that leverage not just a proposal team's capability but also that of the entire organization. Even the Lone Ranger had Tonto; even the sheriff had a posse. The collective knowledge in a Green Team Review process helps overcome one of Murphy's laws: Experience is something you don't get until just after you need it. While Green Team Reviews do not create additional time, they do focus efforts that can be instrumental to better utilize your available time and resources, certainly for the select leads that you really want to win.

The bottom line is this: Green Team Reviews can provide your firm's management with the ability to understand and better support business-development efforts. With the power of today's information technology, your best people from around the world can participate, making the proposal team aware of the knowledge and experience of others in the firm, helping the team members learn what they don't know and what their firm knows. This collaboration, whether in person or virtually, can certainly improve a team's odds of winning, providing some of the two to five points that make the difference between winning and placing second.

By the way, can you think of a more effective professional-development opportunity for training new consultants? "Welcome to Paramount Consulting. . . . We'd like you to watch (or even participate in) a Green Team Review for our lead at ABC."

Proposal Preparation

I f you've done all the work in Parts 1 and 2, you now have a much better understanding of the logics and psychologics of your potential clients' situation. Now, as you'll see, your proposal or presentation is almost ready to write itself slot by slot: SITUATION, OBJECTIVES, METHODS, QUALIFICATIONS, and BENEFITS.

Up to this point, I've shown you how to generate material by dropping it into the right places. While there are no rules, there is a framework for using all the information you've developed and a way to use it both logically and psychologically. You'll see how all the work you've done up to this point will save you considerable time in preparing the actual document or presentation.

But time, of course, isn't the only issue. I wrote this book not just to help you become more efficient but also to help you become more effective so that you can gain the additional points you need to win. By the time you finish Part 3, you'll understand not only how to incorporate the information from the worksheets into the various parts of your proposal but also how to construct and organize these parts so that they result in a persuasive argument—one that is thoughtful, seamless, and compelling.

CHAPTER 9

Writing the Situation and Objectives Slots

n Chapter 1, I said that a well-written proposal isn't a collection of separate sections or chapters or slots but a coherent argument woven throughout the document or presentation. For this reason, it's difficult for me, your potential client, to claim that one proposal slot is more important than another. In some situations, cost could be crucial; in others, your own or your firm's reputation or qualifications; in still others, the methodology, especially when the tasks are numerous and the project's management will be complex.

But let's limit the variables. Let's assume a competitive situation with multiple bidders whose objectives, methods, qualifications, and costs are all similar. Everything else being equal, your competitive edge could lie in the situation slot, which is often formed into a section called "Background" or "Business Issues" or "Our Understanding of Your Situation."

SITUATION is usually my first significant contact with your proposal and, in some cases, with you. It may be my first significant opportunity to sense who you are, what you believe, how strongly you believe it, how knowledgeable and competent you are regarding my problem or opportunity, and how qualified you are to address it.

Later, you probably will discuss your firm's qualifications, but from the first word in SITUATION, you're already displaying (or not displaying) your abilities and projecting (or not projecting) a desirable image of you and your firm. You're already demonstrating (or not demonstrating) that you know my industry, organization, issues, and culture and that you can come into my organization, interact with a wide variety of people, sift through masses of often conflicting information, and achieve our objectives. If you demonstrate all that, by the way, you'll be displaying your qualifications much more persuasively than most qualifications sections can.

Here's an example of a brief background section that contains three components that we'll discuss below:

> A long time ago, in a galaxy far far away, Darth Vader and the evil Empire sought to conquer all of galactic civilization, despite the efforts of the heroic Rebellion to thwart their attempts at every turn. Through the extraordinary efforts of Princess Leia and R2D2, we now have intelligence that the Empire is building a so-called Death Star capable of demolishing an entire planet within minutes. If the Death Star is not destroyed, the Empire will enslave every citizen of the galaxy.
>
> Despite the Death Star's blueprints brought to us by Leia, we still have many questions that must be answered:
>
> - How will the Empire defend the Death Star?
> - What are its defenses?
> - Where are those defenses vulnerable?
> - What fighting force is required to exploit those vulnerabilities?
>
> To answer these questions, we will develop an implementable plan to destroy the Death Star. Subsequent to implementation, the Empire will lose its stranglehold on galactic civilization, the Rebellion will triumph, and Harrison Ford will go on to become a bankable Hollywood star.

As Figure 9.1 illustrates, the background section above contains three components (one per paragraph): Story/S_1, Questions, and Closing/S_2.[1] Each of these components offers you a significant opportunity to convince me that you understand my problem or opportunity and know what it takes to address it.

The Story Component

To describe your understanding of my current situation, your Story Component should tell me a compelling and engaging story by narrating a sequence of events. Why tell a story? Because I and my colleagues like stories and become involved in them. History is a story. So are biographies, plays, movies, novels, newspaper articles, soap operas, and even jokes. I like, read, and need stories so much that even when I sleep I can't help but tell stories to and about myself: I dream. Stories are inherently interesting—I've never met anyone who didn't like them. And inherently interesting to me and everyone else on the buying committee

Component	Content
1. Story/S_1	• What is the history, the external and internal factors (including the triggering event), that caused the problem or opportunity? • What is the problem or opportunity? • What are its effects and "lack of benefits"? • What, if anything, has been done to solve the problem or realize the opportunity? Has this attempt exacerbated the situation?
2. Questions	• What questions must be answered to address or solve the prospect's problem or realize the prospect's opportunity? (derived from deliverables)
3. Closing/S_2	• Transition from Questions Component • Bridge to methods slot • Engagement objective(s) (expression of S_2) • Briefly stated benefits

FIGURE 9.1　The three components of the situation slot

is a story about our organization and our current situation. That situation has a history—a past that led to and a present that is affected by the problem or opportunity and, implicitly, a future that will result in our problem or opportunity being addressed, solved, or realized. We have a sense of immediacy about our story, and we want our potential consultants to share it.

You be the judge. Here are two sentences that began the situation slots in proposals I received when I was working in the health care industry. Which has more power, more force, more reader interest?

* Mercy is a 300-bed hospital in Chicago, Illinois.
* As Mercy grew to 300 beds, its business objectives began to change.

The first sentence contains unnecessary (and redundant) information: I already know that Mercy is a hospital in Chicago, since the proposal was addressed to Mercy in the first place and I went to work there almost every day. That sentence also portrays all the research abilities and problem-solving skills of a fourth-grader. It demonstrates only that you can find information from an annual report or a company brochure; it doesn't offer you a good opportunity to begin demonstrating your understanding of my, the reader's, situation. But even all that doesn't get to the heart of the matter. The plain truth is that the first sentence is dead.

Lifeless. Uninteresting. Boring. Why? Because there's no time in it, no sequence of causes and effects, actions and reactions. It's static. It doesn't move. It's more like a rock, changeless, than an organization that, like my organization and yours, is a living, breathing organism that constantly changes—and whose changes need to be managed, which will be your job if you win the proposed project.

The first sentence, then, is static; the second, dynamic. The first is inanimate, outside of time. The second is animate; it moves because it contains time and the passage of time—like life. The first contains only facts (facts I already know); the second subordinates the facts to a story. As the beginning of a story, the sentence compels my interest because I want to know what will happen next. I want to know the rest of the plot. Your strategy, then, should be to include in your Story Component the necessary information, the facts, about my organization, but to subordinate that information to your story about my problem or opportunity.

Too often, situation slots are written with the goal of feeding back information to me so that I will know that you have listened. But I want you to do far more than just listen. I want you to demonstrate not only that you have listened but that you have understood—that you can take the information I have given you and analyze it, synthesize it, place it in some context, and even educate me in the process. To demonstrate to me that your project won't be a data dump of undigested information, there are four questions germane to the Story Component that you can answer:

- **Causes:** What is the history, the external and internal factors (for example, those related to our markets, competition, costs, and processes), that gave rise to our problem or opportunity?
- **Problem/Opportunity:** What is the problem or opportunity?
- **Effects:** What are its effects on me and my organization (the actual ones of not solving the problem, the potential ones of not realizing the opportunity)?
- **Attempted Solutions:** What, if anything, has been done to solve the problem or realize the opportunity?

Answering the first question, about the background, the history, of the situation, allows you to begin your story as you narrate the events that caused the problem or opportunity. These factors can be internal (new company initiatives, changes in management) or external (aggressive moves by competitors, advances in technology, changes in the economic environment). By discussing the internal factors, you can demonstrate your understanding of my company, people, and cultural issues. By analyzing the external factors, you can demonstrate your knowledge of my industry, projects, markets, and competition. When possible and appropriate, you want to educate me about my organization, my market, and my perspectives on the situation. By sharing nonproprietary, comparative information about these factors, you pique our interest and imply your qualifications.

In answering the first question, as well as the second and third, you must keep in mind that my perception of our current situation, and its causes and effects may be different from the perceptions of others on the buying committee. Your goal is to weave a coherent story that incorporates all the buyers' individual stories. That is, your Story Component needs to narrate the individual perceptions of S_1 and their causes and effects. This isn't an easy task, especially if our individual stories differ significantly. The danger is that the buying committee's lack of agreement could result in your Story Component's lack of coherence or consistency.

Frequently, however, you can turn our lack of agreement to your advantage, since lack of agreement on the buyers' part underscores the problematic nature of our situation and reinforces our need to reconcile disagreement to achieve our desired result, which will remove each buyer's pain or uncertainty. That is, lack of agreement on the buyers' part can reinforce our need for an objective third party sensitive to differing perceptions and desires.

The fourth question, on attempted solutions, applies only if we previously have attempted to move from S_1 to S_2, through either internal efforts or those of consultants. Given that you are being considered for the project, our attempt quite likely was unsuccessful. In this part of the Story Component, you can demonstrate your understanding of what went wrong and, implicitly, what pitfalls therefore need to be avoided.

The following paragraphs contain a brief Story Component from a proposal written some years ago. Note how the writer discusses the external factors that have caused a transition to a deregulated banking environment as well as the opportunities this transition affords. Should she also have discussed the effects? By understanding that the Story Component can contain causes, problem/opportunity, effects, and attempted solutions, you know what you can write into the component, and you can check what you might have unintentionally omitted.

Background

As international standards for capital requirements force liberalization of financial regulations, your organization is challenged by the tremendous transition currently occurring in the Japanese banking industry. Deregulation is leading to heightened competition for domestic banks, and small community and regional banks are threatened by larger, more capital-rich financial institutions. These institutions have already started to increase market share through mergers and acquisitions. To remain competitive, regional banks now face new challenges to obtain new retail customer accounts and to maintain the loyalty of their existing customer base. Through your organization, these regional banks seek innovative ways to differentiate themselves and cope with deregulation to compete profitably against the super-regional Japanese banks.

> With this transition to a deregulated banking environment, your community bank consortium has the opportunity to become more innovative and differentiated among the competition in providing products and services not formerly available in the regulated atmosphere.

Where do you get the content for your Story Component? As you might already have guessed (and as you'll see near the end of this chapter), from Cells 1 and 2 of the Logics Worksheet.

The Questions Component

The Story Component grabs my interest by involving me in a narrative about my organization's current situation and about how we got to where we are today. It also demonstrates your problem-solving skills by presenting your analysis of my organization's problem or opportunity. Now, by your asking questions, the Questions Component helps maintain my interest and continues to demonstrate your analytical skills. This component should answer the following question: What key questions must be answered to address the problem or opportunity?

Questions encourage my interest because they help you create a dialogue with me; they invite my engagement and my participation. A spoken statement such as "It's cloudy today" leaves little room for my response, but a question such as "Is it cloudy today?" invites a response. A statement is convergent; it closes things off. A question is divergent; it creates an invitational pause, allowing me to respond and participate in the dialogue. Because reading or listening is a participatory rather than a passive activity, questions encourage involvement and help me move more thoughtfully through your document or presentation.

One of the most important qualities of a good problem solver (that's one of the characteristics I want you to possess) is the ability to ask the right questions. As long as scientists believed malaria was caused by bad air (in Italian, that's what the word means), they were asking the wrong questions and couldn't determine the cause of the disease. When, however, they asked, "Could it be caused by a microorganism?" they could begin to identify a specific organism and the process of transmission. By identifying the salient issues of our situation and by phrasing them as questions, you demonstrate to me that you can identify those issues and formulate those questions whose answers will help direct us to ensure a successful project.

Questions can provide yet another strategic advantage: They allow you to address a buyer's issue without your having to take a position on that issue. Consider the situation at ABC. Metzger wants to expand at the current site. Of course, you don't know at the proposal stage if expanding there is ABC's best option, but you can let Metzger know that you're sensitive to that option, that you have heard him, if you use a question like this: "How much expansion potential exists at the current facility?"

Collins and Morrison, in contrast, are more concerned about service levels and distribution costs, which probably would improve if ABC built a new facility closer to the company's growing markets. You can let Collins and Morrison know that you're sensitive to their concerns and that you have heard them, if you use questions like these: "Even if resources can be provided at the present location, does it make economic sense to add them there or to make the investment elsewhere? For example, will service levels increase and transportation costs decrease at a new geographic location?" Through these questions, you haven't come down on Metzger's side or on Collins's or Morrison's. You haven't alienated any of them by taking a position. In fact, you likely will have satisfied all of them by demonstrating that you've listened.

Where do you get the questions for your Questions Component? From either of these:

● the deliverables in Cell 5 of the Logics Worksheet
● the logic tree for your methodology

As you saw in Chapter 5, the Logics Worksheet's deliverables likely found their way into your logic tree, each of whose actions need to express a deliverable. So if you have already constructed your logic tree, you can derive your questions from it. For example, consider the logic trees for the proposal to XYZ in Chapter 5 (which I've included again as Figure 9.2).

The second row of the figure implies that you would answer five key questions to achieve the project's objectives:

● What opportunities exist for XYZ in the information service market?
● What capabilities and resources are required to capitalize on those opportunities?
● What gaps exist between those required capabilities and resources, on the one hand, and XYZ's, on the other?
● What actions are required to close those gaps?
● What resources and how much time are necessary to close the gaps?

Note the strategy here. A Questions Component like this not only provides evidence for your problem-solving ability, it also prepares me for your methodology. If I buy into the questions in your situation slot, you have gone a long way toward preselling your methodology.

Of course, this component could include other questions. You may want to use questions that respond to hot buttons, evaluation criteria, and counters to the competition. Even if you don't, you could phrase the questions derived from your logic tree so that they address hot buttons and other thematic material. For example, if

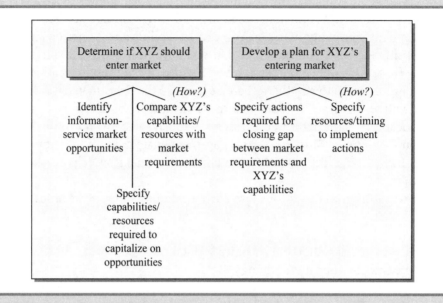

urgency were a theme, the fourth question above could be phrased like this: "What actions are required to close these gaps within the limited time frame required?"

The following passage, which continues the "background" section about the Japanese banking industry, contains a Questions Component:

> However, the transition necessary to change from traditional marketing protocols to new ways of marketing bank services will require a structured investigation that answers the following questions:
>
> ◉ What are the essential customer needs and requirements that will attract new business opportunities for retail banks?
> ◉ What product, pricing, and promotional tools are necessary to implement and support effective marketing plans, new product development, and delivery systems?
> ◉ What types of technology and systems support are necessary to administer new products, services, and marketing efforts?
> ◉ What marketing strategies have successful regional banks in the United States used since deregulation, and what performance levels have resulted from implementing those strategies?

Before I can make the transition from S_1 to S_2, your project will have to answer important questions. Articulating them in the Questions Component suggests to me that you will be able to do that. Framing these questions also forces you to think hard about your project's issues, assumptions, and hypotheses.

* What are the key issues that must be resolved?
* Which issues are crucial, and which are tangential?
* Given the crucial issues, how will your methodology be designed to resolve them?
* In resolving them, what benefits will accrue to me and my organization?

The last two questions suggest an important function of the Questions Component: It helps SITUATION speak to other proposal slots, in this case, to METHODS and BENEFITS.

The Closing Component

The function of the Closing Component is to provide a smooth transition from the text above it to the text below it, to state the project's objective(s), and to conclude SITUATION with a closing oriented toward me, your potential client.

The Closing Component can include briefly stated themes related to hot buttons, evaluation criteria, and counters to the competition. These themes could emphasize your experience, expertise, past performance, or previous relationship with me or others in my organization or industry. Or they could sell certain aspects of your methodology. Depending on the overall length of the proposal, the Closing Component might be two or more paragraphs or a single sentence. Whatever its length, it contains these elements:

* Backward transition from the Questions Component
* Forward transition to METHODS
* Project objective(s)
* Briefly stated benefits if they are not immediately apparent in the objectives

For content related to the third bullet above, your project's objectives, rephrase the overriding question(s) from Cell 4 of your Logics Worksheets or the desired result(s) from Cell 5. For content related to the fourth bullet above, look to the benefits you have included in Cell 6, choosing two to four powerful selling points of your project. Note how the following sentence, which completes the sample background section we have been considering, contains those four elements:

To answer these questions, we have designed an approach for developing a plan that, after implementation, will enable the community retail bank consortium to achieve the benefits of increased competitiveness in the deregulated market.

Putting It All Together: Composing the "Background" Section from Your Logics Worksheet

If you've done all the work in Parts 1 and 2, your proposal or presentation is almost ready to write itself slot by slot. First, I'll show you and explain the "map" (Figure 9.3) for writing your background section. Then, I will follow that map, constructing the first draft of a background section.

For the Story Component
- Create the history of the problem from the content of Cell 1.
- Follow with the triggering event, the problem, and its effects from Cell 2.

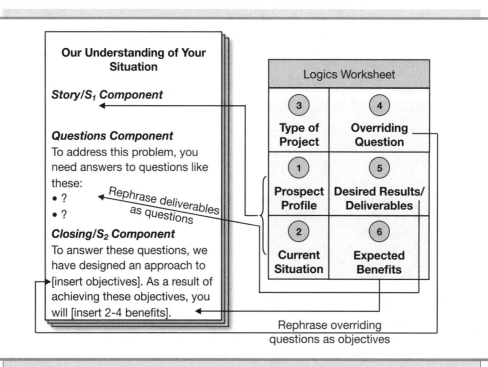

FIGURE 9.3   Using the Logics Worksheet to construct your background section

For the Questions Component

⦿ Turn appropriate deliverables from Cell 5 into questions.

For the Closing Component

⦿ For the objective(s), rephrase the overriding question(s) from Cell 4.
⦿ For the benefits, choose two to four appropriate ones from Cell 6.

By following the map in Figure 9.3, I will "write" ABC's background section in the next six figures (Figures 9.4–9.9). Each figure has two parts: on the left, the information from a cell of the Logics Worksheet; on the right, the part of the background section I'm writing directly from that cell.

Logics Worksheet, Cell 1, "Prospect Profile"	Background Section, Story Component
Major products/markets: Large home appliances (refrigerators, stoves, washers/dryers, etc). **Annual revenue/profitability/trends:** • 20XX revenue = $18B. • Profit increased 22% year over year. • Increasing distribution costs (a major component of landed cost) could begin to erode margins. • Trends?? **Major competitors:** GE, Whirlpool, Bosch. **Market/industry issues:** Fairly stable, mature industry, with only modest growth expected next five years. Demand moving to U.S. South and Southwest. **Strategic Direction:** Unknown **Experience with your competition:** Has worked with one of our major competitors (name unknown) and with two boutiques.	With 20XX revenues of $18B and a 22% year-over-year increase in profits, ABC has continued to gain share against GE, Whirlpool, & Bosch in the large home-appliance market at a time when distribution costs are a major component of landed costs. Despite these successes, two issues concern management. First, in a market projected to grow only modestly in the next five years, demand is moving to the U.S. South and Southwest, away from ABC's major production facilities.

FIGURE 9.4   Writing the Story Component

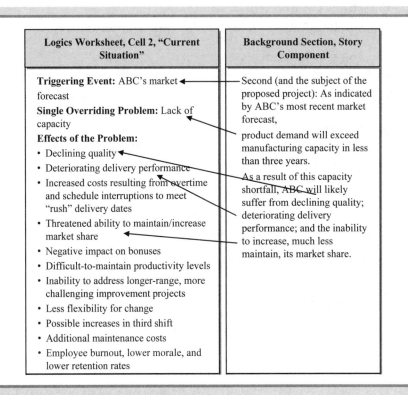

Logics Worksheet, Cell 2, "Current Situation"	Background Section, Story Component
Triggering Event: ABC's market forecast **Single Overriding Problem:** Lack of capacity **Effects of the Problem:** • Declining quality • Deteriorating delivery performance • Increased costs resulting from overtime and schedule interruptions to meet "rush" delivery dates • Threatened ability to maintain/increase market share • Negative impact on bonuses • Difficult-to-maintain productivity levels • Inability to address longer-range, more challenging improvement projects • Less flexibility for change • Possible increases in third shift • Additional maintenance costs • Employee burnout, lower morale, and lower retention rates	Second (and the subject of the proposed project): As indicated by ABC's most recent market forecast, product demand will exceed manufacturing capacity in less than three years. As a result of this capacity shortfall, ABC will likely suffer from declining quality; deteriorating delivery performance; and the inability to increase, much less maintain, its market share.

FIGURE 9.5 Writing the Story Component (cont.)

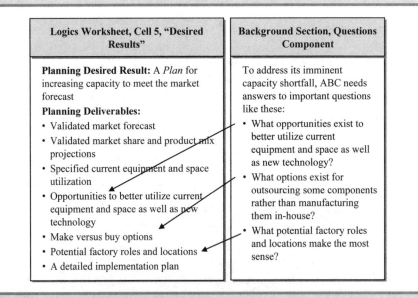

Logics Worksheet, Cell 5, "Desired Results"	Background Section, Questions Component
Planning Desired Result: A *Plan* for increasing capacity to meet the market forecast **Planning Deliverables:** • Validated market forecast • Validated market share and product mix projections • Specified current equipment and space utilization • Opportunities to better utilize current equipment and space as well as new technology • Make versus buy options • Potential factory roles and locations • A detailed implementation plan	To address its imminent capacity shortfall, ABC needs answers to important questions like these: • What opportunities exist to better utilize current equipment and space as well as new technology? • What options exist for outsourcing some components rather than manufacturing them in-house? • What potential factory roles and locations make the most sense?

FIGURE 9.6 Writing the Questions Component

Logics Worksheet, Cell 4, "Overriding Questions"	Background Section, Closing Component
Overriding Planning Question: How best should ABC increase capacity to meet the sales forecast?	To answer these questions, we will develop a detailed plan to increase ABC's capacity to meet its sales forecast.

FIGURE 9.7   Writing the Closing Component

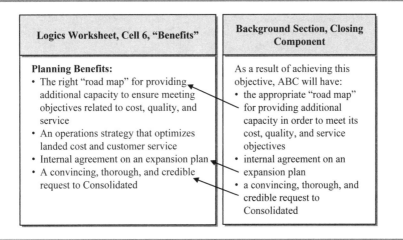

Logics Worksheet, Cell 6, "Benefits"	Background Section, Closing Component
Planning Benefits: • The right "road map" for providing additional capacity to ensure meeting objectives related to cost, quality, and service • An operations strategy that optimizes landed cost and customer service • Internal agreement on an expansion plan • A convincing, thorough, and credible request to Consolidated	As a result of achieving this objective, ABC will have: • the appropriate "road map" for providing additional capacity in order to meet its cost, quality, and service objectives • internal agreement on an expansion plan • a convincing, thorough, and credible request to Consolidated

FIGURE 9.8   Writing the Closing Component (cont.)

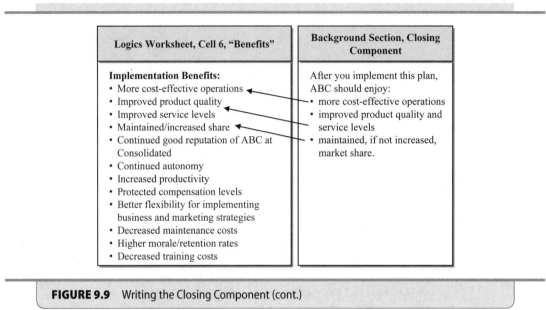

FIGURE 9.9   Writing the Closing Component (cont.)

There you have it: a background section in five minutes! Although what I've written is just a first draft, please note these two important points. First, I could "write" the section as quickly as I did because I wasn't starting from a "blank page." Second, the page I was starting from contained fully aligned, well-strategized information that, together with my map, I could use to construct a persuasive section.

The Situation Slot and Competitive Advantage

The Story, Questions, and Closing Components allow you to present not only an interesting story but, more important, a thoughtful, logical and persuasive argument. They can help you project an image of yourself as competent, organized, logical, analytical, knowledgeable, thorough, relevant, coherent, insightful, and creative. These are generic attributes of a good problem solver, characteristics that can be presented to me long before a logically written METHODS validates them and a relevant QUALIFICATIONS reinforces them. You are showing me, not telling me, your capabilities within the context of my situation. Showing always trumps telling.

Moreover, after using these components in proposal after proposal, you'll find that you can compose the situation and objectives slots more easily and quickly because you will have developed a schema, an internal formula or "script," just as you probably have developed a script for proposals in general. Many proposal writers have difficulty writing background sections because they haven't developed such a formula. The preceding structure supplies you with that formula. While not a rule, it provides a guideline regarding what kind of information to consider and where to place it.

The components also help you make SITUATION speak to other slots in the proposal. The questions you present relate directly to your stated objectives and your approach to achieving them. The three components will provide implied but convincing evidence regarding your qualifications as a problem solver.

Finally, like an overture in a symphony, SITUATION can initiate the themes developed later, in subsequent slots of the proposal. As a result, your situation slot gets you and your proposal off to a good start as you begin at the beginning to convince me of one of your proposal's major claims: You know my industry; you know me; you know my organization and its challenges, problems, and opportunities; and you can address them—maybe not as inexpensively as someone else but better.

CHAPTER 9 REVIEW

Writing the Situation and Objectives Slots

The situation slot has three components that help answer a series of questions, as summarized in Figure 9.10.

Component	Content
1. Story/S_1	• What is the history, the external and internal factors (including the triggering event), that caused the problem or opportunity? • What is the problem or opportunity? • What are its effects and "lack of benefits"? • What, if anything, has been done to solve the problem or realize the opportunity? Has this attempt exacerbated the situation?
2. Questions	• What questions must be answered to address or solve the prospect's problem or realize the prospect's opportunity? (derived from deliverables)
3. Closing/S_2	• Transition from Questions Component • Bridge to methods slot • Engagement objective(s) (expression of S_2) • Briefly stated benefits

FIGURE 9.10   The three components of the situation slot

WORK SESSION 7: Writing the Situation and Objectives Slots for ABC

Before you actually begin to strategize the proposal, Gilmore sends you a memo concerning the formatting, page layout, and other such "requirements" about which he wants you to adhere. You expect this memo because it is his standard operating procedure.

Requirements for the Proposal's "Look and Feel"

In almost every project, you have heard, Gilmore engages one or more of the buyers in a discussion of the quality of writing in the prospect's organization. He does so for two reasons.

First, it allows him to understand the culture better. An organization's documents, he knows, are like cultural artifacts, and embedded in them are important aspects of the prospect's culture. Are their decision-making documents composed in PowerPoint or in Word? How powerful are the Format Police, those individuals, usually in Marketing, who have spent months developing a consistent document "look and feel" that harmonizes rather than conflicts with the organization's attempts to support the firm's branding? To what extent and how often does the prospect, in this case Anil Gupta, use the format requirements, and if he doesn't, why doesn't he? What seems to be the expected length of decision-making documents and the reaction to documents whose length exceeds those expectations? For example, does President Armstrong get frustrated by having to read more than an executive summary (as, in Gilmore's experience, is typical of many CEOs and presidents)?

Second, this discussion invariably leads the prospect to show Gilmore some of the firm's decision-making documents and, if he is fortunate, some proposals and reports submitted by external consultants for previous projects. By having Gupta comment on such documents and their formatting and quality, Gilmore can make strategic decisions about the format and design of your proposal.

Here are the key points from Gilmore's memo to you:

- Although most of the previous consultants' proposals and reports were written in PowerPoint and designed in landscape, as are ours, ABC's internal decision-making documents are in Word and designed in portrait. Their default font appears to be 11 pt. Century Old Style, and the content in their charts appears to be 9 pt. Helvetica Neue. The captions in those charts, however, appear to be 8 pt. Myriad Pro.
- Given the above, we need to write our document in Word and in portrait, with 11 pt. Century Old Style as the "normal" font and 9 pt. Helvetica Neue for

charts and figures and 8 pt. Myriad Pro for captions. As much as possible, our color schemes/palette should harmonize with their own. To help reinforce the good relationships we've developed with ABC's buyers, the document should be a letter proposal that therefore will allow us to address ABC directly and to use second-person pronouns.

- Given the need to adapt the document to different readers with different attention spans (e.g., Armstrong on the short end and the detail-oriented Morrison on the other), we should keep our methods section relatively brief and place our full-blown methodology in an appendix.
- Bottom line: When they read our proposal, we want them to feel as if it's one of their own internal documents, as if we and they are partners sharing the same culture.

In your experience, and to his credit, you believe, Gilmore is the only consultant you know who engages in such strategies. A form of Neuro-Linguistic Programming, these strategies certainly help him avoid situations where the buyers expect parchment and the consultants deliver stone tablets.

Writing the Story Component

Before beginning to write the Story Component, you review the Logics Worksheet that you filled out in Chapter 3, especially Cell 1 (Prospect Profile) and Cell 2 (Prospect's Current Situation). You also consider the large amount of Story Component material from your and Gilmore's notes as well as from the extensive in-house research that you've conducted. From these notes and research, you know, for example:

- Industry unit sales have been fairly stable, and total market forecasts indicate only modest growth.
- Despite stable industry sales, demand for ABC's products has been growing consistently, with associated (though modest) increases in market share, because of well-designed, high-quality, and competitively priced products, as well as good customer service.
- Projected demand will soon exceed available capacity.
- Lack of adequate manufacturing capacity could certainly stall ABC's growth.
- Geographic shifts in both population and households have changed patterns of demand and suggest that to maintain or improve customer service some manufacturing capacity should perhaps be located closer to high-growth areas.
- Several expansion alternatives have been proposed, though little agreement exists among ABC's management.

- A major area of disagreement could be the issue of control versus risk as it relates to expanding at the major facility only, as opposed to increasing capacity at one of the regional facilities or at a new location.
- Consensus exists about ABC's needing a plan and soon.

Your task is to paint a picture of the various buyers' combined perceptions of the current situation as well as their combined perceptions of the related causes and effects. In doing so, you want to be certain that you address several of the buyers' concerns: Collins's on customer service and its impact on market share; Armstrong's on the relationship with Consolidated; Morrison's on distribution costs and potential use of his model; Gupta's on the threat of increased operating costs; and Metzger's on expanding in other than the major facility. You also want to initiate some themes: "Urgency" comes to mind, as does "complexity." After several drafts, and in a fairly forceful voice cognizant of the threats to ABC's market share and position within Consolidated, you come up with the following:

The Situation at ABC

Over the past five years, household appliance shipments by ABC and your competitors have been fairly stable, and only modest growth is projected over the next five years in your mature industry. Despite the relative stability of these shipments industry-wide, ABC has managed to increase its share of the household appliance market primarily by producing high-quality products at competitive costs and by being responsive to customers' needs. As a result, ABC has become a leader in the market and one of the premier divisions within Consolidated Industries.

Your consistent record of success, however, may be threatened. Although your market forecasts indicate that ABC can continue to increase market share, even the conservative forecast clearly shows that projected product demand will exceed your available manufacturing capacity in less than three years. Without adequate capacity, your competitive position will certainly suffer as a result of declining delivery performance, deteriorating product quality, and increasing operating costs.

Complicating the picture, demographic shifts are moving demand farther away from your existing midwestern production facilities. Population and household growth in three geographic regions remote from these facilities have far exceeded that of the Midwest, as well as the nation as a whole.

Undoubtedly, these geographic shifts have contributed to ABC's increased distribution costs, a major factor in the total landed cost of household appliances.

In jeopardy are not only ABC's operating objectives but your status as a premier division within Consolidated.

Recognizing these threats, your management group has suggested several options for increasing capacity, but little agreement exists about how that capacity should be deployed, and no agreement exists about the amount of capacity required. Consensus does exist, however, in two areas: Additional capacity will be needed, and the time when it will be needed is fast approaching.

Writing the Questions Component

The Questions Component, you now know, provides you with an opportunity to demonstrate your qualifications as a problem solver, as someone who can demonstrate the ability to ask the right questions (the better to supply the correct answers). It also provides an opportunity to address key questions that you believe are on the minds of the various buyers. These questions allow you to indicate to each buyer that his or her desires or concerns have been heard without your having to take a position one way or another. Consider the question "How much expansion potential exists at the current facility?" In posing that question, you would address Metzger's desire to expand at the current facility without having to indicate at this point whether such a strategy is desirable. Equally important, the Questions Component "speaks" to and prepares the way for your methodology because this component presents key questions related to deliverables expressed as important actions in your logic tree.

You begin with a transition that continues the themes of "complexity" and "urgency" and that also initiates the themes of "thoroughness" and "comprehensiveness":

Complicating the need to move quickly is the need to carefully develop a thorough, convincing, and comprehensive plan accepted by both ABC's and Consolidated's management. This plan should answer questions like these:

⊛ Based upon the long-term forecast, how much total factory space, equipment, and human resources are required and when?
⊛ What opportunities exist to better utilize current equipment, space, and new technology?
⊛ What manufacturing factory configuration option or options will provide the required space? For example, how much expansion potential exists at the current facility, and what, if any, make/buy scenarios as well as changes in factory roles and locations can provide additional space?

- Even if resources can be added at the present location, does it make more economic sense to add them there or to make the investment elsewhere? For example, will service levels increase and transportation costs decrease at a new geographic location closer to growth markets?
- Which option is most appropriate considering the qualitative and quantitative factors identified in our methodology below?

Writing the Closing Component

The Closing Component is rather simple: a short, prospect-oriented paragraph that

> (*provides a backward transition from the Questions Component . . .*)
> To answer questions like these,

> (*provides a forward transition that anticipates the methods section . . .*)
> I and my colleagues at Paramount Consulting have designed a methodology

> (*states the project's objective . . .*)
> that will develop a manufacturing strategy to provide the capacity necessary for meeting forecasted demand

> (*and ends with some briefly stated benefits . . .*)
> as well as a concrete plan for implementing that strategy to improve your position within the marketplace and solidify your position within Consolidated Industries.

In rereading all the components together, you're reasonably satisfied. You've supplied good transitions to bridge the junctures between components. You've not only initiated the themes, but by doing so, you also have addressed various buyers' hot buttons while attempting to counter the competition. In general, you believe you've been responsive to ABC's needs. You've not only told a good story, you've told *their* story. And, you hope, they will begin to see you as part of it.

CHAPTER 10

Writing the Methods Slot

n Chapter 5, you saw that your methodology includes two kinds of tasks: actions necessary for achieving the project's objective and activities important for planning and communicating. (See Figure 10.1.) Note that both kinds of tasks tell me how you will do things—how you will achieve the project's objectives and how you will plan and communicate with me while doing so.

If you have worked for me before and I trust you explicitly, or if you have discussed your methodology with me and I am satisfied by how you will achieve your objective, or if your leadership style isn't detail oriented, then explaining *how* might be all that you need to do. In many situations, however, *how* isn't nearly enough, as the following example (based partly on the ABC case in Appendix A) ought to illustrate.

Assume the following:

- You are Marcia Collins, and I (switching roles here) am the consultant.
- As ABC's vice president of marketing, you are confident about your market forecast that predicts an imminent shortfall of capacity.
- Because I know that the engagement's success will depend upon a validated forecast, I need to explain to you *how* I will validate that forecast.
- You, of course, believe that such validation would be a waste of time and money.
- I am presenting my proposal to you and your management team.
- Just before displaying the first slide of the methods section, I say: "Our first task will be to validate ABC's market forecast."

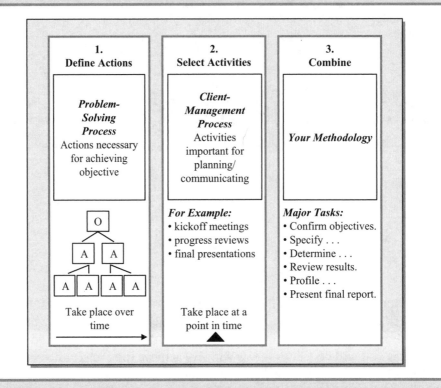

FIGURE 10.1 Your methodology includes both actions and activities.

Now, remember, you are Marcia Collins. How do you feel, Marcia? Angry? Embarrassed? Astonished, threatened, hostile, bitter, disbelieving, undermined? If your receptivity rating was a "single plus," it's now likely a "single minus" (or worse). If it was a "single minus," it's now a "double minus." I made a huge mistake by not having discussed with you, before the presentation, this key task in our methodology. I also failed to use a simple and yet extraordinarily powerful concept that will help you to develop persuasive methods sections. The concept is called PIP, which stands for Persuasion–Information–Persuasion, and the rest of this chapter explains what it is and how to use it.

What Is PIP?

Persuasion primarily involves logical or emotional appeals intended to change beliefs or produce conviction. Information primarily involves facts. The power of the PIP technique rests on these commonsense assumptions:

- Proposals contain both information and persuasion.
- Proposals (and their sections and subsections) have beginning, middle, and ending slots.
- When presented with a three-part sequence (i.e., a beginning, middle, and end), people tend to remember the beginning and ending items much more than those in the middle.
- If you need to be persuasive, as opposed to just informative, your persuasion should go in the first and last slots.

To sense the importance of the first and last slots, consider a sequence of three proposal presentations. If you were one of three bidders, you'd want to arrange to be first or last. As first presenter, you'd have the opportunity to set the tone and create the standard by which later presenters would be judged. As last presenter, you'd have the opportunity to make the last (and, you'd hope, a lasting) impression. The middle presenter risks getting lost in the shuffle, especially in a very close competition.

I call the beginning and ending slots, where you place your proposal's persuasive content, persuasion slots (P-slots). The opening P-slot explains *why* something should be done, and the closing P-slot explains *what* will result (for example, what benefit will accrue) from the doing. Persuasion slots always frame or "sandwich" an information slot, an I-slot, which explains *how* something will be done.

Now let's see how PIP works, or should have worked, in my presentation to Collins and her team. So far, I had filled the information slot, the I-slot, explaining how, in part, I would achieve the project's objective (Figure 10.2).

Now assume that I had provided a rationale for what I was going to do, explaining *why* the *how* should be done. Figure 10.3 shows that rationale along with an improved I-slot.

How do you feel now, Marcia? Of course, you're still angry and embarrassed, because I have still made the crucial mistake of not having discussed this issue with you before the presentation. But notice how you are *less* angry, *less* embarrassed. Why? Because I've explained *why*. I gave you a good reason for why I'd do what I said I'd do. I filled the opening P-slot by providing a rationale.

Slot	Explains	Expresses	Example
I-slot	How	An action/ activity	*We will work with ABC to update its market forecast.*

FIGURE 10.2 The I-slot and what it does

Slot	Explains	Expresses	Example
Opening P-slot	Why	A rationale	*Because ABC's market is changing rapidly,*
I-slot	How	An action/ activity	*we will work with you to update your market forecast.*

FIGURE 10.3 The opening P-slot and what it does

Slot	Explains	Expresses	Example
Opening P-slot	Why	A rationale	*Because ABC's market is changing rapidly,*
I-slot	How	An action/ activity	*we will work with you to update your market forecast.*
Closing P-slot	What	A result/ benefit	*By having the market forecast validated by an outside party, your firm will help convince Consolidated that the project is rigorous and current.*

FIGURE 10.4 The closing P-slot and what it does

If I need to be even more persuasive, I can fill the closing P-slot by explaining what benefits will accrue from the doing, as shown in Figure 10.4.

PIP: Persuasion–Information–Persuasion. Three slots. The first and last are relatively more important and, therefore, include the persuasion. The middle slot is relatively less important and contains the information. That information is almost always necessary, because it states the tasks necessary for achieving your objective. But the information isn't always sufficient. By itself, it might not be as persuasive as it needs to be.

Now that you understand how PIP works, we can talk about how you can use this organizational technique at various levels of the methods section (as well as throughout the entire proposal).

PIP at the Task Level

If necessary or appropriate, each task in your methods section can be organized according to PIP, as suggested by Figure 10.5.

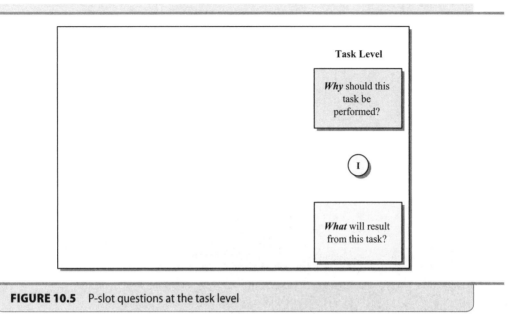

FIGURE 10.5   P-slot questions at the task level

The informational part (the middle I-slot, shown as a circle in Figure 10.5) is the action or activity itself. It explains *how* the task will be performed. If you sense that I want to know *why* you are performing a task, you might decide to provide some good reason, in the form of a rationale, for its performance; therefore, you'd fill the opening P-slot by providing that rationale. If you have a good rationale for conducting the task, it's because the task will produce some definable end product, or benefit, some understanding or knowledge or validation framework or decision point. If that end product is worth mentioning, you can fill the closing P-slot by explaining *what* the task will accomplish or what benefits or value will accrue from its accomplishment.

Imagine the difference in persuasion between a series of tasks that are PIP-ed,[1] like that one in Figure 10.6, and a series that omits all the P-slots. The latter would contain only information related to how each of the tasks would be performed. The PIP-ed series would also explain to me why you are doing what you propose to do and what benefit or value I would receive from your doing it.

Figure 10.6 obviously shows a PIP-ed task in a text proposal. In a slide presentation, you can use PIP as shown in Figure 10.7. The opening P-slot, the task's rationale, is usually spoken, often as an oral transition before you reveal the slide. The I-slot, where you explain how the task in the headline will be achieved, is shown in the body of the slide. The closing P-slot can be revealed as a build in what is sometimes called a "So What?" box at the bottom of the slide.

P–slot (Why?)	**Task 1: Confirm Business Direction** A clear understanding of your company's business, mission, and current and future direction is key to the success of this project. This understanding establishes the context within which all further assessments are made and recommendations are developed.
I–slot (How?)	Therefore, we will review all relevant materials concerning your company's mission and basic strategy. After interviewing members of the board and senior management, we will know exactly how ABC's basic mission and strategies compare with those of similar entities elsewhere.
P–slot (What?)	As a result of completing this task, the project team will clearly understand your business direction and underlying strategies, senior management issues and perspectives, and major areas of focus for the balance of the project. We will document the results of the task in a summary presentation and review it with you to ensure a common base of understanding.

FIGURE 10.6   PIP at the task level

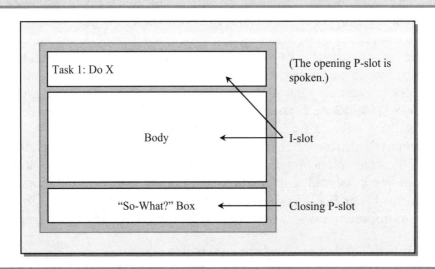

FIGURE 10.7   Using PIP in a presentation slide

Why aren't the tasks PIP-ed in many if not most of your proposals? I can think of three reasons:

1. The tasks just don't have to be PIP-ed. That is, during the business-development process, you have already persuaded me that your methodology is sound; as a result, you don't have to provide me with a rationale for why you are proposing the tasks or with a discussion of the benefits of your completing the tasks.
2. You don't fill the opening and closing P-slots because you fail to consider my needs. Although *you know* why you are completing the tasks as well as the benefits of your doing so, possibly because you have done similar projects dozens of times, *I don't know* what you know.
3. You don't know about or understand the strategic benefits of using PIP.

Now you know.

PIP at the Methods Section Level

Your methods section is more than a collection of tasks. It has a beginning, middle, and end; an introduction, body, and conclusion. Let's focus on the introduction, on the introductions in proposals you've written and read. If your experience is like mine, those introductions begin something like this:

> We recommend the following six- [or five- or ten-] step approach.

Ask yourself: Is that information or persuasion? Of course it's the former. It doesn't provide a rationale for why you have constructed your methodology as you have. It doesn't answer the question, "Why out of a universe of possible methodologies have you chosen this one?" It doesn't, that is, fill the opening P-slot at the methods-section level.

As Figure 10.8 illustrates, all your tasks (all of which could themselves be PIP-ed) form the middle or the body of the methods section. At the methods-section level, those tasks are the I-slot, explaining *how* you will achieve the project's objective. As is always the case, above and below the I-slot are P-slots, which you must decide whether to fill. The entire methods section can be organized according to PIP.

When you write the introduction to your methods section, ask yourself if you have filled the opening P-slot. For example, does your introduction "recommend a three-phase approach" and pretty much leave me with only that information? Or should it go on to explain persuasively that such an approach will be employed because the phases will, for example:

* Allow me to achieve short-term results to make subsequent phases "pay as you go."
* Allow me to address broader strategic issues early on before focusing on more tactical questions.

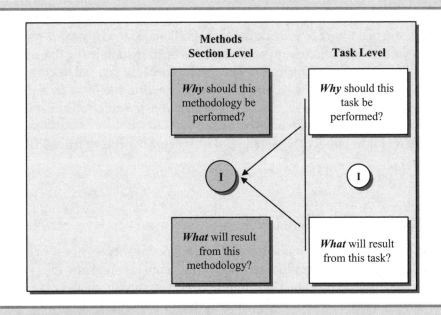

FIGURE 10.8   P-slot questions at the methods-section level

- Continuously build on each other so that decisions reached in earlier phases influence and help screen options in later ones, thus leading to economies because I can choose to limit further evaluation in later phases based on analyses performed in earlier ones.

Does your introduction recommend collaboration between your team and mine and pretty much leave me with that information only? Or should it go on to explain that the study is strategically planned to meet my specific needs by employing a team approach that will, for example:

- Generate enthusiasm and commitment for the project's potential outcomes.
- Keep me informed at every major step of the project.
- Result in jointly developed and better accepted recommendations and action plans.
- Efficiently resolve newly surfaced issues.
- Keep the lines of communication open.
- Efficiently transfer to your team my organization's intimate knowledge of your firm.
- Most efficiently transfer to my people your team's knowledge, technology, and/ or skills.

Your introduction to METHODS provides a great opportunity to sell your methodology, to explain persuasively to me and others on the consultant-selection committee exactly how your methodology contains elements that will lead us to a more successful and beneficial project.

If you have completed a Themes Development Worksheet (TDW) (see Figure 10.9), you already will have generated much of the persuasive content for the opening P-slot of METHODS.

The Situation (S) and Methods (M) columns of your Themes Development Worksheet provide the opening P-slot material, the rationale for constructing your approach as you have. Because those columns' content contains your themes, your opening P-slot implicitly (and often without my realizing it) communicates the following:

> We have designed our methodology as we have because it addresses your hot buttons, meets your evaluation criteria, and counters our competition.

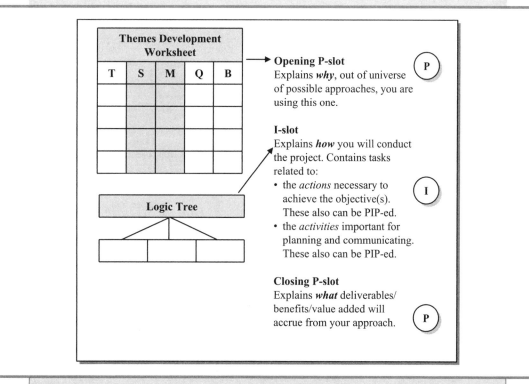

FIGURE 10.9 Your TDW provides the content for the methods section's opening P-slot.

If you have done a good job on your Themes Development Worksheet, your opening P-slot to METHODS *can't not* be persuasive! If you have four themes, you will have four reasons arguing that out of a universe of possible approaches, yours is the best for our situation. The work session at the end of this chapter, which is essential reading, will clearly demonstrate how the TDW's Situation and Methods columns provide most if not all the content for your methods section's introduction.

As Figure 10.8 and Figure 10.9 illustrate, the conclusion to your methods section also contains a P-slot. Rather than ending with a discussion of the tenth task of the third phase—i.e., ending with information—you can persuasively conclude your methods section by itemizing the expected deliverables (if they haven't been identified within the tasks), by summarizing the most important deliverables (if they have been included in the tasks), and/or by explaining to me the value that your approach will add, the benefits that will accrue, during the project.

PIP at the Document Level

I doubt that you have ever seen a proposal whose methods section either began or ended the document. Typically, methods sections reside in the middle of the

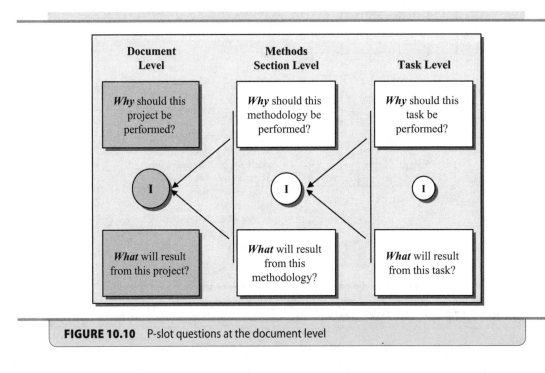

FIGURE 10.10   P-slot questions at the document level

proposal. At the document level, the methods section functions as the document's I-slot. As Figure 10.10 reveals, the document level also contains two P-slots:

- At the document level, the opening P-slot provides a persuasive rationale for why the project itself should be done. That P-slot is SITUATION, which (as Chapter 9 explained) is usually formed into a background section that argues the need for the entire project.
- At the document level, the closing P-slot discusses the benefits that will accrue from the project. That P-slot is BENEFITS, which we will discuss in Chapter 12.

PIP and Proposal Strategy: Determining the Needed Level of Persuasion

Think of the various levels of PIP as a set of Russian nesting dolls (Figure 10.11). Your document is the largest doll, whose opening P-slot *can be* SITUATION and whose closing P-slot *can be* BENEFITS. The next smallest is all the tasks in your methodology, which itself *can be* PIP-ed. The smallest is all of your methodology's tasks, which themselves *can be* PIP-ed. When you use the PIP strategy, you are explaining to me, at every level of the proposal, from one handcrafted doll to another, *why* something must be done, *how* it should be done, and *what* I will receive from your doing it.

When I say that something *can be* PIP-ed, you might be asking an important question: When *should* a P-slot be filled? In this last section of the chapter, we need to discuss that strategic question.

FIGURE 10.11　The various levels of P-slots are like Russian nesting dolls.

Because P-slots exist at the beginning and ending of things, they're easy to find. Once you find them, however, you have to decide whether they should be filled. Your decision will depend on your sense of the situation, which will be different in every proposal opportunity. As a friend recalls a proposal situation some years ago when he was a fairly inexperienced consultant:

> I wrote a proposal that I thought was going to be exactly like another proposal a consultant wrote for another company. Both companies competed in the same industry and manufactured the same products in almost the exact same geographic area. I pulled out that other proposal in order to boilerplate from it. I thought this would be a cakewalk. But by the time I was done, the only thing the other proposal did was to supply some neat ideas for me.
>
> The consultant's earlier proposal was written to a company for which he had done ten previous projects. He knew the president very well (the president's son was also a client), and the company was extraordinarily successful. But the current proposal was for a company where I had never met anybody; the company was in trouble; there was no warm feeling; there was no ten years of experience; there were no previous assignments.
>
> The earlier proposal, according to the consultant, was sort of a "Hey, Stan, this kind of confirms what we will do together, and we will do our best, and if we blow it we will change in midstream, and it has been great seeing you." But the current proposal is, "number one you don't know me, number two I have to establish my credentials and my firm's credentials, number three we are sorry we took so long to respond, because we lost your letter (which is really number four); of all the firms you talked to, however, we are the only one with the exact right qualifications—here they are," and now, suddenly, we have a totally different proposal.[2]

Obviously, the second proposal had to be much more substantial and persuasive than the first; therefore, more of the P-slots had to be filled. But how do you decide just how persuasive your proposal needs to be? I can think of at least three factors you should consider: your relationship with the buyers, the competition, and your sales objective, as shown in Figure 10.12.

The first two categories, "relationship with buyers" and "competition," are fairly obvious. Assume, for example, that the quality of your relationship with me is excellent, that you've done many studies for me and my organization, and that I'm not talking to any of your competitors. No one else is competing for my attention, and, in the past, when you have worked for me, you've done so very successfully. Your credibility is a given; you don't have to acquire it. I've asked you to meet with me to discuss a problem that needs to be solved, and you have convinced me in our two-hour meeting that you understand the problem and have the right people and approach for solving it. We've also discussed costs, and I've agreed to them.

More or fewer P-slots need to be filled depending on . . .		
*Your **relationship** with the buyers* • What is the quality of that relationship? • How many previous studies have you done for their firm, and what was the result? • What studies, known by them, have you done for other firms, and what was the result?	*Your **competition*** • How many firms are competing? • How qualified are the competitors? • To what extent have these competitors worked for the prospect before? • Is one of them the incumbent?	*Your **sales objectives*** • To prequalify for the next opportunity? • To get to the next level? • To win?

FIGURE 10.12   Considerations to determine if and how much the P-slots should be filled

In short, you've sold the job, and I've asked you for nothing more than a confirmation letter. As a result, you need to do very little with the P-slots. On the task level, there might be little need to provide a rationale for each task and to indicate the benefits of completing it. In fact, you might need to do nothing more with the tasks than include them in a Gantt chart. On the methods-section level, there might be little need to discuss the rationale for your specific approach. At the document level, you might not even need to provide a rationale for why the study should be done nor argue the benefits that will accrue from its doing.

Conversely, if five firms are competing and some of them have capabilities equal to yours, and if they, not you, have worked successfully with me, your proposal will have to be very persuasive indeed. Many of the P-slots will have to be filled—and filled well. At each crucial point, you may have to explain why a task is important to perform—and the results of its performance; why you have designed your approach precisely as you have—and the value of your conducting it; and why, from your point of view, the study should be performed—and the benefits to be gained from your performing it.

In this second case, however, you should seriously consider not writing a proposal at all, especially if my issue doesn't play to your strengths or if I am not one of your target clients or am not in one of your target industries. Instead, redeploy your resources for some other battle you have a better chance to win.

The third category in Figure 10.12, "sales objectives," is important because too many proposal writers view the written proposal as having only one sales objective: to close the deal. A good example of this proposal-as-last-effort viewpoint is the requirement at some consulting firms (sometimes by fiat, sometimes by institutional practice) that letter proposals contain signature blocks at the end of the document, prefaced by a sentence such as "If you agree with the terms as set forth in this proposal, please sign in the appropriate space and forward one copy to. . . ." Required even in competitive situations, this procedure views the proposal as a final product rather than as a negotiating tool—one more possible stage in the proposal process to help you get closer to what then could be your best and final offer to me.

In many situations, of course, the proposal is your best and final offer because I won't allow you any other. But in other situations, the proposal-as-final-offer strategy can be most unstrategic, because your document's sales objective is not always to win but to get you one step closer to what can become a "done deal."

That is, sometimes your immediate sales objective is to get to the next stage, the better to sell at the next level or the better to continue to try to sell at the same level. For example, assume that you don't have access to the economic buyer. In that situation, the strategy could be to write a document whose sales objective is not to close the deal but to get buy-in from the technical and user buyers, who then, in effect, become part of your team. At that point, they can coach you to meet the new sales objective, which would be to work together to sell to the economic buyer. The new document or presentation could then be specifically tailored to meet the new sales objective.

Even if you have access to all the buyers, you can profitably choose to view the written proposal or oral presentation as a discussion document. Indeed, many experienced consultants try not to include fees in the written proposal. They label it a "discussion document" so that they can meet with me and my team to hammer out the methodology and our level of involvement; agree on the deliverables; and, of course, establish the trust and chemistry necessary for us to say "yes" with confidence. If by the end of that meeting, they haven't yet sold the work, they're at least closer, and they know even more about me, my team, and my organization's problem or opportunity. Their proposal and our relationship will be better because of it.

On some (certainly less frequent) occasions, the objective isn't to sell on any level at all but simply to get into the game so that you can play the next time around. A friend of mine, an environmental consultant, decided to play on these terms. He did not originally receive a request for proposal (RFP) from a Canadian governmental agency because the agency wasn't aware that his firm did environmental consulting. After finding out about the opportunity through the Internet, however, he asked for and received permission to bid, and did so, even though a dozen other competitors were involved and the job probably was wired to begin with. His sales objective was not to win but to prequalify for future work. His document functioned less like a proposal and more like a response to an RFQ (request for qualifications).

In the work session of this chapter, you'll get a good sense for the level of persuasiveness needed and, therefore, how many of the P-slots need to be filled. You'll begin to see how the Russian dolls fit together, the better to view your handiwork and craftsmanship.

Writing the Methods Slot

1. The methods slot consists of your methodology (as discussed in Chapter 5) plus your good reasons for performing it.
2. These good reasons take two forms: first, a rationale for why you will do what you say you will; second, the results or benefits that will accrue from your doing it.
3. The good reasons can go into persuasion slots (P-slots) that precede and follow information slots (I-slots).
4. The opening P-slot explains *why* you will do something. The I-slot explains *how* you will do it. The closing P-slot explains *what* will result from your doing it. Hence, PIP.
5. PIP can be used to organize the methods section at the task and section levels.
6. How many P-slots should be filled depends on your relationship to the buyers, the competitiveness of the situation, and your sales objective for the document or presentation.

WORK SESSION 8: Writing the Methods Section for ABC

In your estimation, the individuals on the ABC buying team are a rather diverse lot with solid but rather narrow functional capabilities. In evaluating your proposal, some will look for a technically precise methodology that also addresses their individual, varied concerns and needs, that is, one that responds to their different perceptions of ABC's current situation as well as their sometimes similar but often different hot buttons. Your Themes Development Worksheet addresses these hot buttons as well as some of the competition's exploitable weaknesses.

Composing the Opening P-Slot for the Methods Section

In fact, the Situation and Methodology columns of that worksheet provide (as they always do) most of the persuasive material for the opening P-slot to the section. You use those claims and follow them with a statement that forecasts the five major tasks. Your draft of the opening P-slot to the methods section looks like this:

> We have designed our methodology for three important reasons. First, because forecasted demand will soon outstrip capacity and because building new capacity will require long lead times, you need a study that leads to a decision quickly. Therefore, we will involve ABC's management to expedite the retrieval, development, and analysis of relevant information, thus reducing the time for analysis. We will also work with your management team to prepare the final report. This document will be not only a recommended expansion plan

but also an actual proposal to Consolidated that justifies the cost of the expansion by articulating the compelling reasons to move forward with urgency.

Second, because of the many and varied proposed expansion alternatives, you need well-defined and agreed-upon criteria for evaluating them. Therefore, we will conduct strategy sessions with all relevant ABC managers to gain consensus on and establish the proper quantitative and qualitative criteria. Quantitative criteria worth considering include ROI, investment incentives, taxes, and costs related to labor, service levels, distribution, construction, and utilities. Qualitative criteria could include labor supply, union climate, workforce characteristics, productivity, environmental regulations, vocational training capabilities, manufacturing support services, risk, controllability, the ability to develop and promote employees, and the flexibility to react to unanticipated changes.

Finally, because this will be a cross-functional study, ABC needs a senior, multifaceted consulting team with a broad range of business capabilities, including marketing, manufacturing strategy, facilities planning, logistics, financial analysis, and human resources. These capabilities are necessary to ensure that all relevant options are surfaced and evaluated in a practical manner, that the most desirable options and their attributes are clearly identified and defined, and that ABC's management not only has the ability to make the right decision but that Consolidated is convinced of its appropriateness. Therefore, we will form a joint ABC/Paramount study team with ABC's managers playing an integral role, thereby providing the additional benefit of training ABC's management to analyze and plan for additional capacity in the future.

Specifically, our methodology consists of the following five major tasks:

[note to myself: insert Gantt chart here]

Please note that the five-month estimate for completing the study is conservative. Working with your management team, we will make every effort to accelerate the completion of the tasks discussed in greater detail in Appendix A.

After composing this P-slot, you turn your attention to the five major tasks that you developed by using a logic tree. Your purpose is to build persuasiveness into the methodology by providing beginning and ending P-slots for each of these major tasks.

Composing the P-Slots for Task 1: Confirm ABC's Long-Term Product Forecast

The opening P-slot for this task will be particularly important. Without providing a highly persuasive rationale for confirming the forecast, you run the considerable risk of alienating Collins, who not only developed the forecast but also has confidence in its accuracy. You decide to use two key arguments:

- An accurate forecast is critical for determining the magnitude and timing of additional manufacturing resources (that is, it drives the entire analysis).
- An independent confirmation of the forecast will assure Consolidated that ABC's projected growth and timing are real and merit significant capital investment.

Your closing P-slot for this task, where you have the opportunity to explain the results of completing it, will argue that an accurate, authenticated forecast will provide the basis for making a sound first estimate of future resource requirements.

Below is your draft of Task 1. The bullets in the middle of this and subsequent tasks are the I-slot material taken from your logic tree.

Task 1: Confirm ABC's Long-Term Product Forecast

Although ABC already has a forecast by product line, we believe that the engagement must be conducted with Consolidated constantly in mind. Since Consolidated must release the necessary capital funding, it must be convinced of the engagement's rigor and robustness. For that reason, we believe that the forecast must be confirmed by an independent third party. Therefore, we propose to work with ABC's marketing management to confirm or modify the long-term forecast by:

- validating ABC's current overall market forecast
- validating ABC's market share and your geographic and product-mix projections

The consensus market forecast developed in this task will represent the best thinking of your marketing group and the Paramount team. The forecast, used with various manufacturing data, will enable the engagement team to develop future resource requirements over time.

Composing the P-Slots for Task 2: Determine Total Factory Resource Requirements at Alternative Forecast Levels

Your initial meeting with ABC's buying team and Gilmore's description of the current operation have given you a high regard for ABC's capabilities. But you also realize that even competent managers can be so close to their operations that they risk taking them for granted, not fully recognizing opportunities for improvement. You also know that ABC hasn't been involved in planning a new facility for years and probably doesn't recognize that facility needs can be either seriously overstated or understated without first establishing a solid base of effective operations from which to project those needs.

These are points you develop to formulate an opening P-slot for this task. Importantly, the task will involve identifying opportunities to improve current operations and/or outsource various components to establish a solid base that will be used in conjunction with the forecast to accurately project future requirements.

You know that the output from this task will provide an essential ingredient for developing the overall manufacturing facility strategy. Only when future requirements are known can the study team explore viable options for providing these requirements. You convey this important understanding in the closing P-slot.

Your draft of Task 2:

Task 2: Determine Total Factory Space Requirements at Alternate Forecast Levels

An important task of the engagement team will be to use the existing base of production resources (floor space, equipment, and staffing) and modify that base so that it can accommodate the additional future production demands over time indicated by the confirmed market forecast. First, however, the team will carefully evaluate that base to identify improvements or eliminate inefficiencies that might exist today. We don't want ABC to risk adding too much or too little capacity. This risk can be avoided by first establishing a proper base, a "current-improved" base, from which to project future resource requirements. All this will be critical, because determining future needs involves far more than simply an arithmetic extrapolation of today's activities.

We were very much impressed during our walk-through of your main manufacturing facility. You should know, however, that in nearly every similar engagement, we have been able to recommend methods for better utilizing currently available space, thereby making space available for additional equipment to add to manufacturing capacity. To provide additional capacity and/or space without first determining such improvement opportunities could result in unnecessary capital investment.

We will ensure that ABC is making the most effective use of existing manufacturing resources. Specifically, we will:

- document current equipment and space utilization
- determine opportunities to better utilize current equipment and space and to improve material flow

- determine opportunities for utilizing new equipment technology
- specify which products or components, if any, could be made in-house or purchased from suppliers

The modified, effective base of production resources coupled with the confirmed market forecast will enable the engagement team to develop an accurate and credible projection of future resource requirements. At this point, the joint ABC/Paramount engagement team will have a sound basis for identifying, evaluating, and selecting the most viable option or options to provide these requirements.

Composing the P-Slots for Task 3: Define Manufacturing Facility Options to Provide Required Resources

Many different facility configurations could provide ABC's needed additional resources. ABC's management team understands this as well: Metzger felt that the existing facility should be expanded, Gupta thought the same for the satellite facilities, and Collins argued for a "greenfield" site closer to expanding markets. You try several times to write P-slots for this task, but each of them sounds forced and dry. Eventually, you realize why: The fundamental purpose and result of this task are so obvious that opening and closing P-slots are unnecessary. So you introduce this task with nothing more than a transition from Task 2 and end the task's discussion with a transition to Task 4.

Your draft of Task 3 reads as follows:

> **Task 3: Define Manufacturing Facility Options**
> **to Provide Required Resources**
> Once we know how much additional space and equipment are required, we will identify the possible manufacturing options that will provide these additional resources. Accordingly, we will develop and analyze various options and determine which configuration of facilities best meets your objectives.
>
> Specifically, we will:
>
> - determine expansion potential at the current facility
> - specify potential factory roles and locations for increasing capacity
>
> As a result of completing this task, we will have narrowed the field from the possible to the probable, the better to be able to scrutinize the remaining options and to choose the most appropriate.

In rereading your draft, you realize that the second bullet probably should have some discussion under it.

Composing the P-Slots for Task 4: Select the Most Appropriate Option

This task will help eliminate the uncertainty that must be disconcerting to ABC's team. It will reveal whether Metzger's, Collins's, or Gupta's biases are valid. But in the process, you know that a number of "pet" ideas are going to be "shot down." Only considerable agreement among the buying team on the criteria to be used to evaluate the multiple options will avoid hard feelings and assure acceptance of the selected facility option. These thoughts, which also focus on the theme of consensus, help you formulate an opening P-slot.

For the closing P-slot, you focus on two crucial results of completing the task: first, ABC will know precisely how to configure its manufacturing facilities over time; second, the result of proper configuration will allow ABC to meet customer demand throughout the forecasted period cost-effectively and responsively.

Your draft of Task 4 reads as follows:

> **Task 4: Select the Most Appropriate Option**
> Using ABC's distribution model and Paramount's proprietary models for assessing expansion options, the joint engagement team will evaluate thoroughly each potential expansion option and then select the one most appropriate. Although the range of options will have been narrowed, those remaining will quite likely be diverse. Therefore, we will work with ABC management to develop both quantitative and qualitative criteria that will differentiate carefully among the various options, and we will obtain management's agreement on the one most appropriate.
>
> Specifically, to select the most appropriate option, the engagement team will:
>
> - define quantitative and qualitative criteria important to ABC and Consolidated
> - evaluate each option against quantitative criteria such as ROI, landed cost, quality, and customer service
> - evaluate each option against qualitative criteria such as manufacturing flexibility and potential risk
>
> When this task is completed, you will know precisely how to configure your manufacturing facilities over time so that you can meet customer demand throughout the forecasted period cost-effectively and responsively.

Composing the P-Slots for Task 5: Develop a Plan to Implement the Selected Option

Merely defining the best facility option for ABC won't be enough. They will need to know precisely how to implement the selected strategy, and they will look to Paramount to provide that direction. Since space, equipment, new technology, and people probably will be added in stages during the forecast period, ABC will want to know just when and how much new capital and additional manufacturing resources will be needed over that time period. You feel confident that carefully worded statements based on this need will provide an impressive opening P-slot.

Your closing P-slot will stress that completing this task is most important to ABC. It will provide them with an accurate, carefully defined road map showing precisely how to implement the facility strategy in a timely, efficient, and cost-effective manner. The draft of the final task looks like this:

> **Task 5: Develop a Plan to Implement the Selected Option**
>
> Because the additional manufacturing resources required will likely be brought onstream at various times throughout the forecast period, ABC will need a carefully prepared plan to monitor progress during implementation. To that end, we will prepare a plan to ensure that additional manufacturing resources and facilities are in place when and where they are needed to meet forecasted demand. The various steps in our implementation plan will be time-phased so that management will know precisely when additional capacity is required and when other managerial decisions and actions are needed.
>
> Specifically, we will:
>
> - define the tasks necessary to implement the selected option
> - define the resources and responsibilities necessary to complete those tasks
> - develop a critical path to estimate the time required to complete all tasks
>
> As a result of this task, management will know all the tasks required to provide the additional manufacturing resources, when each task should be initiated and completed, and the skills required to complete each task. The implementation plan will provide you with a critical mechanism to monitor overall progress, to efficiently invest required capital and other resources when they are needed, and to take corrective actions if actual market demand differs significantly from that projected.

After completing this task and obtaining your agreement, we will work with you to immediately prepare a capital appropriations request that can be submitted directly to Consolidated for their timely consideration.

Because the closing P-slot for Task 5 discusses some of the project's major outcomes (an implementation plan and a capital appropriations request), you decide to use it as well for the closing P-slot of the entire section.

CHAPTER 11

Writing the Qualifications Slot

'͏ve probably seen more boilerplate in qualifications sections than in a furnace factory, especially from the larger consulting firms, the ones with big research departments. These firms' proposals list everything they can about what they've done and whom they've done it to. There's a better way, and I'll tell you what it is.

The situation and methods slots allow you to demonstrate your qualifications implicitly. In SITUATION, for example, you can display your abilities as a problem solver by demonstrating your understanding of our problem's causes and effects and by indicating your awareness of the important questions that must be answered before this problem can be addressed or solved. Your understanding of these matters can be crucial to the successful conduct of the project, and your clear and accurate presentation can serve as evidence of your experience, expertise, perspicacity, ingenuity, insight, and whatever other characteristics you wish to convey. In SITUATION and METHODS, you're showing your qualifications, implicitly. In QUALIFICATIONS, you're telling them, explicitly. You're explicitly attempting to answer the question "Why are you best qualified for *this* project?"

The answer to that question should focus on abilities and capabilities related to my specific situation. Abilities are qualities of people, such as experience, kind and level of expertise, and personal characteristics. Capabilities are qualities of things, such as your firm or proprietary intellectual capital like methodologies, databases, or models. In a great many proposals, abilities are discussed in résumés (often attached in an appendix) and in staffing sections or subsections that often include brief biographies as well as the roles and responsibilities of those who will play a part in the project. These abilities are certainly part of the qualifications slot, even though they might not be in a section called "Qualifications."

If you are a consultant, you have electronic files filled with descriptions of abilities and capabilities: résumés of your professional staff; a record of the studies your firm has done in various industries, in achieving various objectives; a history of the firm itself and how it has grown and developed; and prepackaged statements about the firm's commitment to quality, effective implementation, and so on. All that boilerplate is important. And everyone else, including each of your competitors, has it too.

So you and they keep using it, especially in qualifications sections. I've read proposals that didn't once mention my organization's name in the qualifications section because that section contained nothing but generic fluff lifted whole cloth from an electronic file. I've read other proposals that did contain the name of a firm, but not my own, because the section was lifted whole cloth from another proposal. And I've even read one document—you won't believe this!—that contained place holders for where my organization's name should have gone, for example: <insert client's name>. Computers are wonderful things, but they're not a remedy for laziness or carelessness or a substitute for logical thinking about why you are, in fact, the best firm to meet my needs.

Persuasion occurs at the intersection of your abilities and your firm's capabilities with my needs. By that definition, a qualifications section that focuses only on abilities and capabilities isn't persuasive, or at least not as persuasive as it could be. It must focus on those abilities and capabilities *as they relate to my needs.*

Many qualifications sections don't address those needs because they are written by someone who doesn't know them, much less understand them. Consider, for example, a typical situation that occurs at some large consulting firms. The firm has four people working on a particular proposal, and they represent four levels in the firm's professional ranks. Though the terms differ from firm to firm, let's call them partner, principal, manager, and consultant.

Although the partner is the only one who has met with the potential client, she will write little, if any, of the proposal. She will, however, review it, though her review will focus primarily on staffing and costs, since she may get the proposal only 15 minutes before it has to go out the door. The principal will manage the proposal-writing effort, composing some of the document's parts and assigning others to the manager. Partner, principal, and manager will have discussed the situation at the prospect's firm and the strategy for preparing the document. The consultant rarely, if ever, writes proposals because he spends almost all his time doing research on the projects themselves; he is not involved in selling work. He has neither met with the potential client nor been apprised of the situation or the study's objectives or possible methodology. Can you guess who is assigned to write the qualifications section?

The consultant finds (he's often instructed to find) several previous proposals written to similar clients, perhaps for similar studies. These proposals were written by others like him, and those qualification sections were written by still others like him. The sections aren't directed to specific readers in specific situations, with specific needs, problems, or opportunities. They are directed to what I call "Generic World." They contain discussions of abilities and capabilities that could be read by almost any reader in almost any situation. They don't focus on the intersection of your abilities and capabilities with my needs or evaluation criteria, and neither will the new qualifications section that the consultant will write—or copy—from the old ones. In this chapter, I'll show you how to write a qualifications section that focuses on that intersection.[1]

Your Qualifications Section Needs to Be an Argument

In Chapter 5, I showed you how to construct a logic tree to develop the actions in your methodology. That logic tree structured an argument to address the key question I wanted your methodology to answer: "How will you achieve the project's objective?" Your qualifications section also is an argument, and it also can be developed with a logic tree. Now, however, my key question is not *How?* but *Why?* Why are you the best-qualified firm, with the best-qualified team, to conduct *this* project? (See Figure 11.1.) The principles in building this "why" logic tree are similar to those used to build the "how" logic tree in the methodology. In a "why" logic tree, each box in one row of the logic tree stakes out a claim you must substantiate, and each group of boxes below it argues why that claim is true.

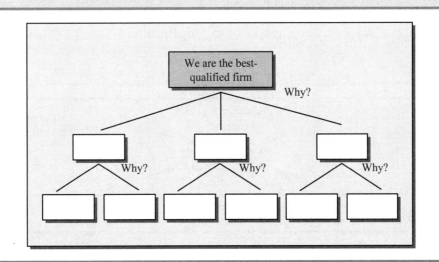

FIGURE 11.1 The qualifications section can be organized by a "why" logic tree.

Typical Qualifications Sections Don't Present an Argument

Qualifications sections written to Generic World can't present an argument whose claim is "We are the best-qualified firm," because *best* implies *in this situation*. Such sections tend to be organized by easy-to-boilerplate categories, as in Figure 11.2, rather than as specific claims that answer the question *Why?*

If I asked you, "Why are you the best-qualified firm?" I doubt that you would answer, "Description of the firm, industry experience, and, oh yes, consulting philosophy." You wouldn't be answering my question. You'd be answering something like, "What *categories* will you use in organizing your qualifications section?" I don't care about that question. I want to know why you believe you're the best-qualified firm so that I can judge for myself.

These categories, you see, focus inwardly only on your abilities and capabilities, not outwardly on their intersection with my needs. Consider the subsection "Description of the Firm." (Yes, this qualifications section was written by the same consultant I previously discussed, and yes, it was part of a proposal sent to me.) The subsection contained information on the history of the consulting firm, the number of employees, and the number and location of offices. Terrific!

All this information could be relevant and persuasive in our situation. For example, assume the proposed project would take one year, require vast consulting resources and expertise, and affect my organization's facilities around the world. In this case, I might want to engage a stable firm that's been around a long time, with vast resources and diverse expertise and with offices and capabilities around the world. However, my proposed project could require only specialized expertise and affect only one of our operations. Of course, that was the case. But the consulting firm's qualifications section was written by someone with scant knowledge of my organization and of my organization's current situation and

FIGURE 11.2 The lower-level boxes don't support the claim of the upper box.

desired result. It didn't matter to the writer that I was reading the section. The section wasn't written to me and my world but to Generic World.

The subsection "Proprietary Methods" began this way: "The general operating practice of QRS Consulting is to develop frameworks and approaches to client-specific problems—not cookbooks that are simply transferred from client to client. . . . We tailor each approach for each client to ensure a unique and competitive solution to that client's specific problem." Would you trust someone who uses boilerplate to assure you that you and your organization are unique? This passage is worse than insincere. It borders on the hypocritical. Don't think I can't smell boilerplate. Don't think I'm stupid. You are the one who comes off not necessarily stupid but insincere, untrustworthy, unthinking, uncreative, uncaring, and unworthy. This is no way to gain two to five points.

Use Your Themes Development Worksheet to Structure Your Argument

Themes are related to the qualities of the seller as they intersect with my needs as the buyer. So if you want to focus on your qualifications as they intersect with me, you need to look to your themes. Specifically, you need to capture the information in the Qualifications column of your Themes Development Worksheet. Why are you the best qualified? Because, as that column will reveal, you can respond to my hot buttons. Because your abilities and capabilities are in line with my evaluation criteria. Because you can counter the competition against these criteria.

Let me be more specific. Assume that I and my organization want from our consultants personal service when and where we demand it and that you are a small firm bidding against two much larger ones. Why are you the best qualified? Because your small size avoids levels of bureaucracy. You can move quickly if I need you quickly. You're lean and fast and therefore attentive. So if I ask you why you're the best-qualified firm, you can give me not a category but a good reason like that shown in Figure 11.3.

Now you can discuss how big your firm is, not in a subsection called "Description of the Firm" but in this one. That is, you will discuss the size of your firm because it is relevant, in this case, to your ability to provide close personal service, which is relevant to this project because it's relevant to me. It's an instance of your qualifications intersecting with my needs. You are describing your firm not simply to describe your firm but to provide evidence for your claim: "We are the best-qualified firm for *this* project, in part because of our relatively small size. . . ." Now, you can also discuss your consulting philosophy, but again, only as it relates to close personal service, only as it provides evidence for your claim. And so on down (and across) the logic tree. A fully fleshed-out logic tree will have many filled boxes, and every

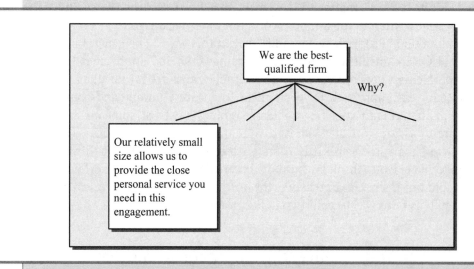

FIGURE 11.3   The lower-level box supports the claim of the upper box.

one is there for a reason, because it supplies a good reason that answers my question: "Why should I select you?"

CHAPTER 11 REVIEW

Writing the Qualifications Slot

1. The qualifications slot explicitly discusses abilities and capabilities as they intersect with the buyers' needs.
  - Abilities are qualities of people, such as experience, kind and level of expertise, and personal characteristics.
  - Capabilities are qualities of things, such as your firm's proprietary methodologies, databases, models, and other intellectual capital.
  - Abilities and capabilities are often discussed in résumés and your project's staffing. This qualifications *slot* material is often not part of the qualifications *section*.
2. The qualifications section is an argument that provides evidence for the claim "We are the best-qualified firm."
  - That claim forms the top box in a logic tree that can be used to organize the section.
  - A "how" logic tree organizes the actions in the methodology; a "why" logic tree organizes the qualifications section to demonstrate why yours is the best-qualified firm for this situation.
3. The content for some if not most of your argument can be gathered from the Qualifications column of your Themes Development Worksheet.

- The TDW expresses your qualifications as they are related to hot buttons, evaluation criteria, and counters to the competition based on those criteria.
- Therefore, that content phrases your abilities and capabilities as they intersect with the buyers' needs. (See Figure 11.4.)

WORK SESSION 9: Writing the Qualifications Section for ABC

You know very well that a solidly argued and well-tailored qualifications section can provide some of the two to five points that make the difference between winning and being an also-ran. Your qualifications section will have to incorporate and reinforce the themes developed and played out in preceding sections of the proposal and also demonstrate clearly and conclusively that Paramount is superior to its competitors in having the resources and the ability to conduct the proposed methodology expeditiously; to produce a more comprehensive and effective plan; and, if necessary, to help ABC implement the selected alternative in a timely manner.

You feel that your own time pressures are building, and you're hopeful that you can draw on materials from previous proposals that responded to similar

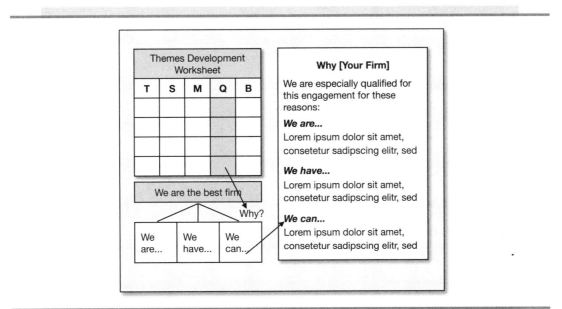

FIGURE 11.4   The TDW's qualifications column can provide the answers to why you are best qualified. These answers can be structured by a "why" logic tree. In turn, the logic tree can structure the argument in your qualifications section.

situations. When you access your firm's database of previous proposals, you find a few that look like they might be helpful, but you're disappointed again—though not really surprised. All the qualifications sections appear interchangeable, and, in fact, you conclude that they pretty much are. They contain some useful and well-written paragraphs on Paramount's history and on its experience within ABC's industry. But they all sound as if they were written by Marketing. They are generic: they use too much boilerplate and never read as though they were written to real readers in specific situations with specific problems. The paragraphs aren't formed into an argument. They won't sufficiently differentiate you from the competition and won't convince ABC that Paramount is the firm that should be engaged for this project.

When you and Gilmore began developing a strategy for the proposal to ABC, you and he spent considerable time preparing a Themes Development Worksheet. You now want to take advantage of the thought that went into that effort, so you review the worksheet's column labeled "Qualifications." You use a "why" logic tree to structure that column's content (Figure 11.5).

In supporting the claim that yours is the best-qualified firm for this project, you write that Paramount has:

- The resources to begin this engagement immediately and to complete the study in as little as four to five months
- Substantial manufacturing, financial, and strategy-development experience within the household-appliance industry

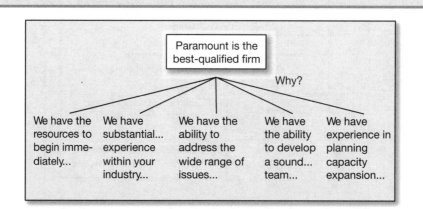

FIGURE 11.5   The "why" logic tree for the qualifications section in the proposal to ABC. The supporting claims come from the Themes Development Worksheet's qualifications column.

- The ability to address the wide range of issues related to this engagement
- The ability to develop a sound, joint ABC/Paramount team
- Proven experience in planning and controlling implementation of the strategy we will develop with you

With that content, you construct your argument, using these five claims as subsections in the body of your qualifications section. The last claim, you realize, provides an opportunity to look ahead to what you hope will be another project at ABC—implementing the plan developed during this planning project.

One group of themes not addressed in your logic tree is that related to comprehensiveness, thoroughness, and complexity. This theme you decide to include in the introduction to the section by stressing that ABC's problem is complex, that the right solution will not come easily, and that ABC doesn't have much time left to conduct a comprehensive study. The results of your efforts are shown in the following:

Qualifications of Paramount Consulting

ABC is faced with a most formidable challenge as it begins the task of providing additional manufacturing capacity to avert the shortfall expected in the next few years. This capacity shortfall should be considered imminent as you examine the numerous tasks that must be completed effectively within the narrow available time frame.

Time will be required for sufficient interchange between ABC and Consolidated to agree on the decision to commit scarce financial, planning, managerial, and other resources needed to implement the selected option. Substantially more time will be needed to put in place additional resources and to provide the necessary training for an effective start-up.

As described in the following paragraphs, Paramount has the diverse capabilities to help you complete this challenging engagement successfully and expeditiously. Specifically, we have:

- The resources to begin this engagement immediately and to complete this project in four to five months
- Substantial manufacturing, financial, and strategy-development experience within the household-appliance industry
- The ability to address the wide range of issues related to this engagement
- The ability to develop a sound joint ABC/Paramount team
- Proven experience in planning and controlling implementation of the strategy we will develop with you

Paramount Has the Resources to Begin and Complete This Project Quickly
Of the nearly 100 consultants in our nearby Midwest office, we have already identified several individuals with the skills and experience needed to help develop a sound plan for increasing capacity. Each of these professionals has worked on similar engagements, is substantially "down the learning curve," and will therefore be able to function effectively at the beginning of the engagement. In fact, several of them have participated in developing this proposal. Our proposed engagement team of four consultants will be drawn from this group, and we would like to introduce this team to you so that you feel as comfortable with them as we do. We will use no subcontractors without your concurrence, and we will be able to begin the engagement immediately after your approval to proceed.

We Have Substantial Manufacturing, Financial, and Strategy-Development Experience Within Your Industry
For almost 40 years, Paramount has served clients with a high level of satisfaction. In fact, over 80 percent of our consulting engagements come from previous clients. Paramount originated with a strong manufacturing and strategy capability that has grown significantly over the years; this strength will enable us to address all the diverse issues that must be resolved during the proposed engagement. In the last five years, we have conducted over 200 manufacturing strategy engagements, of which nearly 25 were conducted for companies within the appliance industry. Furthermore, approximately 60 of those studies specifically involved our developing a broad range of manufacturing capacity plans. Many of them were designed to answer questions similar to yours: "How can we provide additional manufacturing capacity most effectively?"

We Are Able to Address the Wide Range of Issues Related to This Study
The team proposed for this engagement will have expertise in all aspects of this study. We understand the marketing and manufacturing issues from a business perspective so that we can develop various capacity expansion options; evaluate them with your management team, considering each of the team members' individual (and often differing) perspectives; select the most appropriate option; prepare for Consolidated a comprehensive appropriation request; and plan for its successful implementation within your tight time frame.

We Have the Ability to Build a Sound ABC/Paramount Team
Because the staff to be assigned has considerable expertise in conducting similar studies, building consensus, and transferring their knowledge, skills,

and expertise, we have been able to carefully structure our approach so that ABC management will participate actively and become an integral part of the engagement team. Thus, on completion of the engagement, ABC will possess a base of residual knowledge that will be invaluable in addressing future capacity and other strategic manufacturing questions. For example, we believe that ABC members of the engagement team will be able, even more effectively than at present, to monitor sales forecasts, plant productivity, and capacity utilization to project accurately when additional capacity might be needed in the more distant future.

We Have the Ability to Plan and Control Implementation
Once the most appropriate capacity expansion option has been selected, it will be extremely important to implement that plan without delay. Although an implementation phase lies outside the scope of this proposed project, you should be aware that our significant experience in successfully implementing comprehensive plans for increasing capacity could be invaluable to ABC.

Our project teams that work on such implementation projects routinely use a variety of sophisticated project-control software packages. These programs are necessary for properly allocating resources; monitoring task completion and costs, thereby assuring adherence to budget; identifying potential problems or delays; and reallocating resources to maintain schedules and achieve time and cost objectives. These control techniques will ensure that implementation of the selected option will proceed smoothly and will be completed on time and within budget.

Even if we are not actively involved in implementation, we will have developed the new manufacturing plan considering ABC's resources and capabilities. Our goal is not just to produce a plan for increasing capacity but to bring that capacity on line as soon as possible. That is, we are not in the business of just developing plans. We want to see those plans implemented whether or not you decide to engage us to help you do so.

CHAPTER 12

Writing the Benefits Section

began this book with a kind of quiz as a way of introducing the concept of generic structure. I discussed how the generic structure of proposals has six slots, the last of which is BENEFITS. Let's begin this chapter on the benefits section with another quiz, which comprises the three statements in Figure 12.1.

It's eminently clear that benefits play an important part in selling, whether you're hawking beer at the ballpark (or at a cricket or rugby match) or submitting a million-dollar proposal to a Fortune 100 firm.

Let's consider the last major part of one of those proposals, a typical proposal, perhaps one of yours written to me and an organization like mine. Your document begins informally and maintains a friendly and informal "we can work together" tone. It conveys the right chemistry; it's responsive to my needs and contains some benefits; and, yes, it even includes a few themes. But in the last section, call it "Timing and Costs," the tone changes dramatically and becomes abrupt. Although the proposal began in a friendly way, now it seems distant. Although it began informally, even addressing me by my first name, now it seems official and formal, with phrases such as "Invoices are payable upon receipt," and "We are also reimbursed for expenses," and "It is our policy to. . . ."

Of course, you can and should try to change the tone so that your fees slot is more aligned in tone with what has preceded it. But information in that slot will always seem relatively distant and official, and sometimes it will have to be. So

Benefits are important to buyers.	True ☐ False ☐
Buyers buy if they perceive that their organization will benefit.	True ☐ False ☐
Buyers might select one firm over another because one communicates benefits more effectively.	True ☐ False ☐

FIGURE 12.1   A true/false quiz about benefits

except for one or two perfunctory closing statements ("Thanks for the opportunity, please call to clarify, blah, blah, blah"), I am left at the end of your proposal with the distant, the formal, and the official. Your proposal not only ends with straight information (on costs and terms of payment), it concludes with the most distasteful information (unless, of course, you happen to be the low bidder).

A good many proposals don't end with timing and costs; they conclude with a section often titled "Why [Your Firm]." These are really qualifications sections, and, like sections on timing and costs, they are also problematic (see Figure 12.2).

What's most strategic is not to end with "Timing and Costs" by telling me how many pounds of flesh you will extract or to end with "Why [My Firm]," which also focuses on you instead of on me. Focus instead on the benefits, the value I am going to get for the money you're asking me to spend. Your proposal's last

Which section is more effective for ending your proposal?			
Section	*Timing and Costs*	*Qualifications*	*Benefits*
Focus	You	You	The prospect
Characteristics	Provides a dry and unpersuasive close (unless you happen to be the low bidder)	Discusses an input into the change process, not the outcomes	Discusses the good things accruing to the prospect, during and after the project

FIGURE 12.2   The advantages of ending with a benefits section

major element can be much more persuasive by discussing the expected benefits of your efforts and, as I will show you, much more.

The Kinds of Benefits

You have already done most, if not all, of the groundwork necessary to think about benefits and value. As Figure 12.3 reminds us, we've discussed and you've identified in the work sessions four kinds of benefits:

- baseline logic benefits (Logics Worksheet, Cell 6, discussed in Chapter 3)
- individual buyer's benefits (Psychologics Worksheet, Cell 1, Chapter 6)
- hot button benefits (Psychologics Worksheet, Cell 2, Chapter 7)
- themes benefits (Themes Development Worksheet, Benefits column, Chapter 7)

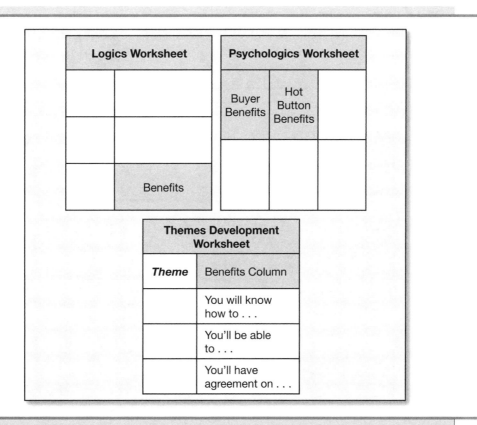

FIGURE 12.3 The four kinds of benefits identified on the worksheets

You are now in a position to reap what you have sown, to summarize for me in a compelling, persuasive finale all the benefits from using your services.

The Function of the Benefits Slot

If you're smart and strategic, you'll discuss benefits throughout the proposal. I've already discussed how the elements of the baseline logic can be formed into a value proposition that can begin your proposal, and I've shown you how the background section's closing component can end with briefly stated benefits (Figure 9.1). That section provides a logical and persuasive movement from a discussion of the current situation, a state of pain or uncertainty or opportunity, to a discussion, however brief, of another outcome, one that is more pleasurable or certain or that has capitalized on the opportunity. And don't forget about the closing P-slots at various levels throughout your document or presentation. They all contain outcomes like deliverables and benefits. (See Figure 12.4.)

You can integrate benefits into other slots as well by considering, for example, the benefits of your methods and of the deliverables accruing from them and

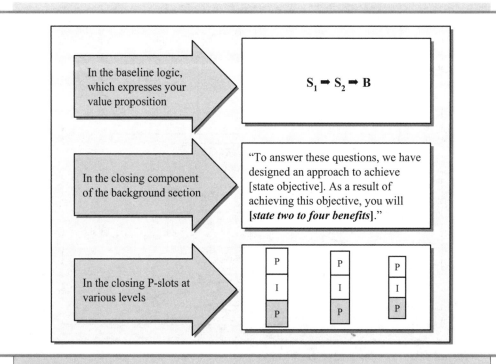

FIGURE 12.4   The benefits slot exists throughout the proposal.

the benefits of your staff's abilities and your firm's capabilities. Your Themes Development Worksheet can help you here. If, for example, one of my hot buttons is urgency, your approach will be beneficial if it will deliver results quickly and your qualifications slot will be persuasive if it argues that you're capable of and experienced in doing so.

But you might not want to leave all the separate strands of benefits scattered throughout the document or presentation, especially since they can make a powerful conclusion to your proposal if you bring them together in one final section or series of summary paragraphs. The overall movement of your proposal will be like this: It will begin by discussing my organization's current situation; it will end by describing how we will benefit from your helping us to achieve our desired result and by summarizing how and why your methods and your qualifications for performing them will best achieve that result. Therefore, you should consider this part of your proposal, whether it's a separate section or not, a persuasive summary—a strategically presented conclusion of your proposal's major selling points. It will be a persuasive *summary* if you summarize the most important elements to us in some of the preceding generic structure slots (e.g., METHODS and QUALIFICATIONS). It will be a *persuasive* summary if you summarize the benefits you have articulated throughout.

CHAPTER 12 REVIEW

Writing the Benefits Section

To structure your benefits section:

- You can generate persuasive content by using the Logics, Psychologics, and Themes Development Worksheets.
- Benefits can exist throughout the proposal (for example, in the closing component of your background section, in the closing P-slots of METHODS, and in QUALIFICATIONS).
- Although they can exist throughout the proposal, benefits can be gathered at the end to form a persuasive summary, a value-laden conclusion to your document or presentation.

WORK SESSION 10: The Content of the Benefits Section

To show you how to compose a persuasive summary of your written or oral proposal, I will complete the last work session of this book.

To organize the large number of benefits captured on the three worksheets, I sorted them into three categories:

1. **Benefits that would accrue during the project:** For this category, I looked especially for benefits related to hot buttons, since by definition hot buttons are desires or concerns that must be addressed during the project. These benefits tend to be expressed in the part of the Psychologics Worksheet related to hot buttons (Cell 2) and in those themes on the Themes Development Worksheet derived from hot buttons. I also examined the Methodology and Qualifications columns of the latter worksheet to try to identify additional benefits related to Paramount's methods and qualifications. Finally, since the benefits section is a persuasive summary, I identified additional content (for example, deliverables) that bore repeating in this last major element of the proposal.
2. **Planning benefits that would accrue after the project has been completed but before implementation:** For this category, I used the planning benefits categorized as such on the Logics Worksheet (Cell 6) and the Psychologics Worksheet (Cell 2).
3. **Implementation benefits that would accrue subsequent to the project:** For this category, I used the same two worksheet cells, focusing instead on the items classified as implementation benefits. As a result, I used a measurable-results orientation.

After sorting the benefits, I identified a claim or proposition for each category so that the entire section would read like a solid argument. I'll state these propositions as if you were talking to me, your potential client:

* You will receive important benefits because of how we will conduct the study to move you from your current situation to your desired result.
* As a result of that transition, these are the benefits you will receive and the value you will be provided related to the plan we will develop.
* As a result of that plan, these are the benefits that can be expected to accrue if or when you choose to implement that plan.

In elaborating on the last proposition/claim, I made certain that I qualified the subclaims, not only using the word *expected* above but also by using other expressions like *if.*

With these three propositions in mind, I spent less than 30 minutes writing the following draft of a benefits section for the proposal to ABC. The writing was quick and relatively easy because I had previously invested the time to organize my thoughts logically and completely on the various worksheets. I hope you'll agree that the section provides a powerful conclusion to, and a powerful persuasive summary of, the proposal. The section begins by addressing Anil Gupta, ABC's vice president of operations, to whom Gilmore directed the proposal.

Benefits

I would like to summarize for you, Anil, some of the most important points we've made to you and to your team in our previous discussions and in this proposal. Then I will describe the benefits we believe you will receive from our developing a capacity plan for meeting ABC's forecasted demand and from that plan's subsequent implementation by ABC (quite possibly with our support).

The Benefits of Leveraging Our Efforts

By forming a joint ABC/Paramount team, with ABC managers playing an integral part, we will be able to leverage the substantial knowledge, expertise, and tools both ABC and Paramount will bring to this project and to develop, sell, and implement the plan as quickly as possible.

This team will hold frequent progress reviews so that various constituencies within the Division (as well as, if appropriate, within Consolidated) will be aware of preliminary conclusions and direction quickly. We plan for these reviews to include strategy sessions, during which we can gain consensus on answers to the wide variety of questions posed in this project and get agreement across various interest areas on the appropriate criteria to be used to select the most effective expansion option. Finally, the team will prepare a final report, which we plan to be a proposal and capital-expenditure request to Consolidated. This strategy will eliminate an entire and possibly time-consuming step in the approval process.

This teaming strategy will work exceptionally well because Paramount's professionals have extensive expertise in building effective client/consultant teams, transferring knowledge, and managing and implementing change. We also understand the range of evaluation criteria important in this analysis and are adept at facilitating discussions to gain consensus on these criteria. We will commit our broad-based team quickly to begin the project immediately after your approval to proceed. Using this team's exceptional expertise in marketing, manufacturing strategy, facilities planning, logistics, financial analysis, and human resources, we will provide ABC with the right "road map" for increasing capacity.

Your Benefits at the End of This Project

Our final report, which we will design as your proposal to Consolidated, will be thorough, comprehensive, and well documented, providing ABC with the basis for making a sound expansion decision that considers and balances all the quantitative and qualitative factors. And because that decision will be based on agreed-to criteria, it will be well accepted by ABC management with different agendas. Just as important, the report will convince Consolidated of the expansion decision's correctness and desirability and answer its "what-if" questions.

In addition to our recommended expansion option, the report will contain:

- a confirmed market forecast as well as market share and product-mix projections
- specified current equipment and space utilization as well as opportunities to better utilize current equipment and space, as well as new technology
- specified make-versus-buy options as well as potential factory roles and locations for increasing capacity
- an implementation plan

Our jointly developed implementation plan will specify the tasks, resources, requirements, and timing necessary to bring additional capacity on line over time in a controlled yet expeditious manner.

Your Benefits Beyond This Project

We are confident that, once implemented, our jointly developed plan will significantly improve ABC's processes; lead to more cost-effective operations, improved service levels, and product quality; and allow you to maintain, if not enhance, your market share. Your productivity should increase, your compensation levels should be protected, and you should realize greater flexibility in implementing your business and marketing strategies. Most important, after subsequent implementation, you should improve your competitive position and maintain your excellent reputation with Consolidated.

◉　◉　◉

Quite obviously, Anil, we believe that Paramount is the right consulting firm for conducting this engagement. We have a comprehensive understanding of your situation and a logical and robust methodology for capitalizing on what we consider ABC's substantial opportunity to continue your growth in the marketplace and solidify your position within Consolidated Industries. Just as soon as possible, we would like to discuss that methodology and how we can best work together with you, President Armstrong, and others so that we can all agree on the proper magnitude of effort, the specific roles ABC and Paramount personnel should play, and the cost of the engagement. This is a

critically important study for ABC, and we look forward to supporting you as
you develop the manufacturing base for continued competitive success.

I, as a potential client, want to achieve a result and the benefits associated with
that result. Because benefits, real or imagined, imply value, they are one of the
most important elements in my decision-making process. And one of the biggest
deficiencies I find in most of your proposals is the lack of in-depth discussion
about how I, my colleagues, and my organization will benefit from using your
services both during and after your proposed project. Never again should you be
unable to provide that in-depth discussion. I've given you three tools—the three
worksheets—that will help you generate persuasive content.

Now you know that you can distribute benefits throughout the proposal, and
you can gather them in a persuasive summary that ends your document or presentation by focusing not on your qualifications or your fees but on the value we
will receive. This orientation toward value should certainly get you a portion of
the additional two to five points you need to win. If you sweep me off my feet
with persuasive benefits from using your services, I'll be less inclined to go with
the lowest bidder, unless, of course, it demonstrates that it can provide similar
benefits.

What a delightful situation this would be for me: comparing consultants based
on their perception of benefits to my organization. How different from my usual
experience: reading or listening to a battle of wits between two unarmed oppo-
nents. By generating, incorporating, and elaborating on benefits, you will have
the arms to win many more battles and to set clearer expectations for the project
after your victory.

CHAPTER 13

Writing the Fees Slot

have a very good friend who played the stock market, timed it well, and made lots of money—more money than most of us will ever see in our lifetimes. He bought a grand house (more like a castle), purchased hundreds of rare books, and assembled a rather significant art collection. By any stretch of the imagination, my friend is rich.[1]

Nevertheless, although he has two cars, the one driven more often is at least 10 years old, the air-conditioning works only sporadically, and the car will never attract the attention of a good thief. Although he serves fine wines and eats well, he uses coupons at the grocery store and reuses paper napkins at meals. His frugality reminds me of other multimillionaires who reduce their utility costs by turning down their thermostats in the winter and living in dimly lit homes.

My friend is like many potential clients, many of your potential clients. What they are willing to spend does not necessarily accord with how much they have. They are not cheap: They might buy a $10,000 rare book. But they are selective: Why buy or use a new napkin when an old one will do? One purchase is an investment (and a wealth of aesthetic pleasure); the other is a cost.

As your potential client, I sense (intellectually, at least) that your professional services are an investment; emotionally, I view your fees as a cost. Your challenge is to determine a price—a pricing strategy, really—considering the value of your proposed services. And this strategy must be as thoughtful, defensible, and well suited to our situation as all the other elements of your proposal. If this strategy is successful, I will view your services not as a commodity but as part of a rich relationship in which we both win. This chapter discusses what you should consider in developing a pricing strategy that will lead to the rich relationship we both desire.

Pricing Considerations After Initial Contact

After our first meeting, possibly even after our first phone conversation, well before you've done all the work to prepare a comprehensive proposal presentation and/or document, you will probably have some preliminary indicators concerning the potential project and the order-of-magnitude fees you believe you might propose. You will have some guidance about how best to proceed if you answer three major questions related to benefits, your contact at the prospect's firm, and your chances of winning.[2]

Are Our Likely Benefits Significant Enough to Warrant Your Services?

I discussed benefits and value in Chapter 12. A quick-and-dirty return-on-investment calculation comparing my organization's order-of-magnitude benefits to your order-of-magnitude fees should yield a multiple of at least 5:1 to 10:1 over the first three years or so after implementation. The logic the other decision makers and I use when purchasing consulting services, especially in implementation projects, is similar to our logic when we consider capital expenditures. Investment, returns, payback periods, and multiples are concepts we use and are comfortable discussing with those willing to compare potential benefits to consulting fees/costs.

We also know that the results of your services may not be as easy to quantify as is purchasing a piece of equipment, especially if ours is an insight and/or planning project. However, you can work with us to make reasonable estimates of the subsequent impact of your work, using whatever measures are agreed to: costs, market share, competitive position, and so on. When you work with us in this way, you are employing a measurable-results orientation. Just as important, when you discuss both tangible and intangible potential benefits with us, you implicitly suggest your and your firm's qualifications. As you relate our particular situation to that of other clients you have served in situations similar to ours, your stories and examples indicate that you have experience and expertise that could be valuable to us. Providing specific references and real-life stories further reinforces the potential value of your services.

What might you do if our overriding question or potential benefits are unclear? Consider a front-end diagnostic to assess the current situation in more detail. This diagnostic gets your foot in the door and gives you and your firm an opportunity to show us how good you are. It also provides you with a higher degree of certainty about the potential benefits, the potential value, of your services. We appreciate consultants who can support their estimates of the potential impact of their efforts.

Is Your Contact at an Organizational Level High Enough to Make or Influence a Decision to Engage You?

You need to be talking to people high enough in my organization to make, or convince others to make, a decision to hire you. If you begin your selling process at a level too low, at worst, you will have little chance of turning your proposed project into real work; at best, you will need to spend significant time and effort to sell upward. If you have a reasonable chance to win, full speed ahead. If not, consider declining to bid with dignity. In either case, file the contact's name and look for ways to build stronger personal relationships, at the right level, while also recognizing that good people get promoted to (or move to another company in) decision-making positions.

As you know, many projects are won years earlier because of personal relationships that have been established and nurtured over time. Your initial contacts provide many opportunities for you to lay the groundwork for a pricing strategy. This foreplay helps build relationships and expectations for a longer-term win-win situation.

What Is the Likelihood of Your Winning This Project?

If you feel uneasy about our situation, believing that you might not have a reasonable chance to win, you could choose to continue cautiously or even politely terminate your efforts, especially if you cannot answer in the affirmative the questions in Figure 13.1. You could say to us, for example: "The people we need to do great work for you are not currently available. Please keep us in mind as your needs evolve, and good luck in this project."

Declining to bid, gracefully, can be perceived favorably. Let me assure you that not many consultants turn down potential work. (By the way, why are your best people almost always available? If they're so good, shouldn't they be gainfully engaged on projects for other clients?) The position you don't want to be in is termed "column fodder," where you are placed among one or another columns of sure losers on the consultant-evaluation matrix. When you're column fodder, this can be said: "Sure, boss, we considered more than one consultant, but we stayed with our current one." And this happens: You never had a fair chance of winning.

> **What is the likelihood of your winning this project?**
> - Given our level of urgency, will you have the right staff available?
> - Do you have the necessary tools and information to answer our overriding question(s)?
> - Do you have the necessary industry/functional expertise?
> - Can you differentiate yourself sufficiently from the competition?
> - Is our budget realistic for the project we are considering?
> - Given the likely evaluation criteria, does our buying committee perceive you as capable?

FIGURE 13.1   Questions to determine your likelihood of winning

Pricing Considerations After In-Depth Analysis

Now let's assume that, based on our initial contact, you've decided to continue discussions with us and to prepare a proposal. This situation suggests that the potential impact on our organization is (or could be) significant and that we appear willing to consider an investment in your services to achieve this impact, this desired result, this value for me and my organization. Let's also assume that given all the information you've collected so far, you are talking to people at a high enough level in our organization and that you believe you have a reasonable chance to win.

You now need a pricing strategy to determine the fees you will quote us. Of course, the easiest and most direct way is to price on the basis of time and material. Here, you would quote a total fee based on you or your team's estimated billable hours multiplied by your team members' respective per-diem billing rates.

Summing up costs for the entire team and adding expenses yields the amount you would receive for the entire project or for a specified period. Now, you know as well as I do that this "rate-based" price is not really a pricing strategy, but some potential clients might accept it. Typically, we dislike time and material pricing, especially if it's not capped, because it is far too open-ended, allowing you to continue working without any agreed-on end point. We like end points and deliverables. We like results—especially those that can be measured.

Accordingly, you often will need to develop a pricing strategy more sophisticated and tailored than time and material, a strategy that you can defend and that can serve as the starting point for negotiation. Elements of this strategy could include at least seven other considerations:

- Our return on our consulting investment
- The strategic value of this opportunity to you
- The potential risk to you and your firm
- The relative capability of you and other consultants to answer our question(s) on this project
- Your and your competitors' relationship with our buying committee
- The desirability of this project to you for internal or tactical reasons
- Your pricing history with us

Some of these considerations will tend to increase your fees above a rate-based price; others will tend to decrease them. Let's discuss each consideration in turn.

Our Return on Our Consulting Investment

Putting yourself into our shoes is almost certain to be a compelling orientation for us. To do this, you would compare our total costs—your proposed consulting fees and expenses—with our likely returns, our value received, our benefits from using your firm's services on this project. "What will be our likely return on our consulting investment?" is the question you would answer, as well as the subordinate questions in Figure 13.2.

As I discussed in Chapter 3, answering this question regarding measurable results is much easier and more direct if we've asked you for a project that includes implementation. In this instance, my company should start achieving measurable results during or immediately after the project because it includes your support in implementation. In this instance, you could argue that our returns, accumulated over three years, plus any one-time returns, could be compared to your consulting charges for achieving those benefits.

For example, if the project's objective were to plan and implement a finished goods inventory reduction program and you estimate $100 million in carrying cost and one-time cost savings over three years, we might consider an investment in your services of $5 million to $10 million. This 10:1 to 20:1 return on investment might look favorable to us as a basis for selecting you. We like working with those who can define compelling and believable value propositions, especially if they can guarantee them.

To formulate such a value proposition, you need to know or to get to know our operations fairly well. The statement "Based on our past experience, we believe that an inventory reduction of 20 to 25 percent is achievable" is not a compelling argument unless you can demonstrate to me and my colleagues that this 20 to 25 percent range applies to our (unique) situation. "Round words" is the term we use to describe your estimates and statements that cannot be substantiated. I'm typically eager to learn about your firm's efforts and results elsewhere, but I need specifics to believe that this level of opportunity/savings is achievable in my situation. Remember, in many cases, I've already tried to reduce inventory, and I am not likely to be impressed by potential savings that you scribble on the back

---

What multiple above your rate-based price is supportable, given my firm's return on investment from this project?

- What measurable results can we expect for the first three years after implementation?

- What one-time impact (cost savings, market share increase, and so on) is is likely to be achieved?

- How do these returns compare with the investment we would incur from using your consulting services?

FIGURE 13.2   Pricing strategy related to ROI

of an envelope. Therefore, you may have to make an investment during the proposal process to learn more about our particular situation. Such an investment, of course, is often perceived favorably by me and my colleagues.

In nonimplementation projects, those that involve only insight and/or planning, your task is even more challenging. Here I have not—or at least have not yet—asked for your assistance in implementation, and so our achieving savings or capitalizing on opportunities is well beyond your direct control. Here, too, however, you can use a measurable-results orientation to compare our potential benefits subsequent to the project. Obviously, the risks of our eventually achieving potential benefits are greater, and some of the benefits may be less tangible, but you can still make a compelling argument—if you take the time to learn about our operations, the current situation, and the desired result. We've had some consultants lead our management team in interactive discussions of potential benefits that we could anticipate subsequent to implementation. Consultants put themselves in our shoes and addressed our potential opportunities and obstacles, based on their previous experience. In some of these situations, we've rewarded the consultants' efforts by asking them to add an implementation phase to their offering.

The bottom line is this: If you are the only consultant that clearly understands our situation in detail, if you make a compelling case defining our likely return on our consulting investment, and if we believe that we can work with you and your team, your odds of winning increase significantly.

However, if several firms know our operations well, each makes a compelling case regarding our likely returns, and we believe that we could work with each . . . then what? Then you need to consider other pricing factors that could determine our ultimate selection of a consultant.

The Strategic Value of This Opportunity to You

If we are one of your target companies or a past client you would like to continue to work with, or if we pose an overriding question that would allow you to make an intellectual-capital breakthrough, or if our industry is a particularly desirable one to you, or if the potential fees are high, or if our proposed opportunity allows you to build desired geographic presence, our project becomes more desirable to you. If our organization and/or issue have high strategic value for you, you can reflect this situation in your fees—that is, you would modify them (in some cases, lower them) to increase your chances of winning. (See Figure 13.3.)

Just as my friend uses coupons and reuses paper napkins, we buy some projects on price, especially when two or more bidders are extremely close on the criteria we use to make our decision. Yes, I know that you have operating expenses, invest considerably to build and maintain intellectual capital, make significant

To what extent will winning this project help you meet your organization's strategic objectives?

- To what extent do you want to work with my organization (for example, because you've targeted us or our industry)?

- To what extent is the overriding problem or opportunity to be addressed desirable (for example, because it will provide you with important intellectual capital or experience)?

- To what extent might the project favorably affect both organizations (for example, because it will provide substantial breakthroughs that could be well publicized)?

- To what extent does the project offer possibilities of future work with my organization?

- To what extent might the project (or potential project extensions) produce substantial fees over time?

- To what extent does the project offer you the opportunity to build a regional or country presence?

FIGURE 13.3   Pricing strategy related to strategic value

investments in technology and technological tools, and expand the capability of your staff through professional development.

I also know that your billing rates are often many multiples of your salaries, that your offices are often lavish, that the cars you park in our lot are often more expensive than my own and my colleagues', and that your firm makes very nice profits. So I know that you make a good deal of money when you sell projects at full billing rates (assuming that you complete the projects successfully and within budget).

So you can choose to reduce your fees when a project has important strategic value to your firm. You can make an investment; you can accept lower profit margins. You can even tell me that a particular project should cost \$X at normal billing rates but that you have reduced this price to \$Y because of strategic reasons. (We consider the same thing when we sell our products.) In many cases, lower fees will break ties between consultants.

The Potential Risk to You and Your Firm

While strategic value is a factor that could cause you to consider reducing your fees, potential risk is one that could suggest that you do the opposite. (See Figure 13.4.) If my company's current financial situation or credit rating is questionable, you might want to put protective terms in your proposal offering, or even increase your fees to protect your firm. Similarly, if my issue/question is one that is not very clear to you—that is, the baseline logic and/or benefits are difficult to define—you might want to reflect that condition by increasing your fees or even declining to bid. If the project becomes a disaster, no pricing level, no matter how high, will protect your firm's reputation.

You could regret not conducting an overall risk assessment, especially if answering our overriding question might result in negative publicity or if our desire for a quick return on our investment results in a "pay as you go" arrangement that will be difficult for you to produce. You also should think long and hard about your pricing strategy and about whether to pursue an opportunity when the project's issue is not a top-management priority.

Previously, I mentioned the risk of your selling too low in the organization. Now, I'm talking about a different situation, one in which individuals are at an appropriate organizational level and have the budgetary authority to hire you but do not place a high priority on the issue to be addressed by the project, especially if the project's results will not help our organization achieve its strategic direction. If my firm's management does not believe the issue is important, you could very well sell a project that was doomed to fail.

In this situation, you could choose to increase your fees, hoping to convince management of the issue's importance. Or you could increase your fees dramatically so that I am more likely to decline your bid. In this instance, you are using your pricing strategy to encourage me to say "No" so that you yourself are not declining to bid. If I say "Yes," you will have a built-in cushion to offset the risks.

How risky is the proposed project?

- Do I and my colleagues fully understand what we need to do to ensure a successful project?

- Do you, I, and my colleagues agree on the benefits that will accrue?

- Is this project a top priority for me and my firm's top management?

- Do I and my colleagues desire a quick return so that the project can be "pay as you go"?

- Are my firm's financial profile and credit in good standing?

- Might this project be seen as a conflict of interest by your other clients?

- Could this project generate negative publicity for you?

FIGURE 13.4   Pricing strategy related to risk

The Relative Capability of You and Other Consultants to Answer Our Question(s) in This Project

You'll note that the questions in Figure 13.5 are really the same questions I suggested you ask when you were trying to qualify the lead. Once the lead has been qualified, you need to ask them again, answering in greater detail.

Have you ever hired a roofing contractor? I'd pay almost anything to have the job done right. Price is seldom the primary factor for critical work where my risk associated with a poor job is significant. I want (and have found) a roofer who is never the lowest bidder, but he does outstanding work. Before he begins the work, he thoroughly inspects the roof (just as you might do a preproposal diagnostic), suggests the appropriate materials (seldom the least expensive) to complete the job well, and takes a holistic view of our home. In fact, he suggests that our house is "talking to him" through its cracks, spots, and coloration. Although he's one of the weirdest guys I've ever met, he knows his trade, his results are consistently excellent, and he stands behind his work.

As a client, I sometimes compare consultants the way I compare roofers. If one consulting firm has significantly more expertise related to our industry and/or our issue, that firm has a leg up. If one firm has proprietary tools and methodologies that suggest a better final product, that firm has a big advantage. If one firm has the right team available or can achieve measurable results substantially faster than others can, that firm is advantaged. If your firm has capabilities that others lack, we will pay a premium.

How does your capability compare with the competition's?

- How urgent is my need to begin the project?
- How quickly can you assemble the right staff?
- How capable are you, relative to the competition, of achieving the project's objective(s)?
- Do you have the proper level of industry and functional expertise?
- What is the quality of your proprietary tools for this project?
- Compared to the competition, how do I and my colleagues perceive your firm's capabilities?

FIGURE 13.5 Pricing strategy related to your competition

Your and Your Competitors' Relationship with Our Buying Committee

Remember when we discussed (in Chapter 6) the five different buying roles played by management on our consultant-selection committee? As regards pricing, these different roles intersect with various human considerations—the intangible, touchy-feely, between-the-lines elements of our organization. Obviously, if you have strong relationships with our buying committee or have done high-quality work for us, you will be in an advantageous position. Conversely, if you are relatively unknown to our buying committee or have not worked for us before, you will be disadvantaged compared with competitors with whom we have established relationships. As you know, the quality of relationships often supersedes and trumps all the logical elements of a proposal opportunity.

The quality and intensity of these relationships could well influence your pricing, as suggested in Figure 13.6. If you and your firm are known to us, you could suggest that we should have a higher degree of confidence in your actually achieving the desired results you propose, and that confidence could justify a premium price. Conversely, if we haven't had a chance to gain confidence in you and your firm, you might reduce your price to get your foot in the door. As is the case with my trusted roofer, price will not bridge a large perceived gap in capability. But it certainly is important when two or more consultants are viewed as comparable.

How do your relationships with me and my colleagues compare to your competitors' relationships?

- How experienced is the buying committee in working with consultants?
- How strong is your relationship with me and others on the selection committee?
- At what organizational level is the economic buyer?
- How involved will top management be in the project?
- How experienced are we in working with you and/or your firm?
- If you have consulted previously with us, how well was your work received?
- How competitive is this proposal situation?
- How strong are the competition's relationships with the selection committee and with others in my firm?

FIGURE 13.6   Pricing strategy related to your relationship with the buyers

Your relationship with the economic buyer is singularly important, and so is that buyer's organizational level. Since the economic buyer is concerned with the bottom line and the overall impact on the organization, an economic buyer higher in the organization will be more likely to consider, and fund, larger projects, while lower-level buyers will lack the authority to approve such projects. For lower-level buyers, your strategy could be to break the project into smaller, lower-cost pieces or phases or to attempt to persuade the economic buyer to elevate the proposed project to a higher organizational level. You should be aware, however, that this "elevation" strategy often triggers a new and different economic buyer if your project's proposed fees exceed the original buyer's financial authority.

The Desirability of This Project to You for Internal or Tactical Reasons

Previously, I mentioned some of the strategic reasons that might increase your desire to win a project—for example, you might want to work for a specific prospect or on a specific issue. Tactical or internal issues also can influence your pricing strategy, often resulting in your lowering your fees because of the benefits that could accrue to you and your firm from performing the proposed project. (See Figure 13.7.) If you have unassigned staff available, the project provides an opportunity to use them. You also might view the project as an opportunity to educate your proposed team members about a key business issue or industry. Or your staff could have an opportunity to work in a desirable location—where they reside, for example, instead of Timbuktu.

To what extent will winning this project help meet your firm's internal objectives, providing you the opportunity to:

- use available staff?
- train available staff?
- meet the individual development needs of members of the assigned project team?
- work in a desirable location?
- meet other potential clients?
- gain valuable publicity?

FIGURE 13.7   Pricing strategy related to potential benefits to your firm

In addition to potential benefits related to the professional or personal development of your staff, you may view our proposed project as an opportunity to meet other potential clients. Marketing, benchmarking, and multiclient studies often have such advantages. Similarly, certain projects might provide an opportunity for valuable publicity in markets or geographies important to you. For any number of reasons, the opportunity to build relationships or gain publicity with key personnel in an industry, geographic area, or functional area may be important to your firm. And if it is, you might choose to reflect this benefit to you in a reduced price for us.

Your Pricing History with Us

People and organizations constantly calibrate their interactions with each other. As a potential client, we are no different. If you have already worked for us, your pricing history (even in another unit or division) may act as a precedent, setting expectations for the proposed project's pricing. (See Figure 13.8.) Moreover, we speak to our colleagues at other firms, and if you have discounted your work for them, you might have to justify why you are not providing a similar discount to us.

We can estimate your billing rates, or at least your blended average daily billing rates, so if your pricing is different for this proposed project, you may need to explain why. If your price is higher, you need to explain, for example, that the project requires a greater percentage of senior people. If your price is lower, you should tell us, for example, not only that you are making an investment but that you are doing so for specific reasons. As a result, you can avoid being constrained when you price future projects.

What historical factors could influence your ability to price this project?

- How have you priced other projects, for other prospects, that addressed this project's overriding problem or opportunity?
- How have you priced other projects for us? For example:
  --rate-based
  --success fee
  --contingency
  --retainer

FIGURE 13.8 Pricing strategy related to your pricing precedents

A Bit of a Summary, and More

In the Introduction, I wrote, "Writing always involves choice, decisions among options, and the more options you consider, the better your chance of selecting the most appropriate one for a given situation." Substitute "pricing" for "writing," and the advice is equally apt. In this chapter, I've discussed seven considerations that can influence your determination of fees:

1. Our return on our consulting investment
2. The strategic value of this opportunity to you
3. The potential risk to you and your firm
4. The relative capability of you and other consultants to answer our question(s) in this project
5. Your and your competitors' relationship with our buying committee
6. The desirability of this project to you for internal or tactical reasons
7. Your pricing history with us

These pricing considerations could make the difference between your winning or finishing second. Remember: What worked well in one situation will not necessarily work well in another. Even if the questions or industry issues are identical. Even if the perceived benefits are comparable. Determining the right price is as strategic an activity as any other element of your proposed offering.

Given all the logical and psychological information you've learned about us, your competitors for this project, and your own strategic and tactical objectives, how should you price a particular proposal opportunity? You certainly know by now that I can't answer that question specifically. But I can suggest a range of pricing options you could consider.

- **Rate-Based Pricing.** The options start with a rate-based price developed by summing up your proposed team members' individual fees based on their planned billing days. Let's equate this rate-based price to a 1.0 on the potential-pricing scale.
- **Investment Pricing (Discounting).** Because of the strategic value of this opportunity to your firm or the desirability of this project for internal or tactical reasons, you could choose to reduce your rate-based price by discounting your rates (e.g., 0.9 or 0.8 times your rate base) or by investing or even giving away your services—for example, in a diagnostic (e.g., 0.9 to 0 times the rate base).
- **Return-on-Investment Pricing (Contingency or Success Fee).** Or you could choose to change your price (most likely by increasing it) by adopting a return-

based arrangement. Using return-on-investment (ROI) pricing, your fees could be a percentage, over some number of years, of my organization's increased savings or sales or whatever measurable result is defined in your proposal. In this case, your fees probably will be some multiple of a rate-based price (e.g., 1.5 to 3.0+), though they are certainly contingent on our actually achieving the results you promise. With ROI pricing, of course, you should be very careful about how our actual achieved results are measured. You might even want to involve your and our legal people and get their buy-in to the arrangement. To paraphrase Robert Frost, "Good fences [and agreed-to accounting procedures] make good neighbors." But by all means, worry more about scoring than scorekeeping.

◉   ◉   ◉

One final word: Don't be offended by questions we might ask about how your pricing was determined. When we ask a serious question, we appreciate an honest answer. (Always remember that our questions might be a test of your ability to interact with us.) We might ask about your daily billing rates, expenses, terms of payments, and guarantees. We know that purchasing qualified professional services is expensive. We know that we wouldn't have solicited your help if we believed we could complete the project successfully ourselves. So we believe (we hope) that outside help will be beneficial. But as an outsider, you must be viewed as someone we can trust and work with well during the project and, quite possibly, beyond. Your goal is an ongoing, long-term, mutually beneficial relationship. So is ours. Use your pricing strategy as another opportunity to build a stronger relationship with us. With this relationship and your great project work, we receive the benefits of a successful project; you receive a fair return for conducting it, as well as the opportunity for continuing work.

Together, we both win.

CHAPTER 14

Summary: The Proposal Development Process

This is the last chapter in *Writing Winning Business Proposals*, though there are many important and instructive appendices to follow. You've come a long way toward helping yourself get the two to five points that make the difference between winning and coming in a close second. Very few people know what you have learned. Although you have gained considerable insight by reading this book and although you now have a plan for increasing your percentage of winning proposals, you know that insights and plans are necessary but not sufficient. They need to be implemented. Therefore, I encourage you to use the insights you've gained and the plan you now have. Use them consciously and often. I've brought you out of the forest and to the water; now you have to drink.

This chapter summarizes the plan I've presented to you in this book, which has helped you understand how to use proposal logics and psychologics to prepare your documents and presentations. This summary provides you with a snapshot of the proposal-development process I've discussed with you, as well as a road map you can use as you develop future proposals.

After the summary, you will find a Rating Guide for Proposals (Figure 14.7 and Figure 14.8). You can use the guide to evaluate your own proposals, since the guide reflects many of the concepts and principles I've been helping you learn. Although the guide is based on a 100-point scale, I've arbitrarily assigned points to its six major sections. The sections related to methods and to costs/benefits, for example, are worth 20 points each, while those related to the situation and to qualifications are allotted 15. Obviously, you should adjust the allotments on the basis of your proposal situation. In a given situation, for example, qualifications may need to be weighted more heavily than methods.

You also may be able to use the rating guide to help me and my colleagues to establish evaluation criteria, if I haven't already done so, or to revise those criteria if it's in your interest to do so. That is, you may find it opportune and helpful to discuss the guide with me. As a result, you may have a clearer idea of what I expect and of what you need to deliver.

In the Introduction, I challenged you to work hard to understand the concepts and principles presented. None of these concepts and principles is particularly difficult to understand. But using them intelligently and well takes effort and practice. Now I challenge you to work hard to practice them, to implement them, remembering that most successful business developers are made, not born. Practice never makes perfect, because perfect doesn't exist. But practice does lead to continuous improvement. You've already improved; continue to do so.

The Proposal Development Process

Note: Many of the following steps are iterative, and many of them are coterminous. And all of the terms used are in the downloadable glossary at http://web .me.com/rfreed/Writing_Winning_Business_Proposals/Home.html.

0. Qualify the Lead by using the explicit criteria referred to in Appendix H as well as those criteria implicitly suggested on the Logics and Psychologics Worksheets.

Proposal Logics

1. Use the Logics Worksheet to create and test the baseline logic ($S_1 \rightarrow S_2 \rightarrow B$). (Chapter 2 and Chapter 3.)
  A. Specify the current situation (S_1), which includes the potential client's problem or opportunity, the triggering event that brought the problem or opportunity to awareness, the effects of the existing problem or the effects of not capitalizing on the opportunity, and the lack of benefits. (Logics Worksheet, Cell 2.)
  B. Given that current situation, specify the desired result or results (S_2) that your proposed project will achieve. S_2 can be one or a combination of three kinds: insight, a plan, or an implemented plan. Your project's objectives always express the desired results (Logics Worksheet, Cells 3 and 5).
  C. Given the current situation and desired result, specify the deliverables that you will produce to achieve the desired result (Logics Worksheet, Cell 5).

D. Given the deliverables and the desired result, specify the benefits (B) likely to accrue from producing deliverables and achieving the desired result (Chapter 12; Logics Worksheet, Cell 6).

E. If the desired result is insight or a plan, use a measurable-results orientation to indicate the benefits likely to accrue after subsequent implementation (Chapter 4; Logics Worksheet, Cell 6).

F. Test the alignment of the elements within the baseline logic by answering the following questions (Chapter 3; Logics Worksheet, Cells 1–6):

- Are the prospect's strategic direction, triggering event, overriding problem, and effects aligned?
- Are the overriding question(s), objective(s), and desired result(s) aligned?
- Is the overriding problem aligned with the overriding question(s)?
- Are the deliverables aligned with the desired result(s)?
- Are the deliverables and desired result(s) aligned with the benefits?
- Are the benefits aligned with the effects/lack of benefits?

2. **Construct the methodology** to define how to achieve the objective (Chapter 5).

A. Clearly identify the objective (or objectives), based on the buyers' overriding question (or questions). If the project will move the buyer one step (for example, from lacking insight to having insight), there will be only one overriding question and objective. If the project will move the buyer two or more steps (for example, from lacking insight to having a plan), there will be two or more objectives.

B. Place the objective at the top of a logic tree that organizes the actions necessary to achieve it. (Be certain each action specifically expresses a result, a deliverable.) Build one logic tree for each objective.

C. Once the logic tree is constructed, list the action-results in sequence.

D. Within that sequence, integrate the activities important for planning and communicating.

E. Consider the elapsed timing of each action to determine the project's duration.

Proposal Psychologics

3. **Identify the role or roles played by each buyer** on the consultant-selection committee, and specify the individual benefits that will accrue to each buyer from achieving the desired result (Chapter 6; Psychologics Worksheet, Cell 1).

A. Classify all the members of the buying team according to the role or roles each will play in making the decision: economic buyer, user buyer, technical buyer, coach, ratifier. Remember that a single buyer can play as many as the first four roles; a ratifier can play only one other role: coach (Psychologics Worksheet, Cell 1).

B. Identify for each buyer the likely benefits that will accrue from achieving S_2, remembering that those benefits will be conditioned by the buyer's role and position in the organization (Psychologics Worksheet, Cell 1).

C. If at all possible, develop at least one coach (Psychologics Worksheet, Cell 1).

4. Identify, select, and develop your themes (Chapter 7 and Figure 14.1).

A. Identify possible themes by considering the following:

- **Hot buttons**—the desires or concerns of individual buyers that, if addressed, will affect your selling process, project organization, and/or project methodology (Psychologics Worksheet, Cell 2).
- **Evaluation criteria**—the criteria developed by the consultant-selection committee often contained in RFPs (Appendix G) and other documents (Psychologics Worksheet, Cell 4).
- **Counters to the competition**—your strengths relative to the competition, especially as those strengths apply to evaluation criteria for this particular project or selling opportunity (Psychologics Worksheet, Cell 5).

B. Select the themes by considering the following (Chapter 7):

- **Hot buttons** of medium- and high-power-base buyers whose receptivity you want to maintain or increase (Psychologics Worksheet, Cells 2 and 3). Power base refers to a buyer's relative influence in this selling opportunity, not to

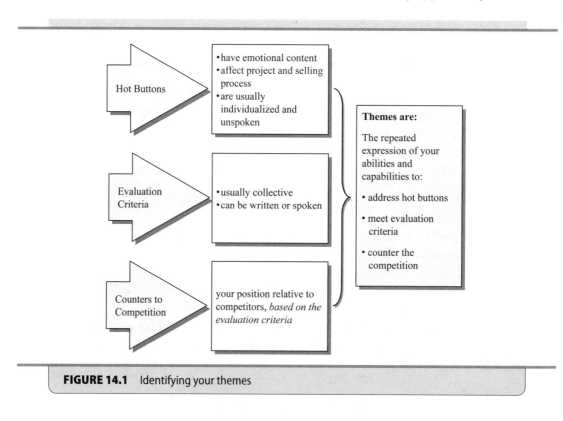

FIGURE 14.1   Identifying your themes

that buyer's general level of influence within his or her firm. Receptivity refers to a buyer's relative reception to your selling efforts to date.

- **Evaluation criteria** on which you believe you rate highly or that the buyers weight heavily.
- **Counters to the competition** that provide you with an opportunity to significantly counter competitors' arguments or moves, remembering that your competition can also include in-house individuals or other initiatives competing for the same limited resources.

C. Develop the themes on the Themes Development Worksheet.

5. **Derive the project's benefits** from the following worksheets:
   A. Baseline Logic Benefits (Logics Worksheet, Cell 6).
   B. Buyers' Benefits (Psychologics Worksheet, Cell 1).
   C. Hot Button Benefits (Psychologics Worksheet, Cell 2).
   D. Themes Development Benefits (Themes Development Worksheet, Benefits column).

6. As you work, **add red and green flags** to your Logics and Psychologics Worksheets: a red flag to indicate a weakness, vulnerability, or gap in information; a green flag to indicate a strength.

7. **Conduct a 40-minute Green Team Review** (Chapter 8) to review your strengths and weaknesses and to identify strategic actions to address them. Conduct one or more Green Team Reviews before investing significant time in proposal preparation. Take whatever actions you and your team believe appropriate (and have the time and resources to implement) to eliminate red flags and leverage green flags.

Proposal Preparation

8. Using the situation and objectives slots, **write a background section** (Chapter 9 and Figure 14.2) that includes:
   A. A Story Component using information from the Logics Worksheet, Cells 1 and 2.
   B. A Questions Component that identifies the key questions that must be answered to eliminate the problem or capitalize on the opportunity. (Use the second and lower rows of the logic tree for the methodology to generate some of these questions; also use deliverables from the Logics Worksheet, Cell 5.)
   C. A Closing Component that states the project's objectives (Logics Worksheet, Cells 3 and 4) and ends with briefly stated benefits (Logics Worksheet, Cell 6).

9. **Write a methods section** that, when necessary and appropriate (Chapter 10 and Figure 14.3):
   A. At the section level, composes the section's opening P-slot from the Situation and Methods columns of the Themes Development Worksheet to provide a rationale that explains why, out of a universe of possible approaches, you will use this approach in this situation.

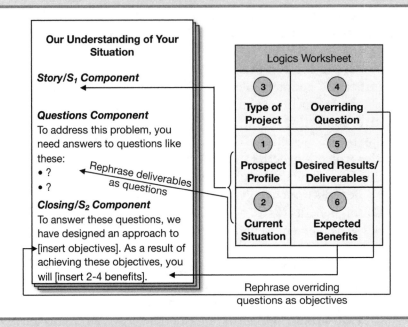

Our Understanding of Your Situation

Story/S₁ Component

Questions Component
To address this problem, you need answers to questions like these:
- ?
- ?

Closing/S₂ Component
To answer these questions, we have designed an approach to [insert objectives]. As a result of achieving these objectives, you will [insert 2-4 benefits].

Rephrase deliverables as questions

Rephrase overriding questions as objectives

Logics Worksheet	
③ Type of Project	④ Overriding Question
① Prospect Profile	⑤ Desired Results/ Deliverables
② Current Situation	⑥ Expected Benefits

FIGURE 14.2 Writing the background section

Approach and Methods

We have designed our approach for three important reasons:

- **Because** [of something in your current situation], **you need** [something related to this theme]. **Therefore, we will** [do something related to that theme].
- **Because** [of something in your current situation], **you need** [something related to this theme]. **Therefore, we will** [do something related to that theme].
- **Because** [of something in your current situation], **you need** [something related to this theme]. **Therefore, we will** [do something related to that theme].

Specifically, our methodology includes the following major tasks:

Themes Development Worksheet				
T	S	M	Q	B

FIGURE 14.3 Writing the introduction, the opening P-slot, to the methods section

B. At the task level, fills each task's opening P-slot by providing a rationale for why the task should be performed; uses a logic tree to fill each task's I-slot (Chapter 4 and Figure 14.4) by explaining how the task will be performed; fills each task's closing P-slot by explaining what will result from performing the task.

10. Write a qualifications section (Chapter 11 and Figure 14.5) that:

    A. Explicitly discusses abilities and capabilities as they intersect with the buyers' needs.

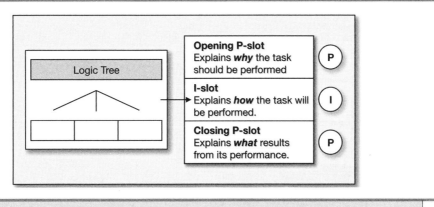

FIGURE 14.4   Using PIP at the task level

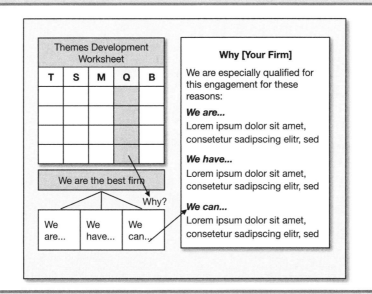

FIGURE 14.5   Writing the qualifications section

    B. Uses a logic tree to develop the claim, "We are the best-qualified firm." (Use the Qualifications column of the Themes Development Worksheet to develop this logic tree.)

11. Write a benefits section summarizing the proposal's major selling points and including, when necessary and appropriate (Chapter 12 and Figure 14.6):

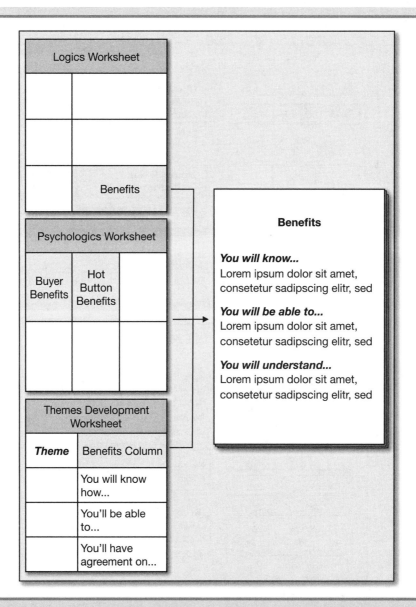

FIGURE 14.6 Writing the benefits section

    A. Baseline Logic Benefits (Logics Worksheet, Cell 6).

    B. Buyers' Benefits (Psychologics Worksheet, Cell 1).

    C. Hot Button Benefits (Psychologics Worksheet, Cell 2).

    D. Themes Development Benefits (Themes Development Worksheet, Benefits column).

12. **Determine the proposed fees** (Chapter 13) considering the prospect's return on consulting investment (and the large number of other measurable as well as nonmeasurable factors influencing the project's value) and the potential risks to you and your firm.

13. **Be certain that your document's sentences and voice are appropriate for the situation** (Appendix E and Appendix F).

14. **Evaluate the proposal** by using the Rating Guide and/or the Lead Qualification Worksheet referred to in Appendix H, making certain to weight the various factors based on the situation while trying to view your efforts from the prospect's perspective (Figures 14.7 and 14.8).

Evaluation Criteria	Points Possible	Your Proposal
This consultancy has established the foundation for a good *working relationship*. • They understand our internal sensitivities. • They can work with our people. • They can and will do what they say they will. • They have been responsible, reliable, and responsive. • They tailored this proposal to our situation, avoiding boilerplate.	15	
They understand our *situation*. • They clearly understand our problem or opportunity. • They know how this situation developed and how it affects us. • They understand the key questions we need to answer. • They understand our issues within a larger business/industry context.	15	
They clearly understand the project's overall *objective(s)*. • The objective(s) expresses our desired result(s) (e.g., insight, a plan, and/or an implemented plan) at the end of this project. • We understand how the objective(s) relates to our problem or opportunity and to the benefits we will receive from achieving that objective(s).	15	

FIGURE 14.7 Rating Guide for Proposals, p. 1

Evaluation Criteria	Points Possible	Your Proposal
They have a logical *methodology* for achieving that objective. • They understand the relationship between the objective(s) and the tasks that will be performed to achieve it. • They provide a clear rationale for their proposed methods in *this* project; I don't sense that theirs is a canned, "off the shelf" workplan.	20	
They have clearly communicated the *qualifications* critical for achieving this project's objective(s). • Given our situation, we understand how their qualifications relate to the objective(s) and to the methods necessary to achieve them.	15	
We believe that the *cost* of the project is justified by the *benefits* articulated. • We understand the benefits we can expect to accrue *during* the project, as a result of how they will work with our people. • We also understand the benefits we can expect to accrue *after* the project, as a result of the project's objective(s) being achieved. • If possible, and within reasonable ranges, they have quantified the tangible benefits likely to accrue.	20	
Total Points:	100	

FIGURE 14.8 Rating Guide for Proposals, p. 2

Paramount Consulting's Proposal Opportunity at the ABC Company

A Case Study

Dramatis Personae

Stan Gilmore, your boss and a partner at Paramount Consulting
Ray Armstrong, President of ABC Company
Anil Gupta, ABC's Vice President of Operations
Marcia Collins, ABC's Vice President of Marketing
Paul Morrison, ABC's Chief Industrial Engineer
Frank Metzger, ABC's Plant Manager

February 1: The First Contact

Stan Gilmore, a partner in Paramount Consulting responsible for the firm's manufacturing practice, just received a letter from Anil Gupta, Vice President of Operations for the ABC Company, a division of Consolidated Industries. The letter states that ABC manufactures and markets a line of major household and commercial appliances, has annual sales of more than US$19B dollars, and has enjoyed a consistent record of growth. Future growth, however, might be curtailed by insufficient manufacturing capacity. ABC, the letter continues, wants to engage a consulting firm to help it answer its questions about manufacturing capacity. Paramount has been recommended to ABC, and if Paramount is interested in pursuing a possible relationship, it should contact Gupta.

Gilmore is eager to pursue this opportunity because he recognizes ABC's brand name as having an outstanding reputation for product quality and delivery performance and knows that ABC holds a significant share of its market. Furthermore, Consolidated Industries is well known for acquiring and developing companies that hold dominant positions in their respective markets. Gilmore is confident that Paramount can help.

Gilmore calls Gupta to affirm that Paramount can indeed provide the needed consulting assistance and welcomes the opportunity to do so. According to Gupta, ABC plans to meet separately with representatives from each of four consulting companies that survived its initial screening. During those meetings, ABC will discuss the need for the study and provide the basic information necessary for the consultants to prepare their proposals. Gilmore asks who will represent ABC at the meeting, and Gupta says that he and the following will attend:

* Marcia Collins, Vice President of Marketing
* Frank Metzger, Plant Manager
* Paul Morrison, Chief Industrial Engineer

They conclude their conversation by agreeing to meet the following week at ABC's division office in a large midwestern city.

February 2: Research

Gilmore calls in one of his group's research associates and tells her he needs background data that will give him a better understanding of ABC's operations. She immediately embarks on a LexisNexis search, a review of Consolidated's annual and 10K reports, a study of S&P's industry reports, and a review of an industry report from the research department of a local brokerage firm.

As they analyze the results of the research, Gilmore can see that Consolidated is indeed a very successful company. Headquartered in New York City, it ranks in the upper quartile on most of the factors used by *Forbes* to measure the success of major industrial companies, and ABC contributes significantly to that success. ABC's products are distributed through a strong national network of distributors and dealers and also to major department store chains that market them under their private labels. Its products enjoy high brand-name recognition and have a well-established reputation for product quality. Moreover, the division is recognized within the industry for providing superior customer service.

Industry forecasts indicate that the overall market will grow modestly over the next several years and that relatively little change in product configuration is expected. The forecasts also show that ABC is expected to retain its share of the market, which is highly competitive. Just four major producers accounted for 86 percent of total shipments the previous year. Because of the favorable characteristics of its product line and its high service levels, ABC has consistently increased its market share and participated fully in a modestly growing overall market driven by replacement demand, residential and commercial construction, and general economic conditions.

One of the concerns of the industry is the increasing cost of distributing its products. Apparently, the configuration of the product and its weight yields a bulk/weight ratio that makes distribution costs a major component of total operating costs. Furthermore, geographic demand for the product is following continuing demographic shifts to the U.S. South, Southeast, and Southwest. Industry reports also show that most of ABC's production takes place in one midwestern city but that the manufacture of some special-purpose units in the product line occurs in two smaller satellite facilities in relatively small midwestern cities.

With this basic understanding, Gilmore looks forward to the meeting to learn more about ABC's situation. He has already decided that he will take along one of his associates: you.

February 9: Meeting with Gupta, Collins, Metzger, and Morrison

At the meeting, Gupta introduces the attendees identified in the phone conversation. He explains that the four of them will serve as ABC's consultant-selection committee along with the division president, who is away that day at Consolidated's headquarters in New York.

Gupta introduces Marcia Collins, VP of Marketing, who sets the stage for the meeting. Collins joined ABC two years earlier after spending four years as director of marketing for a large national grocery products company. Prior to that, she received an undergraduate degree from Northwestern and an M.B.A. from its Kellogg School. Collins's basic discussion document is a chart that shows two market forecasts for ABC, one labeled "optimistic" and the other "conservative." (See Figure A.1.)

Obvious from the chart is that ABC's forecasts assume its ability to continue to increase market share. Most revealing is a horizontal line on the forecast graph that represents the capacity of the existing production facility. It shows that in less than three years, existing capacity is exceeded even in the conservative forecast—beyond that point, the shortfall in production capacity becomes progressively larger.

Gupta next introduces Frank Metzger, Plant Manager, explaining that he has been with ABC his entire career. Metzger worked as an hourly employee in the

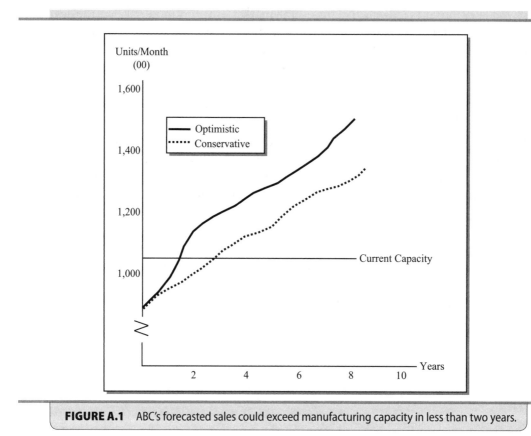

FIGURE A.1   ABC's forecasted sales could exceed manufacturing capacity in less than two years.

press and maintenance departments before becoming press department foreman. Gupta stresses that Metzger was highly successful in the press department
and succeeded him as plant manager three years ago when Gupta was promoted
to VP of Operations. Gupta asks Metzger to describe the current situation related
to utilizing production capacity.

According to Metzger, the plant is meeting its current production schedules by
working two full shifts of operation, with some overloaded work centers working a
third shift. Most scheduled equipment maintenance is also performed on the third
shift so that little overtime premium is incurred because of weekend work. While
showing the group a site drawing of the current facility, Metzger describes how the
site is well utilized with manufacturing and office space, truck docks, and parking areas. "Let me point out," says Gupta, referring to the drawing, "that the site
can't be expanded because it's bounded by railroad tracks in one direction, a major
thoroughfare in another, and by residential areas in the other two directions."

"But," Metzger counters, "there's still some space available within the current site into which the present manufacturing facility could expand. Most of ABC's additional capacity requirements could be met by expanding the current facility into the space remaining." He suggests, however, that to meet the projected forecasts they would probably have to operate a full third shift.

"Are there any downside risks to operating a three-shift schedule?" Gilmore asks.

"It would be a challenge," Metzger admits, "because maintenance work would have to be done on the weekends, in which case, we'd incur additional overtime costs."

Gilmore pursues the issue: "Could productivity and quality on the third shift be expected to attain the level of the other two shifts?"

They would undoubtedly experience additional absenteeism and turnover, according to Metzger, and might even have some difficulty in recruiting for that shift. But even if operating costs are higher, ABC's capital investment would be considerably lower by expanding the existing facility:

"It's also possible," Metzger says, "that we could hold expansion space to a minimum by using outside storage for raw materials and finished goods, if necessary."

Gupta introduces Paul Morrison, ABC's Chief Industrial Engineer, to apprise the group of the manufacturing capacity situation. Morrison has an undergraduate degree in industrial engineering from Michigan and a master's in that discipline from Georgia Tech, where, as a graduate assistant, he taught undergraduate courses in quantitative methods. He joined ABC three years ago, and one of his recent projects was to develop a computer model to enable the division to improve its distribution methods and to track and control those costs, which are an important part of their total operating costs.

According to Morrison, he and his department have not studied the capacity situation to any great extent because they have been occupied in helping the production departments maintain productivity levels so that they can meet increasing schedule demands. However, after examining current work center loads to judge the amount of new equipment that will be required and estimating the amount of additional storage space that will be needed for higher production levels, he questions whether the space available on the existing site is adequate:

"Even though investment costs might be lower, I would be hesitant to put all of ABC's eggs in one basket, giving us no protection against natural catastrophes or labor difficulties. Furthermore, ABC's markets are growing faster outside the Midwest."

He suggests that even if the projected forecasts could be satisfied at the present site, if they were able to increase market share further, or if the overall market grew more rapidly than expected, they would be facing the same dilemma again in the near future:

"In my view, the consultants must carefully define what ABC needs in terms of additional manufacturing capacity, develop logical alternatives to meet these needs, and then quantitatively and qualitatively evaluate those alternatives."

Gupta thanks them all for their input and remarks that one of Morrison's points is especially important—that virtually all of ABC's production occurs at this facility, which makes ABC somewhat vulnerable. He also expresses some surprise that no one has mentioned another possible option:

"What about our two satellite manufacturing facilities? Neither one is on a site large enough to accommodate our full expansion requirements, but maybe one of the product lines could be relocated to one of these sites, thereby freeing up space at the existing facility."

However, he agrees with Morrison that they will look to the consultants to develop possible alternatives and that those alternatives will have to be analyzed very thoroughly and convincingly, especially since ABC most likely will have to make a major capital investment.

Gupta asks Gilmore what else they can provide that will help him prepare the proposal. Gilmore requests copies of the site plan; the market forecast data; samples of various productivity, work center loading, and scheduling reports; equipment lists; and manning tables. He also asks Gupta to identify the other three consultants who will bid on the project. Gilmore recognizes one of Paramount's competitors, which has strong, diversified consulting capabilities. Not recognizing the other two, he wonders if Gupta will tell him a little about them. According to Gupta, they are local companies that specialize in facilities planning, plant layout, materials handling, and productivity improvement. One of them helped ABC with a materials handling problem in the past.

"How satisfied were you with their work?" Gilmore asks.

Gupta responds briskly, but not curtly: "Satisfied enough to ask them to bid."

Gilmore knows that the materials he requested will provide him a good understanding of ABC's current situation related to manufacturing capacity. In addition, to make certain that Paramount's proposal will be entirely responsive, Gilmore remarks, he would like to meet individually with each of the people present to understand their perspectives better and to probe the advantages and disadvantages of the alternatives they had discussed as well as some others that might be worth considering. During that visit, he would also like an extensive tour of the manufacturing operations.

Gupta is pleased with Gilmore's willingness to take the additional time to do this and, after polling his group, suggests that the following week would be convenient. He also mentions that Ray Armstrong, ABC's president, will be back in the office then and Gilmore probably could meet with him. Gilmore says he will call each person to schedule a specific time. He spends the balance of the meeting telling the group about Paramount's overall capabilities, history, and reputation; its specific expertise in the areas relevant to the proposed study; and the capabilities of its staff. He then describes some consulting assignments in which Paramount had been successful in helping clients with similar problems.

The two of you leave the meeting feeling that you have a good preliminary understanding of ABC's capacity situation and that you have established a reasonable rapport with the group. However, you recognize that you need to know much more about ABC's operation to scope the proposal properly. This, you both feel, can be accomplished through Gilmore's interviews. You also agree, however, that a major objective of the interview process should be to better understand the people on the selection team, including their interests and perceived study objectives, and how the results of the study could affect them. That will enable you to make the proposal responsive to the needs of each member of the team.

February 14: Individual Meetings with the Major Players

"I believe that your market forecasts will play a major role in the proposed study." Gilmore is talking to Collins. "So I would like to understand better how they were developed."

"Most of my data," she says, "come from reports published regularly by the industry trade group, the Association of Home Appliance Manufacturers, in which ABC participates. These data were supplemented by others from *Appliance Design* surveys, Standard & Poor's industry surveys, and ABC's own historical data." Because there is a good deal of consistency among the data from the different sources, Collins is confident that her conclusions on the overall industry forecasts are valid.

"However," she points out, "my development of optimistic and conservative forecasts is based on my interpretation of ABC's position in the market."

She explains that the division's steady increases in market share are due to its ability to control costs, maintain quality, and provide a high level of service to its customers:

"The optimistic forecast assumes that ABC will be successful in maintaining those positions; the conservative forecast assumes some slippage in market share."

According to Collins, maintaining or increasing market share is important to ABC's success:

"Not only does it affect our operating results, it is also a performance measure in our bonus plan. Furthermore, it affects the level of autonomy we enjoy as well as the ease with which we can obtain capital funds from Consolidated."

Gilmore asks Collins to assess the various possibilities for expanding capacity that were discussed the previous week. Collins isn't really knowledgeable about manufacturing operations, she says, and has little sense of just how many additional resources would be required. However, she is concerned about adding capacity entirely at the existing site:

"High service levels are important to increase market share, and ABC's current service levels could be jeopardized if all manufacturing were in one location."

Her reasoning appears sound. First, as she says, ABC's major markets are shifting away from the Midwest, resulting in increased delivery times; second, if there should be a fire or another catastrophe, its reputation for good service would certainly deteriorate.

"I feel so strongly about maintaining or improving current service levels that I think service levels should be a major criterion for evaluating the various alternatives for expanding capacity."

Metzger's office is centrally located in the manufacturing area of the facility. As Gilmore enters, Metzger immediately apologizes: He has to delay their meeting for at least an hour to meet with his maintenance, press, and assembly department foremen. One of the major fabrication lines has broken down, and they have to find a way to complete a production run because the customer's trailers are waiting at the shipping dock. In the meantime, he asks his assistant to give Gilmore a tour of the plant.

Gilmore is immediately impressed with the excellent housekeeping in the plant. Aisles are clear and well marked, storage areas are orderly with good use of clear height, individual work areas are clean and well organized, and there are many examples of point-of-use storage where materials are stored close to and are easily available to the production operators. The assistant explains that each operator is responsible for his own workplace—that housekeeping personnel are used only to maintain major travel aisles. Gilmore is also impressed with the production equipment, which appears reasonably state of the art. The assistant remarks that the industrial engineering group has an aggressive program to continually evaluate and upgrade equipment and that the plant engineering department is adept at designing and installing special-purpose equipment.

When Metzger returns, he again apologizes profusely and explains that they were able to make some equipment substitutions that will minimize the downtime on the assembly line as well as increase the rate of delivery of the finished product to the customer's trailers. Gilmore compliments Metzger on the general appearance of the manufacturing facility and comments that it could be a model for many of his clients' facilities. He asks Metzger to expand a bit on his background as portrayed the previous week at the initial meeting.

Metzger augmented his high school education with numerous in-house courses offered by ABC. He broadened himself beyond those offerings by taking courses in human relations, shop supervision, quality control, and advanced shop math at the local community college. Those efforts served him well because he was promoted to maintenance group leader and then succeeded the press department foreman when that individual became ill. As he explained last week, he was fortunate to be selected to replace Gupta as plant manager when Gupta was promoted.

Gilmore would like to hear more about Metzger's concept of increasing capacity at the existing site. Metzger replies that although he doesn't know just how much additional capacity would be needed, there is quite a bit of land available on the present site for expanding the manufacturing building. Although some of that space is now used for employee parking, he thinks this could be overcome by double-decking the remaining parking area. If the present facility were expanded, he would have the opportunity to promote some well-deserving first-line supervisors into positions of greater responsibility. The capital requirements for that option would probably be less, and he has heard that Consolidated is becoming less generous in releasing funds to the competing divisions.

In Morrison's office, located in the same area, Gilmore remarks that the caliber of the equipment he saw on his plant tour was evidence of his group's successful program to continually monitor and upgrade major production equipment. Morrison thanks him and shows him a stack of reports Gilmore had requested at last week's meeting. They discuss the reports in some detail, and Morrison suggests that the documents could be very useful in determining ABC's capacity requirements. Gilmore readily agrees.

Gilmore compliments Morrison about some of Morrison's comments last week: Several of the factors that would have to be considered in the proposed study were, in Gilmore's experience, right on the mark. But Gilmore wonders about a factor not discussed:

"What about distribution costs?" he asks. "Distribution costs are a major component of total operating costs throughout the industry."

"These are very important to the division," Morrison says, "and you're right—they weren't sufficiently discussed last week. Because of the weight and configuration of our product, these costs are virtually the same as those for fabricating and assembling our product. They are such a concern," he adds, "that my group worked with the information systems and distribution managers to develop a computer model. This model enabled us to analyze different logistics strategies, select the best, and then monitor the costs of distributing product to our nearly 150 demand points on an ongoing basis."

Morrison explains that this model had been properly validated and could be used to determine distribution costs for different manufacturing capacity alternatives. The model had been developed because Armstrong was concerned about escalating distribution costs and their potential impact on profits. Learning that Armstrong planned to engage a consultant to develop the model, Morrison discussed with the systems and distribution managers the possibility of developing such a model in-house. They agreed that it could be done if Morrison, because of his academic background, would lead the project. They subsequently met with Armstrong and convinced him that the in-house project was feasible and cost-effective. Armstrong also saw that the project would provide a beneficial learning experience for his managers, and so he gave his approval to proceed. Morrison's team overcame a number of problems (which he had anticipated) and successfully completed the project, although it took four months longer than expected.

"I should tell you," Morrison confides, "that I recommended to Armstrong that ABC also conduct the capacity expansion study in-house. But Armstrong believed that I and my group were stretched too thin, that additional staff would have to be hired, and that the division needed to address its capacity issues without delay. Armstrong acknowledged that my group had proven capabilities for the study, but he held firm to his decision to use outside consultants. At this point, I am only interested in seeing the study done, done right, and completed expeditiously."

He thinks the study will be complicated because there are many different alternatives, each with its own devotee. And yet these alternatives are being tossed around without the knowledge of just how much additional capacity is needed.

"So let me repeat what I said last week: One of the initial major tasks of the consultants will be to carefully define capacity requirements. Then, alternatives for satisfying those requirements can be developed and evaluated. The development of sound, agreed-upon evaluation criteria would be very important, too, to overcome any built-in prejudices that people might have in favor of their own ideas." Gilmore tells Morrison that he completely agrees.

Gilmore mentions that he is meeting with Armstrong later that afternoon and asks if Morrison can tell him a little about Armstrong's background. Armstrong, it turns out, was recruited from outside the company and has a marketing and financial background. Armstrong became vice president of marketing at a large manufacturing company and was recruited away from that position by a search firm to fill a CEO spot at another company. A few years after that, Consolidated recruited him to head ABC. Morrison doesn't really have that much involvement with Armstrong but thinks him open-minded, analytical, and firm in his decisions once he has heard and thoroughly considered all sides of an issue.

Gupta's office is near the conference room in which they had met last week. He receives Gilmore very cordially and asks him about his interviews and plant tour. They were very informative and helpful, Gilmore responds, and he is beginning to get a good "feel" for ABC's operation, its organization, and its manufacturing capacity situation—background that will help Paramount prepare a responsive proposal.

Gilmore adds it would be helpful if he knew something more about the vice president's background. After graduating with a degree in industrial engineering from Purdue, Gupta replies, he joined ABC's I.E. Group. During his several years in that group, he worked in many different manufacturing areas, including plant layout, process engineering, equipment justification and selection, wage incentives, and job evaluation, among others. When the incumbent plant manager announced his retirement, he was offered the position, which he readily accepted. As plant manager, he set several goals for the plant, including meeting the continually increasing production schedules, controlling costs by improving manufacturing methods and processes, maintaining and improving product quality levels, and fostering harmonious employee relations. He believes he has been reasonably successful in meeting those goals; apparently, so did top management because after about five years, he was promoted into his current position and became part of the president's management team.

Gilmore asks Gupta to tell him about ABC's satellite manufacturing operations since he mentioned them last week during their discussion of capacity expansion alternatives.

"They are relatively small operations in two rural cities," he says, "producing certain low-volume, special-purpose units in the product line. Both of the facilities are on plant sites large enough to accommodate some building expansion."

But the manufacturing workforce in both cities is rather small and might not support a major expansion. His supervisory groups there are relatively thin and would have to be "beefed up." But an expansion to accept a limited part of the product line in addition to expansion at the existing facility probably would enable ABC to meet its forecasted demand for several years.

Gilmore finds Armstrong to be very congenial, with a demeanor that reflects his guidance of a key and successful division at Consolidated. They spend some time discussing business conditions generally and Consolidated and ABC in particular. Armstrong asks Gilmore to tell him about Paramount, which he is pleased to do since Armstrong hadn't attended the previous week's meeting.

Gilmore then leads the discussion to the proposed study. Armstrong believes a sound, comprehensive study is critical to the future of the division. Only by providing manufacturing with the resources it needs to operate cost effectively and to maintain and improve product quality and service levels can the division hope to maintain its reputation, compete effectively in the marketplace, and assure success for the company and its employees. He wants to initiate the study quickly because he knows that if, for example, a new facility is required, it probably will be close to two years before it reaches full production. And, he points out, some critical work centers are already operating on a third shift. Gilmore replies that Armstrong's time estimates are realistic and that Paramount can initiate the study quickly.

Armstrong again emphasizes that the study would have to be thorough and convincing. He tells Gilmore that although he operates ABC with a great deal of autonomy and that although ABC is very successful, it—like other Consolidated divisions—has to compete for funds "at the company trough."

"Therefore, as you've probably been told, the study will have to be well documented and the returns from the investment clearly defined, because an expansion project of this probable magnitude will require capital funding by Consolidated, and our request will receive close scrutiny at corporate headquarters."

Others had remarked about the study needing to be thorough and convincing; this was an additional reason why.

Gilmore asks Armstrong what deliverables he expects from the study. Armstrong and his management team have given considerable thought to that topic; indeed, the depth and diversity of their discussions convinced him they would need outside assistance. He goes on to say that the team agreed that the study would definitely have to answer at least the following questions:

- What will it take in terms of space, equipment, and manpower to meet both the conservative and optimistic forecasts?
- How many of those resources can be provided by expanding the current facility?
- Even if those resources can be added at the present location, does it make economic sense to do that or to make the investment elsewhere?
- Can service levels be increased and transportation costs reduced at a new geographic location to provide greater leverage in selling to mass-marketed customers?
- What ROI will result from the substantial new investment?
- Which alternative generates the greatest profit during the forecast period?

Gilmore responds that these are important and realistic questions and that in judging different alternatives, certain qualitative analyses also would have to be made regarding labor supply, union climate, available technical training assistance, and the like. Armstrong acknowledges this and says he wants to leave Gilmore with one additional point before they end their discussion. He explains that even though they are seeing a shift in market demand away from the Midwest, they have no intention of relocating the existing facility because of its central geographic location and experienced workforce, the significant cost involved in relocating many pieces of equipment and numerous personnel, and the large "sunk cost" in land, building, and fixed equipment.

Gilmore says he appreciates that comment because in the back of his mind he had considered these factors. He thanks Armstrong for his time and tells him that he can probably have a proposal to him by the end of the following week. Armstrong instructs him to send the proposal to Gupta, who is heading the selection committee.

February 15: Next Steps

When he returns to the office the following day, Gilmore meets with you to brief you on his second visit to ABC. Gilmore wants you to spearhead the preparation of the proposal, which he will help you with as time is available.

Worksheets

This appendix contains the 6 individual cells from the Logics Worksheet and the 6 individual cells from the Psychologics Worksheet. These 12 cells as well as the complete worksheets (which contain the individual cells in strategic order) can be downloaded from http://web.me.com/rfreed/Writing_Winning_Business _Proposals/Home.html. The Themes Development Worksheet is also available at the site.

Logics Worksheet — Cell 1

Prospect Profile

"How would you characterize the prospect?"

- Major products/markets
  _____
  _____

- Annual revenue/profitability/trends
  _____
  _____

- Major competitors
  _____
  _____

- Market/industry issues
  _____
  _____

- Strategic direction
  _____
  _____

- Experience with your competition
  _____
  _____

FIGURE B.1   The Logics Worksheet, Cell 1

Logics Worksheet — Cell 2

Prospect's Current Situation (S_1)

"What is happening today that the prospect would like to change?"

Prospect's Triggering Event, Problem, and Its Effects
(Including Lack of Benefits and Downside Risk of Doing Nothing

Triggering event: _____

Single overriding problem:* _____

Effects of problem: _____

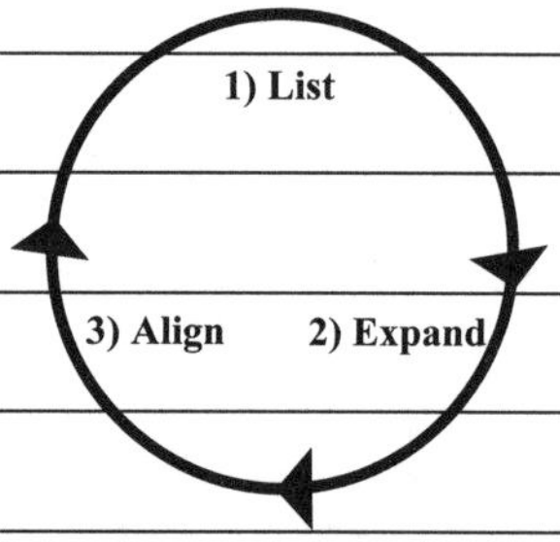

1) List

3) Align   2) Expand

* Align with the dominant overriding question in Cell 4

FIGURE B.2   The Logics Worksheet, Cell 2

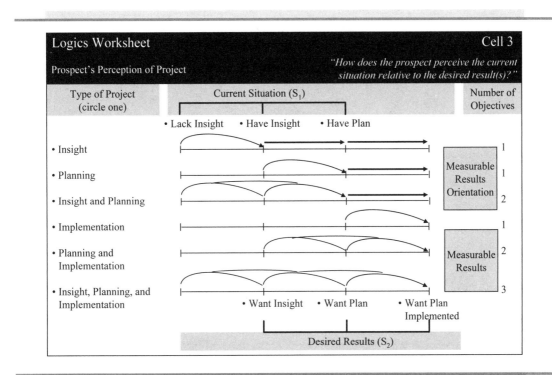

Logics Worksheet — Cell 3

Prospect's Perception of Project

"How does the prospect perceive the current situation relative to the desired result(s)?"

Type of Project (circle one)

Current Situation (S_1)

Number of Objectives

- Lack Insight   • Have Insight   • Have Plan

- Insight — 1
- Planning — 1
- Insight and Planning — 2

Measurable Results Orientation

- Implementation — 1
- Planning and Implementation — 2
- Insight, Planning, and Implementation — 3

Measurable Results

- Want Insight   • Want Plan   • Want Plan Implemented

Desired Results (S_2)

FIGURE B.3 The Logics Worksheet, Cell 3

Logics Worksheet — Cell 4

Prospect's Overriding Questions

"Given the number of objectives (noted in Cell 3), what overriding question(s) does the prospect want answered to improve the current situation?" (List one overriding question per objective.)

Prospect's Single Overriding Insight *Question**	Prospect's Single Overriding Planning *Question**	Prospect's Single Overriding Implementation *Objective†*
■ _____ _____ _____ _____ ?	■ _____ _____ _____ _____ ?	■ _____ _____ _____ _____

*To state the project objective, rephrase the overriding question, using an active verb.

†Implementation projects have no overriding question.

FIGURE B.4 The Logics Worksheet, Cell 4

Logics Worksheet · Cell 5

Prospect's Desired Results

"What does the prospect desire instead of the current situation?"

Prospect's Desired **Insight** Result (to be achieved after Insight Question is answered)	Prospect's Desired **Planning** Result (to be achieved after Planning Question is answered)	Prospect's Desired **Implementation** Result (or Measurable-Results Orientation, if not an Implementation Project)
■ *Insight*/knowledge regarding . . .	■ A *Plan* to/for . . .	■ An *Implemented Plan* to/for . . .
Deliverables	**Deliverables**	**Deliverables**

FIGURE B.5   The Logics Worksheet, Cell 5

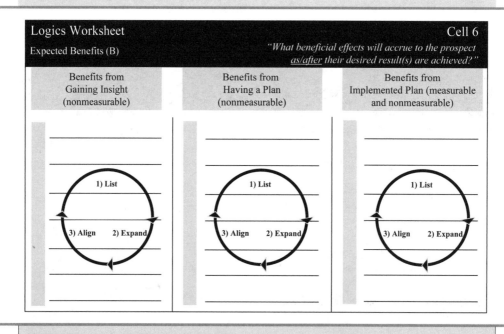

Logics Worksheet · Cell 6

Expected Benefits (B)

"What beneficial effects will accrue to the prospect as/after their desired result(s) are achieved?"

Benefits from Gaining Insight (nonmeasurable)	Benefits from Having a Plan (nonmeasurable)	Benefits from Implemented Plan (measurable and nonmeasurable)
1) List 2) Expand 3) Align	1) List 2) Expand 3) Align	1) List 2) Expand 3) Align

FIGURE B.6   The Logics Worksheet, Cell 6

Psychologics Worksheet — Cell 1

Individual Buyers' Titles, Roles, and Benefits

"What benefits will accrue to each buyer as/after the desired result(s) are achieved?"

| Buyer/Title | Buyer Role(s) | | | | | Based on their respective roles, each buyer's . . . | |
	E	U	T	C	R	Benefits from *Insight* or *Plan*	Benefits from *Implementation**
1							
2							
3							
4							
5							

*If proposed project does not involve implementation, use Measurable-Results Orientation to indicate tangible benefits buyer could achieve subsequent to implementation.

FIGURE B.7 The Psychologics Worksheet, Cell 1

Psychologics Worksheet — Cell 2

Hot Buttons

"What desires or concerns of each buyer must be addressed?"

Buyer's Hot Buttons*	How Addressed	SA	M	PO	Benefits to Each Buyer from Addressing His/Her Hot Buttons
1					
2					
3					
4					
5					

*Hot button: process-related desire or concern of a buyer that will affect your sales approach (SA), project's methodology (M), and/or project organization (PO); often personal, having emotional rather than technical content. Use single words or short phrases such as:

- Thorough, integrated, balanced, or flexible approach
- Urgency (e.g., to get quick results)
- Creativity
- Control
- Fear or change
- Project complexity
- Objectivity
- Sensitivity to . . .
- Involvement
- Teaching/training

FIGURE B.8 The Psychologics Worksheet, Cell 2

Psychologics Worksheet — Cell 3

Buyer Receptivity

"How receptive is each buyer to your efforts to date?"

	Power Base			Receptivity				Rationale for Your Ratings
	L	M	H	– –	–	+	+ +	
1								
2								
3								
4								
5								

FIGURE B.9   The Psychologics Worksheet, Cell 3

Psychologics Worksheet — Cell 4

Evaluation Process/Criteria   *"What process/criteria will the buying committee use, collectively?"*

"What is the prospect's budget for this project?"	
"How will the selection decision be made?"	

"What collective evaluation criteria will be used?"	Knockout	Relative Weighting
1		
2		
3		
4		
5		
		100%

FIGURE B.10   The Psychologics Worksheet, Cell 4

Psychologics Worksheet — Cell 5

Competition

"Based upon the evaluation criteria, how does the prospect compare you with competitors?"

Competitors	Considering the Prospect's Evaluation Criteria for *This Opportunity . . .*	
	Competitors' Strengths	Competitors' Weaknesses
• In-house/other initiatives		
•		
•		
	Your Strengths	Your Weaknesses
• You		

"How might you counter competitors' strengths or exploit their weaknesses?"	"How might competitors counter your strengths, exploit your weaknesses, or redefine the overriding question?"
•	•
•	•
•	•

FIGURE B.11   The Psychologics Worksheet, Cell 5

Psychologics Worksheet — Cell 6

Themes

"What repeated messages best characterize the prospect's story and/or differentiate you?"

	Themes Come from Hot Buttons, Evaluation Criteria, and Counters to the Competition
1	
2	
3	
4	
5	

FIGURE B.12   The Psychologics Worksheet, Cell 6

Themes Development Worksheet

Prospect: _____ Date: ___ / ___ / ___

1) Selected Theme		2) Situation	3) Methodology	4) Qualifications	5) Benefits
"What repeated messages will increase your probability of winning?"		*"Given the current situation, what do the buyers need related to this theme?"*	*"Given this need, how have you designed your methodology or project organization to meet it?"*	*"Given those methods, how are you qualified to perform them, related to that need?"*	*"Given those methods and qualifications, how will the buyers benefit by your meeting that need?"*
Theme	Source* HB EC CC	State as prospect's needs... (focus on the prospect)	...which will be met by you (focus on you)	State as good reasons (focus on you)	State as good reasons (focus on the prospect)
1		Because . . . , you need . . .	Therefore, we will . . .		
2		Because . . . , you need . . .	Therefore, we will . . .		
3		Because . . . , you need . . .	Therefore, we will . . .		

*HB = hot buttons; EC = evaluation criteria; CC = counters to competition

Example: Urgency	**Because** forecasted demand will soon outstrip capacity, and because adding new capacity will require long lead times, **you need** a study that produces a decision quickly.	**Therefore, we will** involve management in preparing the final report, which will be the proposal to Consolidated, thereby eliminating one step in your decision-making process.	**We** will immediately commit a project team with the practical experience to develop and execute a work plan that will minimize the study's elapsed time.	By our conducting this study expeditiously, **you** will have time for detailed planning and implementation, which will allow maintained customer service during the transition.

FIGURE B.13 The Themes Development Worksheet

Paramount's Proposal Letter to the ABC Company

Proposal to ABC Company
February 29, 2XXX

Paramount

Paramount Consulting
401 East River Run
Chicago, Illinois 606XX

Mr. Anil Gupta, Vice President   February 29, 2XXX
ABC Company
234 Raintree Road
Midwestern, Illinois

Dear Anil:

Thank you for the time you and your colleagues have spent with us to describe in detail ABC's urgent need for additional capacity to meet anticipated market demand. We have given your situation considerable thought, which we have reflected in this proposal to develop a manufacturing strategy, the implementation of which will provide the capacity necessary to meet forecasted demand. Our proposal presents our understanding of your situation, our proposed methodology for developing the most appropriate capacity plan, our qualifications for supporting you, and the benefits we believe you will realize from our participation in this most challenging engagement. As you requested, we have submitted separately our estimated fees, the résumés of our proposed team, and references from similar projects.

The Situation at ABC

Over the past five years, household appliance shipments by ABC and your competitors have been fairly stable, and only modest growth is projected over the next five years in your mature industry (Figure 1).

Despite the relative stability of these shipments industrywide, ABC has managed to increase its share of the household appliance market primarily by producing high-quality products at competitive costs and by being responsive to customers' needs. As a result, ABC has become a leader in the market and one of the premier divisions within Consolidated Industries.

Your consistent record of success, however, may be threatened. Although your market forecasts indicate that ABC can continue to increase market share, even the conservative forecast clearly shows that projected product demand will exceed your available manufacturing capacity in less than three years. Without adequate

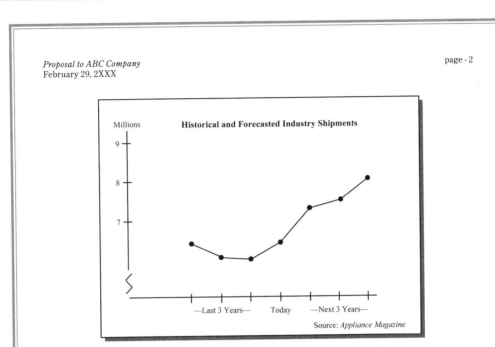

FIGURE 1   Industry forecasts show modest growth over the next three years.

capacity, your competitive position will certainly suffer as a result of declining delivery performance, deteriorating product quality, and increasing operating costs.

Complicating the picture, demographic shifts and exports are moving demand farther away from your existing Midwest production facilities (Figure 2). Population and household growth in three geographic regions remote from these facilities has far exceeded that of the Midwest, as well as the nation as a whole. Undoubtedly, these geographic shifts have contributed to ABC's increased distribution costs, a major factor in the total landed cost of household appliances. In jeopardy are not only ABC's operating objectives but your status as a premier division within Consolidated.

Recognizing these threats, your management group has suggested several options for increasing capacity, but little agreement exists about how that capacity should be deployed, and no agreement exists about the amount of capacity required. Consensus does exist, however, in two areas: additional capacity will be needed, and the time when it will be needed is fast approaching.

Complicating the need to move quickly is the need to carefully develop a thorough, convincing, and comprehensive plan accepted by both ABC's and Consolidated's management. This plan should answer questions like these:

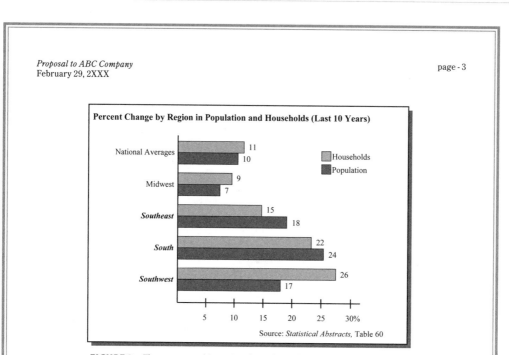

FIGURE 2   Three geographic regions have household and population growth exceeding the national average and growth in the Midwest.

- Based upon the long-term forecast, how much total factory space, equipment, and human resources are required and when?
- What opportunities exist to better utilize current equipment, space, and new technology?
- What manufacturing factory–configuration option or options will provide the required space? For example, how much expansion potential exists at the current facility, and what, if any, make versus buy scenarios as well as changes in factory roles and locations can provide additional space?
- Even if resources can be added at the present location, does it make more economic sense to add them there or to make the investment elsewhere? For example, will service levels increase and transportation costs decrease at a new geographic location closer to your growing markets?
- Which option is most appropriate considering the qualitative factors and quantitative factors identified in our methodology below?

To answer questions like these, my colleagues at Paramount Consulting and I have designed a methodology that will not only develop a manufacturing strategy to provide the capacity necessary for meeting forecasted demand but also a concrete plan for implementing that strategy to improve your position within the marketplace and solidify your position within Consolidated Industries.

Our Proposed Methodology

We have designed our methodology as we have for three important reasons. First, because forecasted demand will soon outstrip capacity and because building new capacity will require long lead times, you need a study that produces a decision quickly. Therefore, we will involve ABC's management to expedite the retrieval, development, and analysis of relevant information, thus reducing the time for analysis. We will also work with your management team to prepare the final report. This document will not only be a recommended expansion plan but also an actual proposal to Consolidated that justifies the cost of the expansion by articulating the compelling reasons to move forward with urgency.

Second, because of the many and varied proposed expansion alternatives, you need well-defined and agreed-upon criteria for evaluating them. Therefore, we will conduct strategy sessions with all relevant ABC managers to gain consensus on and establish the proper quantitative and qualitative criteria. Quantitative criteria worth considering include ROI; investment incentives; taxes; and costs related to labor, service levels, distribution, construction, and utilities. Qualitative criteria could include labor supply, union climate, workforce characteristics, productivity, environmental permitting and regulations, vocational training capabilities, manufacturing support services, risk, controllability, the ability to develop and promote employees, and the flexibility to react to unanticipated changes.

Finally, because this will be a cross-functional study, ABC needs a senior, multifaceted consulting team with a broad range of business capabilities, including marketing, manufacturing strategy, facilities planning, logistics, financial analysis, and human resources. These capabilities are necessary to ensure that all relevant options are surfaced and evaluated in a practical manner, that the most desirable options and their attributes are clearly identified and defined, and that ABC's management not only has the ability to make the right decision but that Consolidated is convinced of its appropriateness.

Therefore, we will form a joint ABC/Paramount study team with ABC's managers playing an integral role, thereby providing the additional benefit of training ABC's management to analyze and plan for additional capacity in the future.

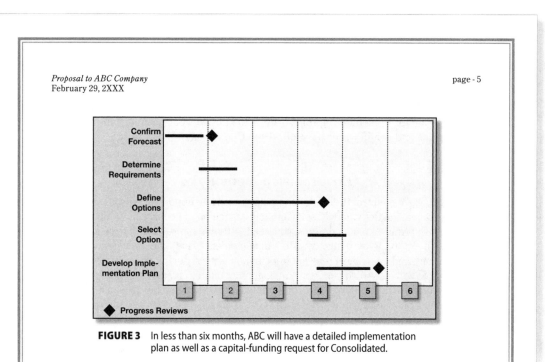

FIGURE 3 In less than six months, ABC will have a detailed implementation plan as well as a capital-funding request for Consolidated.

Specifically, our methodology consists of the five major tasks shown in Figure 3 and discussed in detail in Appendix A. Please note that the five-and-one-half-month estimate for completing the study is conservative. Working with your management team, we will make every effort to accelerate the project's completion.

Qualifications of Paramount Consulting

ABC is faced with a most formidable challenge as it begins the task of providing additional manufacturing capacity to avert the shortfall expected in the next few years. This capacity shortfall should be considered imminent as you examine the numerous tasks that must be completed effectively within the narrow available time frame.

Time will be required for sufficient interchange between ABC and Consolidated to agree on the decision to commit scarce financial, planning, managerial, and other resources needed to implement the selected option. Substantially more time will be needed to put in place additional resources and to provide the necessary training for an effective start-up.

As described in the following paragraphs, Paramount has the diverse capabilities to help you complete this challenging engagement successfully and expeditiously. Specifically, we have:

- The resources to begin this engagement immediately and to complete this project in four to five months
- Substantial manufacturing, financial, and strategy-development experience within the household-appliance industry
- The ability to address the wide range of issues related to this engagement
- The ability to develop a sound joint ABC/Paramount team
- Proven experience in planning and controlling implementation of the strategy we will develop with you

Paramount Has the Resources to Begin and Complete This Project Quickly

Of the nearly 100 consultants in our nearby Midwest office, we have already identified several individuals with the skills and experience needed to help develop a sound plan for increasing capacity. Each of these professionals has worked on similar engagements, is substantially "down the learning curve," and will therefore be able to function effectively at the beginning of the engagement. In fact, several of them have participated in developing this proposal.

Our proposed engagement team of four consultants will be drawn from this group, and we would like to introduce this team to you so that you feel as comfortable with them as we do. We will use no subcontractors without your concurrence, and we will be able to begin the engagement immediately after your approval to proceed.

We Have Substantial Manufacturing, Financial, and Strategy-Development Experience Within Your Industry

For almost 40 years, Paramount has served clients with a high level of satisfaction. In fact, over 80 percent of our consulting engagements come from previous clients. Paramount originated with a strong manufacturing and strategy capability that has grown significantly over the years; this strength will enable us to address all the diverse issues that must be resolved during the proposed engagement.

In the past five years, we have conducted over 200 manufacturing strategy engagements, of which nearly 25 were conducted for companies within the appliance industry. Furthermore, approximately 60 of those studies specifically involved our developing a broad range of manufacturing capacity plans. Many of them were designed to answer questions similar to yours: "How can we provide additional manufacturing capacity most effectively?"

We Are Able to Address the Wide Range of Issues Related to This Study

The team proposed for this engagement has expertise in all aspects of this study. We understand the marketing and manufacturing issues from a business perspective so that we can develop various capacity expansion options; evaluate them with your management team, considering each of the team members' individual (and often differing) perspectives; select the most appropriate option; prepare for Consolidated a comprehensive appropriation request; and plan for its successful implementation within your tight time frame.

We Have the Ability to Build a Sound ABC/Paramount Team

Because the staff to be assigned has considerable expertise in conducting similar studies, building consensus, and transferring their knowledge, skills, and expertise, we have been able to carefully structure our approach so that ABC management will participate actively and become an integral part of the engagement team. Thus, on completion of the engagement, ABC will possess a base of residual knowledge that will be invaluable in addressing future capacity and other strategic manufacturing questions. For example, we believe that ABC members of the engagement team will be able, even more effectively than at present, to monitor sales forecasts, plant productivity, and capacity utilization to project accurately when additional capacity might be needed in the more distant future.

We Have the Ability to Plan and Control Implementation

Once the most appropriate capacity expansion option has been selected, it will be extremely important to implement that plan without delay. Although an implementation phase lies outside the scope of this proposed project, you should be aware that our significant experience in successfully implementing comprehensive plans for increasing capacity could be invaluable to ABC. Our project teams that work on such implementation projects routinely use a variety of sophisticated project-control software packages. These programs are necessary for properly allocating resources; monitoring task completions and costs, thereby assuring adherence to budget; identifying potential problems or delays; and reallocating resources to maintain schedules and achieve time and cost objectives. These control techniques will ensure that implementation of the selected option will proceed smoothly and will be completed on time and within budget.

Even if we are not actively involved in implementation, we will have developed the new manufacturing plan considering ABC's resources and capabilities. Our goal is not just to produce a plan for increasing capacity but to bring that capacity on line as soon as possible. That is, we are not in the business of just developing plans. We want to see those plans implemented whether or not you decide to engage us to help you do so.

Benefits

I would like to summarize for you, Anil, some of the most important points we've made to you and your team in our previous discussions and in this proposal. Then I will describe the benefits we believe you will receive from our developing a capacity plan for meeting ABC's forecasted demand and from that plan's subsequent implementation by ABC (quite possibly with our support).

The Benefits of Leveraging Our Efforts

By forming a joint ABC/Paramount team, with ABC managers playing an integral part, we will be able to leverage the substantial knowledge, expertise, and tools both ABC and Paramount will bring to this project and to develop, sell, and implement the plan as quickly as possible.

This team will hold frequent progress reviews so that various constituencies within the Division (as well as, if appropriate, within Consolidated) will be aware of preliminary conclusions and direction quickly. We plan for these reviews to include strategy sessions, during which we can gain consensus on answers to the wide variety of questions posed in this project and get agreement across various interest areas on the appropriate criteria to be used to select the most effective expansion option. Finally, the team will prepare a final report, which we plan to be a proposal and capital-expenditure request to Consolidated. This strategy will eliminate an entire and possibly time-consuming step in the approval process.

This teaming strategy will work exceptionally well because Paramount's professionals have extensive expertise in building effective client/consultant teams, transferring knowledge, and managing and implementing change. We also understand the range of evaluation criteria important in this analysis and are adept at facilitating discussions to gain consensus on these criteria. We will commit our

broad-based team quickly to begin the project immediately after your approval
to proceed. Using this team's exceptional expertise in marketing, manufacturing
strategy, facilities planning, logistics, financial analysis, and human resources, we
will provide ABC with the right "road map" for increasing capacity.

Your Benefits at the End of This Project

Our final report, which we will design as your proposal to Consolidated, will be
thorough, comprehensive, and well documented, providing ABC with the basis for
making a sound expansion decision that considers and balances all the quantitative
and qualitative factors. And because that decision will be based on agreed-to
criteria, it will be well accepted by ABC management with different agendas. Just
as important, the report will convince Consolidated of the expansion decision's
correctness and desirability and answer their "what-if" questions.

In addition to our recommended expansion option, the report will contain:

- a confirmed market forecast and market share and product-mix projections
- specified current equipment and space utilization and opportunities to better
  utilize current equipment and space as well as new technology
- specified make-versus-buy options as well as potential factory roles and
  locations for increasing capacity
- an implementation plan

Our jointly developed implementation plan will specify the tasks, resources,
requirements, and timing necessary to bring additional capacity on line over time
in a controlled yet expeditious manner.

Your Benefits Beyond This Project

We are confident that, once implemented, our jointly developed plan will
significantly improve ABC's processes; lead to more cost-effective operations,
improved service levels, and product quality; and allow you to maintain, if
not enhance, your market share. Your productivity should increase, your
compensation levels should be protected, and you should realize greater flexibility
in implementing your business and marketing strategies. Most important, after
subsequent implementation, you should improve your competitive position and
maintain your excellent reputation with Consolidated.

● ● ●

Quite obviously, Anil, we believe that Paramount is the right consulting firm for conducting this engagement. We have a comprehensive understanding of your situation and a logical and robust methodology for capitalizing on what we consider ABC's substantial opportunity to continue your growth in the marketplace and solidify your position within Consolidated Industries. Just as soon as possible, we would like to discuss that methodology and how we can best work together with you, President Armstrong, and others so that we can all agree on the proper magnitude of effort, the specific roles ABC and Paramount personnel should play, and the cost of the engagement. This is a critically important study for ABC, and we look forward to supporting you as you develop the manufacturing base for continued competitive success.

Sincerely yours,

Stan Gilmore, Partner

Appendix A: Methodology

Below, we explain in more detail the five major tasks contained in the methods section.

Task 1: Confirm ABC's Long-Term Product Forecast

Although ABC already has a forecast by product line, we believe that the engagement must be conducted with Consolidated constantly in mind. Since Consolidated must release the necessary capital funding, they must be convinced of the engagement's rigor and robustness. For that reason, we believe that the forecast must be confirmed by an independent third party. Therefore, we propose to work with ABC's marketing management to confirm or modify the long-term forecast by:

- validating ABC's current overall market forecast
- validating ABC's market share and your geographic and product-mix projections

The consensus market forecast developed in this task will represent the best thinking of your marketing group and the Paramount team. The forecast, used with various manufacturing data, will enable the engagement team to develop future resource requirements over time.

Task 2: Determine Total Factory Resource Requirements at Alternate Forecast Levels

An important task of the engagement team will be to use the existing base of production resources (floor space, equipment, and staffing) and modify that base so that it can accommodate the additional future production demands over time indicated by the confirmed market forecast. First, however, the team will carefully evaluate that base to identify improvements or eliminate inefficiencies that might exist today. We don't want ABC to risk adding too much or too little capacity. This risk can be avoided by first establishing a proper base, a "current-improved" base, from which to project future resource requirements. All this will be critical, because determining future needs involves far more than simply an arithmetic extrapolation of today's activities.

We were very much impressed during our walk-through of your main manufacturing facility. You should know, however, that in nearly every similar engagement, we have been able to recommend methods for better utilizing currently available space, thereby making space available for additional equipment to add to manufacturing capacity. To provide additional capacity and/or space without first determining such improvement opportunities could result in unnecessary capital investment.

We will ensure that ABC is making the most effective use of existing manufacturing resources. Specifically, we will:

- document current equipment and space utilization
- determine opportunities to better utilize current equipment and space and to improve material flow
- determine opportunities for utilizing new equipment technology
- specify which products or components, if any, should be made in-house or purchased from suppliers

The modified, effective base of production resources coupled with the confirmed market forecast will enable the engagement team to develop an accurate and credible projection of future resource requirements. At this point, the joint ABC/Paramount engagement team will have a sound basis for identifying, evaluating, and selecting the most viable option or options to provide these requirements.

Task 3: Define Manufacturing Facility Options to Provide Required Resources

Once we know how much additional space and equipment are required, we will identify the possible manufacturing options that will provide these additional resources. Accordingly, we will develop and analyze various options and determine which configuration of facilities best meets your objectives. Specifically, we will:

- determine expansion potential at the current facility
- specify potential factory roles and locations for increasing capacity

As a result of completing this task, we will have narrowed the field from the possible to the probable, the better to be able to scrutinize the remaining options and to choose the most appropriate.

Task 4: Select the Most Appropriate Option

Using ABC's distribution model and Paramount's proprietary models for assessing expansion options, the joint engagement team will evaluate thoroughly each potential expansion option and then select the one most appropriate. Although the range of options will have been narrowed, those remaining will quite likely be diverse. Therefore, we will work with ABC management to develop both quantitative and qualitative criteria that will differentiate carefully among the various options, and we will obtain management's agreement on the one most appropriate. Specifically, to select the most appropriate option, the engagement team will:

- define quantitative and qualitative criteria important to ABC and Consolidated
- evaluate each option against quantitative criteria such as ROI, landed cost, quality, and customer service
- evaluate each option against qualitative criteria such as manufacturing flexibility and potential risk

When this task is completed, you will know precisely how to configure your manufacturing facilities over time so that you can meet customer demand throughout the forecasted period cost-effectively and responsively.

Task 5: Develop a Plan To Implement the Selected Option

Because the additional manufacturing resources required will likely be brought onstream at various times throughout the forecast period, ABC will need a carefully prepared plan to monitor progress during implementation. To that end, we will prepare a plan to ensure that additional manufacturing resources and facilities are in place when and where they are needed to meet forecasted demand. The various steps in our implementation plan will be time-phased so that management will know precisely when additional capacity is required and when other managerial decisions and actions are needed. Specifically, we will:

- define the tasks necessary to implement the selected option
- define the resources and responsibilities necessary to complete those tasks
- develop a critical path to estimate the time required to complete all tasks

As a result of this task, management will know all the tasks required to provide the additional manufacturing resources, when each task should be initiated and completed, and the skills required to complete each task. The implementation plan will provide you with a critical mechanism to monitor overall progress, to efficiently invest required capital and other resources when they are needed, and to take corrective actions if actual market demand differs significantly from that projected.

After completing this task and obtaining your agreement, we will work with you to immediately prepare a capital appropriations request that can be submitted directly to Consolidated for their timely consideration.

Internal Proposals (Make Certain They're Not Reports)

Let's consider a situation that might have occurred at the ABC Company, the appliance manufacturer we've discussed throughout the work sessions. Let's assume that Marcia Collins, Vice President of Marketing, has completed her market forecast and therefore believes that ABC will soon run out of manufacturing capacity. Consequently, she has several meetings with Paul Morrison, the Chief Industrial Engineer, to discuss manufacturing and distribution costs, customer service as it relates to capacity utilization, and various scenarios for increasing capacity. As a result of these discussions, Collins decides to "propose" a different way of utilizing existing capacity, and so she meets with Anil Gupta, Vice President of Operations, to discuss her ideas. Very much interested in and intrigued by that discussion, Gupta suggests that Collins develop a proposal that the two of them could present to President Ray Armstrong.

Gupta suggested a proposal. Will Collins, in fact, be preparing one? To answer that question, we need to understand the major difference between proposals and reports. Proposals argue: "This is how we would go about answering your overriding question." Reports (more specifically, final or recommendation reports) argue: "This *is* our answer to your overriding question." That is, proposals *look ahead* to a methodology that *will be* performed; reports *look back* to a methodology that *has been* performed. Therefore, to determine whether the product of Collins's efforts will be a proposal or a report, we need to know what Armstrong's overriding question is and whether Collins's presentation will answer it or already has answered it.

Let's assume that Armstrong's overriding question is similar to the one Paramount Consulting has defined: "How should ABC provide the additional manufacturing capacity needed within the next few years to meet forecasted demand?" Will Collins's presentation answer that question? Because she has already determined "a different way of utilizing existing capacity," the answer is "Yes." Armstrong's question is "How?" Collins's answer is, "This is how." Collins will be preparing a report, not a proposal.

Why is all of this important to you? Because proposals and reports are tools that attempt to achieve very different purposes: for proposals, to explain how you will answer a question; for reports, to present the answer. You would no less want to write a proposal that actually answers a reader's overriding question than you'd want to use a chain saw to pound in a nail. Unfortunately, many people confuse these two common genres (or kinds of communications) for at least three reasons.

First, the two genres share several common elements. Proposals and reports both contain situation, objectives, methods, and benefits slots, though the tense in these slots is different. For example, a proposal presents me with your understanding of what the situation *is*; a report reminds me what that situation *was*. A proposal presents the objective *yet to be achieved*; a report reminds me what that objective *was*. A proposal describes the methods *that will be used* to achieve the objective; a report describes the methods *that were used* to achieve it.

People also confuse the two genres for a second reason: the similarities between the terms *propose* and *recommend*. You can propose a solution, and you can recommend a solution. However, given the concepts we have discussed throughout this book, you can't really "propose" a solution; you can only recommend one. If you propose a solution, you've already found one, and therefore you're not proposing at all; you're reporting. You are recommending, on the basis of some analysis or study that you have already completed, the answer to a question. You are not, as you would be in a proposal, proposing a method—before a study—that will derive the answer. Because of the similarities between the terms *propose* and *recommend*, many managers ask their subordinates for a proposal even though they are, in fact, requesting a report. So if you're asked to prepare a proposal, as Gupta asked Collins to do, consider whether your task is to cut down a tree or to sink a nail. Then you can decide whether you need a chain saw or a hammer.

Third, people confuse the two genres because although they have completed a study and answered an overriding question, they're often not aware of having done so. For example, suppose that you work in my firm and our organizational structure is less effective than you believe it could be. In your spare time, you've been thinking about this problem off and on for months—as you daydream at work, when you shower at home, and so on. And over these months, you've doodled several possible organizational structures, one of which you believe is better than the current one. You decide to write a document to me that "proposes" the new structure.

I didn't tell you to do your little study; no one did. And you really didn't tell yourself to do it, either. You "studied" our current organizational structure by having lived within it. You observed it and analyzed your observations, and you did so probably without realizing that you had. But clearly, you have answered a question: "How can my company more effectively organize itself to achieve our various goals?" If that is also my question and you can support your answer logically and persuasively, you have a good chance of convincing me of your report's recommended solution. But you'll be less successful if you try to write a proposal. To take just one example, you'll spend much time trying to figure out how to construct a methodology that will answer the overriding question you've already answered.

In summary, then, reports and proposals are different because they serve different purposes, but they are also similar enough that people sometimes request one when they really want the other, and writers sometimes try to write one when they ought to be composing the other.

Now that we understand how reports differ from proposals, you probably want to know how to write them better. Unfortunately, that would require another book, something like *Writing Winning Business Reports*. I don't have time to write that book right now. But I can offer you some tips that build on the concepts I've already presented to help you logically structure proposals.

Organizing the Body of Your Report: The Single Recommendation

You already know the best tool you can use to organize your report: a logic tree. As we discussed in Chapter 5, a "how" logic tree can be used to organize the actions in your proposal's methodology. As we discussed in Chapter 11, a "why" logic tree can organize a qualifications section. Reports use both kinds of logic trees. Whereas logic trees can be helpful in organizing a proposal's entire qualifications section or a part of the methodology, a single logic tree can help you structure the entire *body* of a report. The examples in this appendix all use "why" logic trees. Be aware, however, that although most recommendation or final reports support their claims by answering "Why?" at the top level of the logic tree, lower levels can answer other questions, such as "How?" and "What kind of?"

To understand how to build a logic tree for a report, let's assume that Collins has decided to recommend that ABC increase capacity at the current site by expanding the current facility (call this Option A). As Figure D.1 illustrates, the entire body of her report could be a "Why?" logic tree organized to provide evidence and support for that recommendation.

The logic tree is designed to answer Armstrong's questions as he engages in the report's dialogue. His first question is the overriding one, related to how best to provide additional capacity. The top box, the report's major recommendation, supplies the answer: "Expand the current facility to increase capacity." This recommendation, however, generates another question: "Why?" In Figure D.1, the boxes on the next line provide the answer, in the form of three good reasons. The report's major argument, then, comprises the recommendation and the good reasons that justify and support it. Each of these good reasons, however, probably necessitates an additional argument, because in his dialogue with the report, each good reason again causes Armstrong to ask "Why?" for justification. If Armstrong needs no further justification, the logic tree below will suffice. If he does need further justification and desires to search more deeply for the underlying rationale, the report would continue building arguments at lower levels. When do the arguments end? When Collins believes that all of Armstrong's questions have been answered.

No matter how far down the logic tree goes, each box on every level contributes to validating the logic tree's major claim: Option A is the most appropriate possible recommendation.

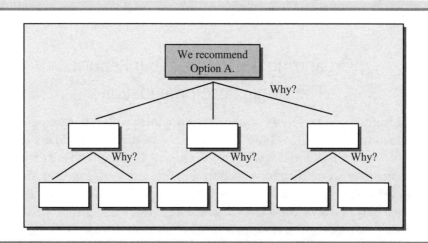

FIGURE D.1   In a report, the top lines of a logic tree usually answer the question "Why?"

Now, let's look at a much more traditional and frequently presented structure that I have seen in many reports submitted to me and that, perhaps, you have used. Note how this reporting structure, in Figure D.2, is much more difficult to understand using the writing patterns typically found in most reports.

Here, the boxes on the second level don't answer any clear-cut question that could be posed after hearing or reading the recommendation. The body of the report contains separate buckets for findings, conclusions, and recommendations. The findings bucket typically consists of a data dump of facts and figures. The conclusions bucket usually contains a large number of conclusions that are difficult to connect to the previously discussed findings. To make matters worse, in reading some reports, I don't even know the recommended answer until I've been overwhelmed with findings and conclusions. Then I'm subjected to a recommendations bucket and forced to tie together previously presented information to determine whether the recommendation is supported.

When you use a logic tree, however, the categories of findings and conclusions are irrelevant. Instead, you just focus on answering at any level my question on the level above. Embedded within the argument may be the notion of "better" or "best." That is, Option A may be preferred because it is at least better in some ways than other options, and overall it's the best of all possible options. Therefore, the boxes on your second line, as shown in Figure D.3, might express these comparisons: "A is *more* cost-effective" or "A is *easier* to implement." Even if your argument is that "A is cost-effective," the implication may remain that Option A is more cost-effective than something else. Therefore, you should be certain that the argument supporting the claim "A is cost-effective" considers the relative, not just the absolute, value of the recommended alternative.

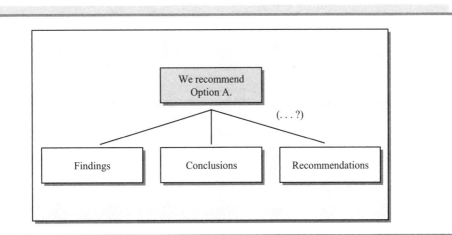

FIGURE D.2   The traditional structure of a report

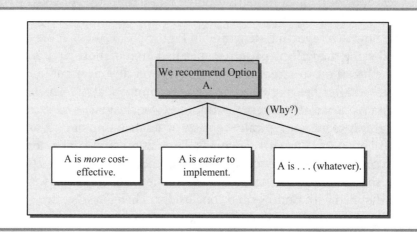

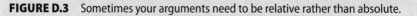

FIGURE D.3   Sometimes your arguments need to be relative rather than absolute.

Organizing the Body of Your Report:
Multiple Recommendations

Let's assume that Collins's answer to Armstrong's overriding question is not to increase capacity at the current facility only. Instead, her recommendation has three parts: Increase capacity at the current facility, increase capacity at one of the satellite facilities, and outsource certain components from suppliers. Faced with this three-part recommendation, Collins may have a tendency to build a logic tree like the one in Figure D.4.

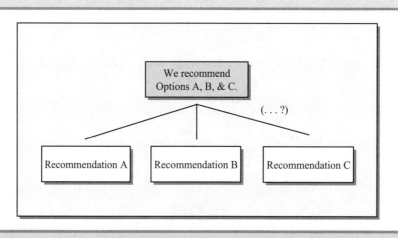

FIGURE D.4   An illogically constructed logic tree for a multipart recommendation

Here, the same problem exists that affected the logic tree organized by findings, conclusions, and recommendations: The logic tree provides Armstrong with no clear answer after he reads or hears the recommendation. This logic tree could prove the validity of Recommendation A, the validity of Recommendation B, and the validity of Recommendation C. However, it does not answer the question, "Why the *combination* of A, B, and C?" That is: "Why this *combination* of actions?" The logic tree in Figure D.5 does provide an answer.

Organizing the Whole Report

As Figure D.6 illustrates, every logic tree row after the recommendation organizes the *body* of your report, not the whole document or presentation. The recommendation itself, along with its supporting claims, can end the introduction. When the supporting claims are bulleted, they provide a good forecast of the content and organization of the body, which in a longer report would contain sections corresponding to each of the claims on the second row of the logic tree. Before the recommendation, other slots typically are provided in what can be considered the report's introduction. These slots explain the problem or opportunity necessitating the study, as well as the study's objectives and methodology. The concluding part of the document or presentation can restate the recommendation and summarize the benefits of acting on it.

Many of the techniques and strategies we've discussed relative to proposals are also useful in preparing reports. Generally speaking, a proposal attempts to "sell" a future service; a report "sells" the ideas gained from that service having been

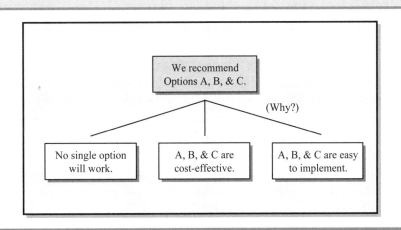

FIGURE D.5   A logically constructed logic tree for a multipart recommendation

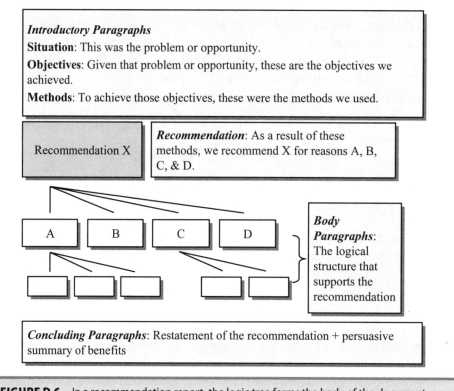

Introductory Paragraphs
Situation: This was the problem or opportunity.
Objectives: Given that problem or opportunity, these are the objectives we achieved.
Methods: To achieve those objectives, these were the methods we used.

Recommendation X

Recommendation: As a result of these methods, we recommend X for reasons A, B, C, & D.

A   B   C   D

Body Paragraphs: The logical structure that supports the recommendation

Concluding Paragraphs: Restatement of the recommendation + persuasive summary of benefits

FIGURE D.6   In a recommendation report, the logic tree forms the body of the document or presentation.

provided. Therefore, you still have buyers, not of your proposed future service (because that's been performed) but of the ideas generated by that service having been performed. As in proposal situations, these buyers play different buying roles in evaluating your report, and they will perceive different benefits based in part on their different roles. These buyers also will have hot buttons, and they will use various criteria to evaluate your recommendation. You might even have competition, in the form of alternative initiatives being recommended by others in your organization: These initiatives might be competing for the same funding you are seeking. In short, in preparing your report, you should find helpful the same concepts and some of the same worksheet cells that are so useful in completing a proposal. There is no magic in writing effective reports. The key is a logical structure that answers the overriding question.

A Few Comments About Writing Effective Sentences (and Paragraphs)

This chapter isn't at all about how to write correct sentences—about avoiding misplaced modifiers, dangling participles, run-on sentences, superfluous commas, or comma splices. And it's far less than comprehensive in discussing effective sentences, so you won't find topics like sentence variety, subordination, and emphasis. What you will find is a few reasonably brief comments about strategies you can use and problems you can avoid when writing proposals.

If you want more information (either about writing correct sentences or effective ones), consult an English handbook, which most people find as enjoyable as memorizing a telephone directory, though considerably more useful. Buy a good handbook and consider it a business expense. Consider it part of your business to know what a comma splice is and how to fix one—or how never to write one in the first place. (Please don't tell me that you've never been able to understand a comma splice. If you're reading this book, you're a very smart person. Trust me: You can understand comma splices.)

If you study the handbook, you won't have to use a computer grammar checker, which can find a comma splice easily enough but hasn't the foggiest notion (despite its fog index) about context. To understand what I mean, type out a stanza or two of Lewis Carroll's "Jabberwocky," a nonsense poem by the author of *Alice's Adventures in Wonderland* and *Through the Looking-Glass*:

'Twas brillig, and the slithy toves
Did gyre and gimble in the wabe:
All mimsy were the borogoves,
And the mome raths outgrabe.

Your spell checker will go crazy, of course. But you will score very well on the "fog index." The sixth-grade level will suggest that your prose is clear and understandable.

Your grammar checker can't understand context, and context determines whether you should or could write a sentence fragment or use the passive voice. Occasionally, fragments are effective, and sometimes the passive voice is necessary. You know all that because I've been telling you since the Introduction. The rest of this appendix will try to reinforce the importance of situational context because, as I provide some guidelines for improving the effectiveness of your sentences, I'll phrase most of the guidelines as questions rather than statements. The guideline "Prefer the Active Voice?" really means, "In this situation, given these readers and your attempt to achieve this purpose, should you consider using the active voice?"

Avoid Abstract Nouns in the Subject Slot?

When you were six years old, you didn't need to know the rules of grammar to be able to speak a perfectly grammatical sentence. Similarly, you don't need to know much about grammar to write good. (Just joking! I know it should be "write well.") It is helpful, however, to be able to identify the sentence's subject, predicate (i.e., the verb), and main clause. If you can, you will know how to fix the problem in the following sentences. Each of these sentences contains examples of the worst, most prevalent, and easiest-to-fix problem that affects your writing style (in certain contexts!)—abstract nouns in the subject slot:

1. A new *approach* to the air flow problem has made ACME a major player in the design and construction of complex commercial buildings.
2. New *regulations* from the state and tighter *building codes* from the city are taking up more and more of the engineers' time.
3. The *shortage* of support staff and the *absence* of proper control systems are causing inefficiencies in your operation.

The italicized words are the grammatical subjects in the sentences, and each word is what I call an abstract noun. Now, it's true that, given certain contexts, some of these words could be considered concrete rather than abstract. For example, if the paragraph or document containing sentence 2 were about regulations, then the word *regulations* would be concrete within that context. Or, for example, if you were writing part of a methods section, the word *methods* would be concrete in that context. Generally speaking, however, concrete nouns are people and places (including organizations like businesses), not things. Each subject in the preceding sentences is a thing. What's wrong with placing "things" (i.e., abstract nouns) in the subject slot?

Abstract subjects tend to increase the distance between the subject and verb, making the text more difficult to comprehend and remember. When you read, you don't process text letter by letter or word by word. If you did, you'd have considerable difficulty remembering the content even of short sentences. Instead, you process text in chunks like phrases and clauses. Because a clause is a group of words with a subject and a predicate, you can't process the clause until you get to the verb. When a sentence begins with a subject and takes a long time to get to the verb, the reader has to keep a great deal of information in short-term memory until the clause is complete.

Abstract subjects tend to increase the distance between subject and verb because you have to explain the abstraction. Take the abstract noun *shortage* in sentence 3. Because it's an abstraction, you have to concretize it, you have to tell the reader *what kind of* shortage it is, before you can explain what it does. That requires the prepositional phrase *of support staff* that separates noun and verb. Just one prepositional phrase isn't bad. But an abstract subject is often responsible for more difficult-to-read sentences, like this one:

> The urgent *request* for all employees of our company to submit their time sheets at the same time *is being made* so that the Accounting Department can more efficiently do its work.

In this case, the writer's answer to the question "what kind of request?" takes three prepositional phrases and 15 words.

The previous example illustrates another problem with abstract nouns as subjects: they tend to take passive verbs (e.g., "is being made"), because abstractions can't act. The effect is lifeless prose, because the sentence's most important slots (subject and predicate) are filled with a noun that can't take action and a verb that can't express action.

Eliminating abstract nouns is fairly easy. And once you get the hang of it, you won't write many of them even in an initial draft. Here's what to do:

- Look carefully at the subject slot to see if it contains, not a person or an organization, but a thing.

- If you find an abstraction, look elsewhere in the sentence to see if the subject (the topic) you're discussing really is explicitly or implicitly about a person or people or an organization. Sentence 1 is about ACME. Sentence 2 is about engineers. Sentence 3 is about business operations.
- Place the subject you're discussing into the subject slot of the sentence.
- See if the sentence is trying to express a causal relationship (a large number of sentences with abstract nouns try to do so). If the sentence is trying to express a causal relationship, use a sentence structure that immediately announces to your reader that such a relationship will be drawn: for example, "Because of X, Y occurs" or "As a result of X, Y occurs." By following these steps, you can easily revise the three problem sentences:

1. Because of its new approach to the air flow problem, *ACME has become a major player* in designing and constructing complex commercial buildings.
2. Because of new regulations from the state and tighter building codes from the city, *the engineers are less efficient.*
3. Because of the shortage of support staff and the absence of proper control systems, *your business is less efficient.*

I've italicized the main clauses (or parts of the main clauses) to illustrate the effects of these transformed sentences. Notice that the subjects and verbs are closer together and that the main clauses, the groups of words that really contain and emphasize your message, are clear and emphatic. The message in sentence 2 is no longer that "new regulations from the state and tighter building codes from the city are taking up more and more of the engineers' time," but that "the engineers are less efficient." The original sentence focuses on regulations and codes; the revision, on engineers and their problems. The original talks about things; the revision discusses a problem that people have.

The Subject Slot in SITUATION, METHODS, and BENEFITS

The generic structure slots SITUATION, METHODS, and BENEFITS each in their own way call for concrete nouns in the subject slot. In SITUATION, the subject (the topic, the idea you're writing about) is an organization's problem or opportunity. Therefore, a good many of the sentences in SITUATION should take as their grammatical subjects the name of the organization or pronouns that refer to it. Consider these paragraphs from the first draft of a situation slot in the ABC proposal:

> For many years now, *ABC* has grown by increasing its share of the modestly expanding household and appliance market, primarily by producing high-quality products at competitive costs and by being very responsive to the needs of its customers. As a result, *ABC* has become one of the premier divisions within Consolidated Industries. . . .
>
> Recognizing these threats, ABC's *management group* has suggested several alternatives for increasing capacity, but little *agreement* exists about how that capacity should be developed, and no *agreement* exists about the amount of capacity required. *Consensus* does exist, however, in two areas: Additional capacity will be needed and the time when it will be needed is fast approaching.

Here, the first three subjects (the ABC organization itself or a group within it) are all concrete. The next subject (*agreement*) is abstract, but the following two (*agreement* and *consensus*) are concrete because of the context established by the first use of *agreement*.

By using concrete subjects in SITUATION, you focus on *my* question: "What is your understanding of *my* problem?" rather than some anonymous question like "What is the problem?"

In METHODS, similarly, you usually don't want to answer, "What will be done?"; you probably want to answer "What will *you* (or *your firm*) do?" The first question calls for an anonymous answer, with an abstract noun as subject: "In Phase I, the resources that are required will be specified." The second question calls for a concrete noun as subject, "we" or the name of your firm: "In Phase I, we will specify the resources required to. . . . "

In BENEFITS, you should try to place either the benefactor (you) or the beneficiary (me) in the subject slot. That is, the template sentence should be either "We will give this to you" or "You will receive this from us." In either case, the subject slot will contain a concrete noun.

Problems are only problems to people or organizations; they aren't abstractions floating in the air affecting no one or some anonymous others. Too many proposals I've read describe my organization's problems or opportunities as if they weren't mine, as if I weren't affected by them. The situation slots tend to address some situation, but not one that's concretely and recognizably mine. Similarly with benefits. When proposals I've read include benefits, they sound like generic blandishments—and bland ones at that—not benefits that I sense can be mine or that are written with me in mind. In almost all cases, the problems described and the benefits articulated seem abstract because the proposal's sentences don't include me and my organization as grammatical subjects.

Change Nouns into Verbs?

The original sentence that follows contains an abstract noun in the subject slot; in the revised sentence, I've corrected that problem and improved the sentence further by changing nouns into verbs:

> **Original:** The *understanding* of design can be helpful in the *construction* of attractive buildings.
> **Revised:** By *understanding* design, you can *construct* attractive buildings.

Some words like *understanding* are spelled the same in their noun and verb forms, and the vast majority of words ending in *-tion*, *-sion*, and *-ment* have verb or *-ing* verb forms. *Construction* can be *construct* or *constructing*. *Dissension* can be *dissent* or *dissenting*. *Development* can be *develop* or *developing*. Note what happened when I changed the nouns to verbs in the preceding sentences: I could delete the article (*the*) before the noun as well as the preposition (*of*) that follows. "The understanding of" becomes "understanding"; "the construction of" becomes "construct." My revision contains fewer words, and the sentence is less noun heavy, less formal, and more active.

Prefer the Active Voice?

In an active voice sentence, the subject does the acting: "John hit the ball." In a passive voice sentence, the subject is acted upon, i.e., passive: "The ball was hit by John." Note that in this instance, the passive sentence takes 50 percent more words to express the same basic idea. If conciseness is your overriding objective, you ought to prefer the active voice.

Of course, we can reduce the second sentence by two words if we eliminate "by John." This construction is sometimes called the anonymous passive because nothing in the sentence explains who (or what) acted. If avoiding blame or attribution is your overriding objective, you ought to prefer the anonymous passive. In some situations, that is, you might prefer "A poor decision was made" to "The CEO screwed up."

As with everything else in writing, your decisions ought to be defined by the situation, by your strategy, by your analysis of your intended readers or listeners and their relationship to you. You and those readers or listeners exist in a context. By the way, if that context happens to be a scientific one and you are writing within a scientific culture, then you will likely be using the passive voice quite often, simply because that's the way things are done, that's how writers are expected to write and how readers expect to read.

Combine *There, It, That, Which,* or *Who* with *to Be?*

When words like *there* and *it* are combined with a form of the verb *to be*, they often signal wordiness. As with the first two sentences below, the only revision needed is a simple deletion. The third sentence requires a little more.

- A problem exists with the air-conditioning system ~~that was~~ recently purchased.
- When the system crashes, those employees ~~who are~~ working on the system have to reenter their data.
- ~~There are likely to be~~ thousands of people [will likely be] laid off at the automobile plant.

Avoid *There is … that* and *It is … that?*

When a sentence begins with *there* or *it*, takes a form of the verb *to be*, and contains a following *that* or *which*, you can very easily revise by eliminating all the offending words:

- ~~It is~~ the lack of space, however, ~~that~~ is the problem.
- ~~There is~~ one other disadvantage ~~that~~ makes renovating an unattractive option.

Use Parallelism?

Do you like swimming, fishing, and hunting? Or do you like swimming, to fish, and hunting? If you focus not on the activities but on the sentences, I hope you say that you like the first sentence rather than the second. The first places similar ideas (in this case, things you might like to do) within similar grammatical structures (in this case, *-ing* verbs). The second sentence places similar ideas within nonparallel structures. That's why the sentence probably sounded strange to you; if you had written it, you would sound strange and perhaps unintelligent to your reader. So one good reason to use parallelism is that you avoid sounding stupid. Another good reason is that your writing (and speaking) will sound more coherent. Incoherent writing, like incoherent behavior, appears random and disconnected:

> I like swimming. Fishing is another enjoyable activity to me. You know, to go out and hunt really enlivens your senses.

Someone who speaks like that, you might conclude, can't quite get all his thoughts together. Nothing seems to "flow." When you say that a paragraph doesn't flow, you mean that it lacks coherence. Compare the preceding paragraph to this one:

> I like swimming because it's invigorating. I like fishing because it's enjoyable. I like hunting because it enlivens my senses.

This paragraph is coherent because it contains three related ideas, and each idea is expressed in the same way: "I like X because. . . ."

In your proposals, I most often see problems with parallelism in lists. By convention, a list is a group of related ideas, and, therefore, the ideas need to be expressed similarly. Usually, a list is preceded by a string of words that end with a colon. These words are called "determiners" because they determine how the items in the list need to be phrased. If, for example, the determiner were "I like," then your list might go like this:

- swimming because it's invigorating
- fishing because it's enjoyable
- hunting because it enlivens my senses

If, on the other hand, the determiner were "I like to," then you'd have to change all the *-ing* words to verbs like "swim."

Even writers who do a good job of using parallelism within a list sometimes have trouble with lists within lists. The text below, taken from a slide in a presentation, contains not one list but three, signaled by the appropriate numerals I've added:

1. Costly administrative organization:
  2. Three separate and fully equipped companies exist in a fairly small market
  2. Considerable overlap occurs in administrative responsibilities

1. Logistics are costly:
  3. Long chain of distribution from production to customer
  3. The tonnage is small
  3. Many small customers
  3. Low rate of turnover in stock

To check for parallelism in text like the above, read each list separately to be certain that all items *within* each list are parallel. In that way, you can quickly and clearly determine that the two items in the first list are out of sync. The first one is a fragment; the second a complete sentence. To correct the parallelism, make both into fragments or both into sentences. Although the items in the second group are parallel to each other, the third group contains an item not parallel with the others. Again, the solution is to make all four items into complete sentences or to make all four into fragments. No problem would exist if the #2 list contained all sentences and the #3 list contained all fragments, because each group is a separate list. (By the way, although the usage varies, it's not always necessary to include end punctuation—for example, a period—after each element in a list because the list itself can be a form of punctuation.)

So far, I've given you two reasons to use parallelism: You can avoid sounding stupid, and you can ensure that your writing flows, that it's coherent. There's a third reason: You can increase the stylishness of your sentences. Now most business documents are written in what's called a plain style because documents need to be used efficiently. But that doesn't mean that you can't incorporate some flourishes, occasionally and judiciously. Effective parallelism can help avoid monotony by creating interesting rhythms, as Thomas Jefferson knew so well:

> In matters of principle, stand like a rock; in matters of taste, swim with the current.

If Jefferson isn't to your taste, at least in a business context, perhaps the following is:

> Most important, we will ensure that simple things get done correctly: that all workers are doing their jobs, that routine responsibilities aren't falling through the cracks, that simple maintenance and housekeeping are provided, that there are proper controls of raw materials and work in process, that scheduling is done effectively, and that all activities are aimed to flow as smoothly as possible during the transition.

Here we have what I call the persuasive force of style. Perhaps just as important as the content in this long sentence is the long string of clauses that suggest a flurry, a whirlwind, of activity. Whether you're writing or speaking, *how* you express yourself can be just as persuasive as *what* you say. Good parallelism can be the "how" that lets the "what" sing.

Write Coherent Paragraphs

As I said in the last section, when you read a paragraph that flows, it has coherence. The ideas move one from the other smoothly, and you don't get lost because you always seem to know, in the flow of ideas, where you've been, where you are, and where you're going. As we've seen, parallelism is one technique you can use to achieve coherence. There are at least four others:

- Pronouns
- Forecasting
- Transitions
- Key repetitions

The paragraphs in Figure E.1 use these techniques (as well as parallelism). Read the paragraphs; then we can talk about them.

1. Top Notch Corporation's **goal** is to maintain or enhance its position of
2. market leadership by being the best producer in the industry. To achieve
3. **this goal**, you have adopted **three overall strategies**:
4. • Improve customer service and quality
5. • Become the low-cost producer
6. • Increase market share through differentiated positioning
7. **All three of these strategies** have significant implications for Top Notch's
8. distribution strategy.
9. ***
10. Top Notch Corporation has attempted to become more **flexible** by
11. developing **partnerships** with customers, such as the Excel-Mart
12. "electronic-links" relationship, the Superway exclusive provider program,
13. and various hospital contractual **relationships**. *However*, **these partner**
14. **relationships** still work best when the customers agree to follow **the Top**
15. **Notch system**. *Unfortunately*, **Top Notch's system** is not **flexible** enough
16. to meet the diverse value-added requirements of individual customers.
17. This **flexibility** will be a prerequisite for future success in this changing
18. market.

FIGURE E.1   Achieving paragraph coherence through parallelism, pronouns, forecasting, transitions, and key repetitions

Pronouns contribute to coherence because they have antecedents (nouns that come before them). Therefore, a pronoun in one sentence that refers to a noun in a previous sentence helps to "glue" the two sentences together. The pronoun *this* (line 3) refers to *goal* (line 1). Similarly, *these* (7) looks back to *strategies* (3), and *these* (13) refers to *relationships*, which ends the previous sentence. Note how the writer is careful to follow every *this* or *these* that begins a sentence with the word it refers back to. In that way, the reader doesn't have to stop reading to look back at the previous sentence to find the antecedent.

Forecasting tells readers where you're taking them, what you're going to be discussing. The bulleted list (lines 4–6) serves to forecast the next three paragraphs (which I haven't included). Each of these paragraphs discusses in turn one of the three overall strategies.

Unlike forecasting, which lets readers know where they're going, *transitions* provide a bridge from one juncture to another. *However* (line 13) and *unfortunately* (line 15) are good examples. They prepare readers for a change in thought that will be expressed in the sentences that the transitions begin.

Using *key repetitions* is one of the most effective techniques for increasing the coherence of your paragraphs. Like pronouns, key repetitions tend to glue sentences together, especially when a word or phrase at the end of one sentence is picked up at the beginning of the next one. The sentence ending on line 13, for example, concludes with the word *relationships*, which is repeated near the beginning of the next sentence. That sentence, in turn, ends with the phrase *Top Notch system* (line 15) and is followed, at the beginning of the next sentence, by *Top Notch's system*. The writer also achieves coherence by using *goal* (line 1) and *goal* (line 3); *strategies* (line 3) and *strategies* (line 7); *flexible* (line 10), *flexible* (line 15), and *flexibility* (line 17); and *partnerships* (line 11) and *partner* (line 13). These key repetitions contribute to the paragraphs' flow.

A fine line exists between key (or "good") repetitions and redundancy (i.e., "bad" repetitions). Key repetitions create cohesion and focus. Redundancies are, well, repetitive. Because writing is an art rather than a science, it's impossible to pinpoint where that fine line is. Only your ear can tell you whether you have crossed it.

◉　◉　◉

I've tried to present some of the important techniques that you can use to write more effective sentences. Like all things related to writing, these techniques take some practice to master. But once you've mastered them, they don't go away: From then on, you simply write better from first draft to last. Your sentences will be crisper, clearer, cleaner, and livelier. Most important, your more effective sentences will convince a reader that you can analyze problems, formulate methods to solve them, and articulate the benefits that will accrue from their solution. Your sentences will contain many of the characteristics of the previous sentence in this paragraph, which has a concrete noun as a subject, little distance between the subject and verb, an active verb, and coherence created by parallelism, pronouns, and key repetitions.

Using the Right Voice

Determining How Your Proposal Should "Speak"

Some years ago, I came across a good illustration of rhetorical voice, a writer's or presenter's construction of her persona, the character she plays in a particular message.[1] When you and I are talking face-to-face, we unconsciously adjust our manner of speaking so that we project the appropriate sides of ourselves to achieve our goals. You don't speak the same way to me, your potential client, as you do to your spouse or your children or your acquaintances or the taxi driver who delivered you to my door. You project certain aspects of yourself that you want me to see or hear. You speak in a certain "voice." When I'm reading your proposal, however, you're no longer there, but your voice is, speaking through the words on the page. If I've come to know you as hard-working, ambitious, and fast on your feet, I'd be taken aback if the voice in your proposal were entirely different.

The good illustration I'm referring to came in the form of two drafts of a progress report a consultant shared with me. The consultant was engaged in a five-week feasibility study. Because of the study's urgency, her proposal had contained a workplan with well-defined deadlines and progress reviews. Despite careful planning, however, after three weeks, the study was three days behind schedule, in part because questionnaires submitted to employees had not been returned on time. Here are two sentences from an early draft:

> **Earlier Draft:** Although we will receive some questionnaires later than we had anticipated, we are tallying those already received. When more responses trickle in, we can simply integrate those data into what we have compiled.

Apparently, the earlier draft's intention was to communicate a message, to speak in a voice, that suggested the following: "Don't worry. This isn't that big a problem, and everything will be all right soon." The voice might be characterized as "laid back" or "unperplexed."

After reading her draft, the consultant must have decided that, although the situation might not be problematic to her as the consultant, it might be seen as a big problem to her reader, who was anxious to have the project completed on time. Where she intended "laid back," the reader might have inferred "lazy." Where she intended "unperplexed," the reader might have read "reactive." So she used a different voice in a later draft—call it "aggressive," "on top of the situation," or "proactive." Even a simple change from *receive* (which suggests passivity) to *collect* (which suggests activity) makes a big difference:

> **Later Draft:** Although we will ~~receive~~ *collect* some questionnaires later than we had anticipated, we are *already analyzing* ~~tallying~~ those ~~already~~ received. *Just as soon as* ~~When more~~ *the remaining* responses ~~trickle in~~ *do arrive*, we ~~can simply~~ *will immediately* integrate those data into what we have *already* compiled.

How important is voice in the proposals you write? Vitally. When I try to decide between your proposal and a competitor's, I feel like I'm listening to a debate. Each proposal not only presents different content, each "speaks" that content in a different voice as it attempts to convince me. You're no longer there, but your voice is, even in your absence. What the voice says reveals a lot about your character and your personal characteristics. The voice can project you as sympathetic or hard-nosed, as structured or flexible, as detail-oriented or global. Your written voice shouldn't be the same from proposal to proposal any more than your speaking voice is the same from situation to situation.

Adjusting your speaking voice is much less difficult than adjusting your written voice. You are well practiced in playing different roles as you speak. You're not the same to a superior as you are to a subordinate; not the same at the office as you are at a sporting event or a cocktail party. You know, somehow, that in any of these situations you're still "yourself," only a different side of yourself, of your many-sided personality. So you don't think very much—you don't have to think very much—about how you present different sides of yourself in these different situations. Every day, you play so many different roles, speak in so many different voices, that you're probably not even aware of doing so.

Despite your being relatively different across different situations, you're relatively the same in similar ones. This consistency within similar situations is important in many relationships. When someone you thought you knew acts differently than you would have predicted, you often feel that you didn't really know her at all or that you didn't know her well enough. This change in behavior might surprise you, and it might even unsettle you.

Consider the common newspaper story of the good husband or boy scout who, beyond anyone's prediction, turns out to be a bigamist or mass murderer. Those events make news because they're so surprising and unsettling. When you try to sell to me your proposal, I don't want any surprises, either. If I come to know you during our initial meetings as energetic and animated, I'd be surprised by a proposal that's leaden and dull. If I know you as analytic and careful, I'd be surprised if the proposal's voice were speculative and incautious. Similarly, if you have established good chemistry and rapport with me but the proposal's voice is neutral and generic, I'd probably suspect that your proposal is boilerplate and thus that your study will be also. So the "you" that you project during the preproposal meetings needs to be the same voice that speaks in the proposal.

Here's how one of my friends, an experienced consultant named Donald Baker, strategically adjusted the voice in his proposal to match the image of himself projected during the client call:

> Baker had been trying for about four years to secure business with this potential client, a leader in the building-materials industry, so when they finally did need a study done, Baker was the one called in first. And he was the only one called, apparently because Baker convinced the company president that the consultant's firm "wouldn't scare the daylights out of" the divisional vice president with whom Baker would be working.
>
> The company's president was a dynamic, aggressive, Harvard graduate. Although the proposal was addressed to him, the primary decision maker was the divisional vice president. Unlike the president, the vice president was not at all polished. He had worked in the mills all his life, was practical and direct, and did not wear a jacket to work. The decision was the vice president's because the company was "totally decentralized." The president had told Baker that if the vice president said yes, he would say yes (though the vice president did not know that). Thus, Baker needed to write a proposal responding to the vice president's practical sensibilities, but he also wanted the document to be responsive to the action-oriented president, who had

never before seen Baker's work and whom Baker wanted to impress for whatever future business might be in store.

To respond to the vice president's needs, Baker used a lot of straight talk, telling him what specific deliverables he would have at the end of the study and how the resulting cost savings would end up paying for the project. Thus, Baker expressed a strong bottom-line orientation: "The proposal, almost by its nature, had to have some boring recapitulation of data that really is not even relevant to the study such as costs and numbers of workers and how big the plant is and how they were organized over the years." Moreover, Baker used headings such as "Sales Effectiveness," "Customer Service," and "Organizational Effectiveness" rather than generic headings such as "Background" or "Methods." He did not "want to sound like a heavy consultant" but rather wanted to place himself in a "sort-of-good-ol'-boy kind of role." In addition, since the vice president was a Southerner whose plant was located in a small deep-South town, Baker brought with him to the meetings a highly experienced colleague who spoke with a strong Southern accent.[2]

This example not only illustrates how Don Baker strategically projected the right voice for a given situation, it also suggests how he adapted his document to respond to that situation because he fully understood his relationship to his readers, his buyers. The questions Baker asked and the answers he received while meeting with the prospect helped him determine what image to convey, what voice to speak in, to satisfy the needs of his readers to make them feel comfortable and persuade them to accept the proposal.

You might have noticed that I have been using adjectives to characterize a specific voice, like *proactive, laid back, analytical,* or *cautious.* Other adjectives could be used to describe characteristics of a good consultant, for example, *confident, energetic, hard-working, responsible, knowledgeable, culturally sensitive, experienced, organized, efficient,* and *reliable.* As a result, many if not most of your proposals will need to project these attributes. Some occasions, however, will demand that you convey not only these characteristics but also specific attributes that respond to these occasions.

How do you decide which characteristics are relevant, which adjectives to use? Figure F.1 shows you how.

Your voice depends in part upon the kind of project you're proposing to do because different kinds of studies might require different roles. But defining your role alone isn't enough. If you are doing a Planning Project for me and I need you to be a visionary, you need to decide what kind of visionary you need to be. That decision depends upon my hot buttons, my selection committee's evaluation criteria, and your counters to your competition. That is, the decision depends upon your themes.

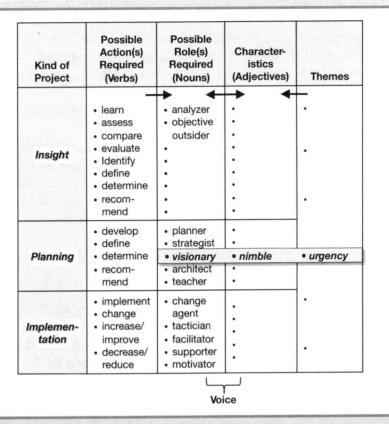

Kind of Project	Possible Action(s) Required (Verbs)	Possible Role(s) Required (Nouns)	Character-istics (Adjectives)	Themes
Insight	• learn • assess • compare • evaluate • Identify • define • determine • recom-mend	• analyzer • objective outsider • • • • • •	• • • • • • • •	• • •
Planning	• develop • define • determine • recom-mend	• planner • strategist • *visionary* • architect • teacher	• • • *nimble* • •	• *urgency*
Implemen-tation	• implement • change • increase/ improve • decrease/ reduce	• change agent • tactician • facilitator • supporter • motivator	• • • • •	• •

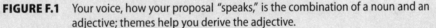

Voice

FIGURE F.1   Your voice, how your proposal "speaks," is the combination of a noun and an adjective; themes help you derive the adjective.

For example, if one of my hot buttons (and one of your themes) is urgency, I wouldn't want a visionary who contemplates his navel; I would want someone who can envision a strategy quickly. You would need to be a combination of an adjective and a noun: a quick-thinking visionary, for example, or as Figure F.1 suggests, a nimble visionary. A visionary might do, and perhaps a visionary is what your competitor will be. But a specific kind of visionary may be more persuasive to me, and if you're capable of being that kind, you ought to be.

In summary, then (and I'm reading right across the columns in Figure F.1), your voice is controlled by the kind of project you're proposing (first column) and by the verbs related to the results you propose to deliver (second column). These verbs, the overall actions required, phrase your project's objectives. These actions, in turn, require a specific set of skills common to a specific role or roles (the nouns in the third column). These nouns, however, are further modified (fourth column) by the kind of person you need to project yourself as. These modifying adjectives are regulated by themes (for example, the hot buttons to which you need to respond) (fifth column). The result, the voice you need to convey, is a combination of the nouns in the third column modified by the adjectives in the fourth column.

So to determine your voice, you need to ask three important questions:

- Given this kind of project (that is, Insight, Planning, and/or Implementation), what verbs characterize the outcomes, the desired results expressed as your project's objective(s)?
- Given that kind of project and those verbs, what nouns (e.g., architect/planner/ strategist; tactician/facilitator/motivator) describe the character you should play to best achieve the desired results?
- Given that character, what adjectives (related to your themes) describe the characteristics you should convey?

The third question should be asked not just for me but for each member of the selection committee.

Because the projects you propose often require you to work closely with me and my people, within my company's culture, your proposal's voice has to demonstrate that you can work with me and my colleagues and adapt to our culture. By consciously defining your relationship to us, you'll be able to determine precisely how you should "speak" and, therefore, what side of yourself is essential to project in your document. Just as I am a complex personality whom you can't totally know, you are a many-sided individual whom I can't completely know. So you must decide what side of yourself your proposal will convey—what personal characteristics and attributes, what persona, you'll project as your proposal speaks to me and my colleagues on the selection committee.

Once again, we see the importance of themes. Voice is controlled at the word level, by your decision, for example, to use the word *receive* or the word *collect*. And your themes not only embody your larger strategy to address hot buttons, evaluation criteria, and counters to the competition; they govern your tactical choices, word by word, so that your document speaks, not with a lisp or a stutter, but fluidly, as it reflects my story and helps me to see how you can become a part of it.

Reading RFPs

If you want a quick sense of how many different kinds of proposals there are, you should search Amazon.com using the key words *proposal writing*, as I did a few months ago.[1] Thirty-three of the three dozen bestselling books, including this one, focused on specific kinds of proposals: business proposals, consulting proposals, sales proposals, grant proposals for university researchers, grant proposals for not-for-profit community organizations, and dissertation proposals. You'd be amazed at the specific focus of these books—for example, an entire book on obtaining funding for nursing research and another on obtaining funding for spatial science research. These last two books were among the *top-36 bestsellers*! Many more scholarly nurses and spatial scientists must exist than I (and, I bet, you) ever imagined.

Only three books focused on proposals in general. One was clearly marketed as a textbook rather than a trade book. Another, *The Zen of Proposal Writing*, focused on a particular approach for writing proposals as well as, we can assume, everything else.

A good reason exists for the large number of books that focus on specific kinds of proposals rather than on proposals in general: Although all proposals have the generic structure slots SITUATION, OBJECTIVES, METHODS, QUALIFICATIONS, COSTS, and BENEFITS, the subgenres are very different. *Writing Winning Business Proposals* is incredibly helpful in writing business (and, more specifically, consulting) proposals, but only about 80 percent of this book's content would help you write various kinds of grant proposals. Generalizations about proposals can be useful. They can also be dead wrong.

The same can be said for books and articles that generalize about requests for proposals (RFPs). A book on responding to guidelines from the National Institutes of Health, the National Science Foundation, or the National Endowment for the Humanities won't be much help to you if you are a consultant who wants to know how to respond to an RFP from a prospective client. Books and articles that focus on specific kinds of RFPs in specific situations tend to overemphasize the importance of RFPs. The author of one of those books believes that by simply receiving an RFP, a firm is so advantaged that it should ask, why *wouldn't* we devote the necessary resources to respond?

Well, for many reasons, not the least of which is that selling consulting work via RFPs is a *relatively* low-value, high-risk exercise. As an example, consider these two scenarios, in both of which you are a consultant. In Scenario 1, you build a trusted relationship with a senior-level potential client, working closely for weeks if not months with the prospect's team to develop custom-made objectives and methods for addressing one of the firm's agreed-to problems or opportunities. At the same time, you are creating barriers to entry for other consultancies, many of whom are unaware of this particular sales process in the first place. The eventual proposed engagement has a price tag of more than US$1M. If you win (and your hit rate in such situations is greater than 70 percent), you can expect considerable follow-on work because your pricing strategy builds in "face time" during the engagement to deepen your relationships, allowing you to uncover additional opportunities, perhaps none of which will require competitive bidding.

In Scenario 2, your consultancy receives on Monday an RFP "over the transom." Not until Wednesday does that document get to you, the subject-matter expert who can address the objectives indicated in the RFP. Not until Friday can you assemble a team whose responsibility is to respond. Because the proposal is due the following Monday, your team writes it over the weekend and delivers it without a single conversation having taken place between you and the potential client. You are one of 15 bidders. The RFP was written by the incumbent, who tailored the requirements to the incumbent's strengths. You and 13 other bidders are column fodder. That is, on the prospect's evaluation sheet, the incumbent is listed in column one; every one else owes their existence to due diligence or legal requirements. Those consultancies in the other columns have little chance of winning. The engagement will be a "one off" with little likelihood of follow-on work. All the consultant-selection team are middle managers, and there will be no opportunity to sell upward, either during the current engagement or during subsequent ones, should they even exist. Given the relatively low-level scope of the work, your bid will be less than US$60K, and given the large number of competitors, your hit rate in such situations is at best less than 25 percent.

Of course, these are extreme scenarios, but they are not unlikely ones: They happen all the time, and I hope you've had considerable experience with the first one. Nevertheless, there *are* many reasons for responding to an RFP. First, business might be in a lull, and you have many people on the beach (i.e., unengaged) with little to do; therefore, you want them to acquire proposal-writing experience. Second, the RFP might have come from a firm that knows little about your consultancy, and although your odds of winning this opportunity are small, you wish to respond, using the proposal as a marketing tool. Third, assuming the Pareto Principle (the 80/20 rule), 80 percent of your revenues likely come from 20 percent of your clients (like the prospective client in Scenario 1), and much of that remaining 20 percent of revenues—in my experience, anyway—is RFP-driven (as in Scenario 2). Those revenues keep the lights on and get the garbage collected. Finally, RFPs have become increasingly important in consulting.

In the late 1990s, one of the consulting industry's most lucrative "products" was strategic sourcing, which helped clients to source required components through competitive bidding, thereby reducing costs for products and material they did not make in-house but outsourced from a variety of suppliers. The vehicle by which those components was sourced was the RFP. Ironically, during the first decade of this century, businesses began to apply to consultants similar practices taught them by the consultants themselves. Long a function in government contracting, procurement (which suddenly included procuring consultants) became an important function in the corporate sector.[2]

Given the growing importance of consulting RFPs, you need to learn how to respond to these documents and, therefore, how to read them strategically. I'll show you how, if you'll follow these three steps:

- Read for the logics.
- Read for the psychologics.
- Strip all the requirements, including those not named as requirements and not in the RFP's section on requirements, and test your proposal's content against those requirements.

Step 1: Read for the Logics

As you know, having read the first section of this book, the logics will involve many of the technical elements of the RFP and your team's response to them in the proposal. I'm not going to talk about this step, for an obvious reason: If you don't have the subject-matter expertise to understand and respond to the RFP's technical requirements, you're whistling in the dark and have little reason to bid.

Step 2: Read for the Psychologics

As you also know, the psychologics includes those elements of persuasion other than logic itself—the heart rather than the head, the emotional rather than the technical—and a key element of the psychologics is your buyers' hot buttons, which I have defined as an individual's desires or concerns that can affect the engagement. In Scenario 1 above, as in the ABC case, hot buttons are not often written and not always articulated. You have to intuit them, ferret them out, read between the lines of the spoken.

In RFPs, your buyers' hot buttons can be identified thematically as repeated words and phrases that express their desires or concerns. Here's an example:

> A European office of a major consultancy, call it ACME, was doing poorly, and many of its consultants were on the beach. A nearby teaching hospital had issued an RFP to 15 firms, but not to ACME, which had no health-care practice. Hearing about the RFP by chance, ACME decided to bid, for two reasons. First, many of its currently unengaged consultants would acquire important experience in proposal writing. Second, the office's strategic direction involved establishing a health-care practice; if, by chance, they were awarded this lucrative contract (more than US$1M), they would be able to hire sufficient experts to build a practice.
>
> In reading the RFP carefully, ACME's consultants noticed a subtle but frequent refrain suggested by phrases like *professional development* and *knowledge transfer*. Recognizing that a hot button can be addressed by changing the project's methodology and/or its project staffing, they built into their methodology significant training and knowledge-transfer components, and they included in their project staffing two U.S. subject-matter experts who would relocate during the entire engagement.
>
> Several years and millions of dollars of follow-on work later, ACME asked why their initial proposal was accepted. Because, they were told, none of the other 15 bidders had proposed a methodology with such a comprehensive professional-development component. This hot button had been expressed in the RFP; ACME had not made it up. But everyone else had failed to see it.

In just a minute, we'll analyze in some detail how one consulting team responded to an RFP, but first some caveats. When reading an RFP, it's important to think of yourself as an anthropologist and to consider the RFP document a cultural artifact. You need to ask, "Whose culture?" and "Whose artifact?" That is, addressing possible hot buttons could create serious problems if:

- The RFP was written by lower-level staff whose desires and concerns are different from those of the buyers.

- The RFP was written by an incumbent, and the document reflects the incumbent's rather than the buyers' culture.

Only if the RFP is written by the buyers, or by those who correctly express the buyers' desires and concerns, can you be relatively sanguine that identifying and analyzing the hot buttons will help you. That was the case in the RFP we'll talk about now, as we examine what the consultants did—or didn't do—in responding.

The RFP requested consulting support for a pharmaceutical company that wanted to improve the analysis of its marketing mix (in this case, its portfolio of drugs) so that its brand teams (those responsible for selling the drugs) could use their resources (for example, their sales teams) to maximize sales.

The 11-page, single-spaced RFP included the following elements:

- the history of the existing problem and the ongoing attempts to solve it (pp. 1–3)
- the existing problem and its ramifications (pp. 3–5)
- the engagement's objectives (pp. 5–7)
- the requirements to be met, divided into five sections, such as "project administration" and "products to be covered" (pp. 7–11)

Some of the possible hot buttons were "consistency," "empowerment," and "collaboration," and they could be combined into this narrative: The consultants had to work *collaboratively* with the buyers to develop a *consistent* framework across the organization that would *empower* the brand teams to make effective decisions in allocating their resources. These words and their variations (for example, *empowering, collaborative,* and *consistent*) occurred on the following pages, none of them among the sections listing requirements:

- consistency: pp. 2, 3 (twice), 4, 5, 6 (twice)
- empowerment: pp. 3, 4 (twice), 5
- collaboration: pp. 2, 3 (twice), 4 (twice), 5, 6 (twice)

You already know that such hot buttons can be developed into themes and placed strategically throughout your proposal: for example, in the background section, the expression of the need for consistency; in the opening P-slot of methods, a rationale for how the methodology is designed to ensure consistency; and similarly for the qualifications and benefits sections.

Step 3: Strip All Requirements in the RFP, and Test Them Against the Proposal

In this step, you need to identify every requirement in the RFP, including requirements not labeled as such, and "strip" them from the RFP by placing them in the first column of a spreadsheet similar to the table in Figure G.1. In additional columns, you can include the RFP's page number(s) where the requirements are listed and the degree—high (H), medium (M), low (L), or not at all (X)—to which they are emphasized in the draft of your proposal and, if appropriate, in the slide deck for the oral presentation.

All but Figure G.1's first row and its last three contain requirements from the RFP's actual requirements sections (which, in total, included more than 50 requirements). The first row's content comes from the RFP's objectives section. The last three rows contain the three hot buttons and their degree of emphasis (which was "not at all"!) in the proposal. I've added those three rows to illustrate these points:

- Although hot buttons aren't *technical* requirements important for executing a successful project, they *are* (de facto) requirements, not only for conducting the project but for selling it, even if the RFP's writers don't consider them requirements.
- The consulting team should have considered them as requirements and addressed them in their proposal.

As mentioned often in this book, on a hundred-point scale, the difference between winning and coming in second is frequently as little as two to five points. If the consultants had considered the prospect's hot buttons as requirements, would they have gained a few points? If they had addressed those hot buttons, would they have won? (They didn't.)

These questions don't have easy answers, but this one does: Would it have been worth the consultants' time and effort to address the hot buttons, thereby increasing the likelihood of their winning and decreasing the odds of their placing a close second?

In the consulting game, even great proposals lose, and even awful proposals win. In fact, in situations like Scenario 1—that is, when RFPs are not involved—great business developers will tell you that proposals themselves rarely win. They either clinch or lose, because the engagement should have been won, or substantially won, before the proposal was even submitted, as a result of relationships and upfront selling. In such situations, the proposal is pro forma, in effect, a legal document serving as a contract. In RFP situations, however, proposals play a

Requirement	Page Number	Emphasis
Objectives		
Within-channel mix optimization		
Within-brand mix optimization		
Decision-support tools for within-brand and channel		
Cross-portfolio mix optimization		
Web-based marketing mix repository		
Details on methodologies and models		
Outline of promotion channels modeled		
Prelaunch channels approach		
Intellectual property rights		
Previous experience for this work		
Bios of team members		
Time line		
Workplan		
Data and IT needs from company		
Consistency	2, 3 (2X), 4, 5, 6 (2X)	X
Empowerment	3, 4 (2X), 5	X
Collaboration	2, 3 (2X), 4 (2X), 5, 6 (2X)	X

FIGURE G.1   An example of requirements, even those not labeled as requirements, stripped from an RFP

critical role in winning the work. As I mentioned above, they also can be responsible for much of the 20 percent of the revenues that keep on the lights. And we know how important that is, since only very few things get done in the dark.

A Worksheet for
Qualifying Your Lead

Many people believe that lead qualification is a single step in the business-development process that occurs early on. Once the lead is qualified, according to this belief, and the decision is "Go" rather than "No go," it's full speed ahead and never look back. Of course, that belief is mistaken because the quality of a lead is always in flux. What once appeared a done deal can quickly become a dead deal. New competitors could enter the picture. The economic buyer could change. One of your key subject-matter experts might find herself otherwise engaged. A new and negative buyer could join the consultant-selection committee. In short, relationships are always changing, and situations are never preserved in amber. As a result, you must keep qualifying to determine how to apply your limited resources most effectively.

To help you qualify your leads, I've developed three worksheets based on the concepts in this book. Most likely, you have your own criteria for qualifying leads, and these worksheets are not intended to replace those criteria but to augment them. The worksheets are automated in Excel via some truly elementary programming and can be downloaded at: http://web.me.com/rfreed/Writing_Winning_Business_Proposals/Home.html. As with all the downloadable materials, feel free to modify the worksheets as you please.

One worksheet focuses on the logics of the situation—that is, for example, on the overriding problem and questions and on deliverables and benefits. Another worksheet focuses on the psychologics of the situation—that is, for example, on your positioning in relation to the economic buyer and his or her team's evaluation criteria, as well as to your competition. A summary worksheet calculates your score, providing a "forecast" of your positioning and some strategies you might employ based upon that positioning.

Keep in mind that, like the weather, forecasts always change, and you must be ever alert to how quickly today's sunshine can give way to tomorrow's storms. Regarding lead qualification, you must focus, not just on what is happening today, but on what could happen tomorrow. As Steve Jobs famously said, paraphrasing what Wayne Gretzky famously said, ". . . skate to where the puck is going to be, not [to] where it has been."

Notes and Citations

Preface

1. The term *buyer* refers to decision makers or decision influencers—those people who must agree that you are the right choice to support them in a proposed project. Therefore, a buyer is your potential client, whether that person exists within or outside your organization. Chapter 6 examines this concept of buyers.

2. Throughout this book, the terms *proposal-development process* and *business-development process* are often used synonymously. In conventional usage, the former term is viewed as less comprehensive than the latter because *proposal-development process* usually refers to the set of activities that begin with composing the proposal document or presentation. However, my conception of "the proposal" is much broader. *Proposal* includes the set of activities beginning with the first discussion between the consultant and potential client and ending with your potential client saying "Yes" or "No." That is, "the proposal" is not the document itself but the entire courtship.

Also note that above I have used the term *potential client* rather than *client*. Even if you have worked for your "client" on dozens of projects or engagements, for *this* project he or she does not become your client until the project has been authorized. By using the phrase *potential client*, you will constantly remind yourself that the proposed engagement has *not yet* been sold.

Chapter 1

1. A great many people and a great many textbooks on writing confuse proposals, which propose a method for answering a question, and recommendation reports, which provide an answer to that question. That's why I've written Appendix D, which discusses these two different kinds of documents and gives you some pointers on writing reports.

2. From here on, I will use small caps to designate generic structure slots. That is, I'll refer to the methods slot either by calling it that or by writing it in small caps: METHODS. I'll refer to the methods section either by calling it that or by writing "Methods."

Chapter 3

1. As indicated on the Logics Worksheet, Implementation Projects do not have an overriding question.

2. I recognize that in many of your past projects, you have used more than one, two, or three objectives. Logically, however, as we have seen in Chapter 2, you can have at most three objectives. If you have more than one objective for each desired result, the other so-called objectives are likely deliverables or benefits. If you receive an RFP that specifies a whole host of objectives, you might very well use all those objectives in the final draft of your proposal. However, to make certain that you provide a logical foundation for your proposal and project, as well as a sound methodology, be certain that, in your thinking and in your prior drafts, you use the process described in this book.

3. You might be interested in reading "Deliverables and Benefits" at http://web.me.com/rfreed/Writing_Winning_Business_Proposals/Home.html.

Chapter 5

1. I should have written the word *objective(s)*, since depending on whether your project takes me one step along the continuum or more than one step, your project will achieve one objective or more than one. But I'm getting tired of writing the word that way, and you're probably getting tired of reading it. So from here on, I'll occasionally use the plural *objectives* even when I might also be referring to the singular. What this loses in precision it gains in lack of distraction.

2. The Pyramid Principle is a system for logical thinking and writing developed by Barbara Minto when she was at McKinsey. Minto's methods have been taught to major consulting firms and other businesses around the world. For a fuller explanation of pyramid logic, see Barbara Minto, *The Minto Pyramid Principle: Logic in Writing, Thinking, and Problem Solving*, Minto International (1996). Minto is primarily a logician, believing that logic alone is sufficient for persuading readers. As demonstrated throughout the psychologics part of this book, you need to be more like a rhetorician, for whom logic is, of course, necessary but certainly not sufficient. Logic and rhetoric as well as grammar were "the three ancient arts of discourse," the

foundational courses in the medieval university's liberal arts education. Aristotle defined *rhetoric* as "the faculty of observing in any given case the available means of persuasion." Beginning with the next chapter, you will be focusing on those means, the ends of which will be a proposal that sells.

Chapter 6

1. Robert B. Miller, Stephen E. Heiman, et al., *The New Strategic Selling* (New York: Warner Books, 2005).

2. Glenn J. Broadhead and Richard C. Freed, *The Variables of Composition: Process and Product in a Business Setting* (Carbondale, IL: Southern Illinois University Press, 1986), 52–53.

3. As with the Logics Worksheet, the Psychologics Worksheet as well as its individual cells can be downloaded from http://web.me.com/rfreed/Writing_Winning_Business _Proposals/Home.html.

Chapter 7

1. See Appendix E on writing effective sentences for a discussion of this important technique.

Chapter 8

1. DeBono's website calls him "the leading authority in the field of creative thinking, innovation, and the direct teaching of thinking as a skill."

2. You can download a handbook for conducting 40-minute Green (or Red) Team Reviews from http://web.me.com/rfreed/Writing_Winning_Business_Proposals/ Home.html.

Chapter 9

1. So that you don't get tired reading them and I don't go nuts writing them, for the rest of this chapter, I will refer to the Story/S_1 Component as the Story Component and the Closing/S_2 Component as the Closing Component.

Chapter 10

1. I pronounce it "pipped."

2. Broadhead and Freed, *The Variables of Composition*, 58.

Chapter 11

1. Why is it so often the case that the consultants (or associates or whatever the title might be) are assigned to write the qualifications section, even though they know next to nothing about the prospect's situation? Here's at least one reason: The partners or vice presidents don't believe that section is particularly important. They believe that prospects don't even read that section or, if they do, that their eyes glaze over as they read because all the qualifications sections pretty much sound the same. And in some, maybe many, but certainly not most situations, they may be right. However, I've asked more than three dozen people to rate the importance of qualifications sections. Before they were hired by a consultancy, half of them worked in organizations where they had to evaluate consultants' proposals. The other half worked as consultants from the get-go. More than 80 percent of the former believed qualifications sections were important. Of those consultants who had never evaluated proposals on "the other side," less than a third believed qualifications sections were important.

Chapter 13

1. I hope you're wondering why this chapter on fees follows the chapter on benefits, especially after I argued that ending a proposal with a benefits section is almost always more strategic than ending with one on costs or fees. Here's the reason for this chapter's placement: You need to have some idea of the potential client's benefits before you can determine your fees, using the variety of possible approaches discussed in this chapter.

2. Also see the lead-qualification criteria in Appendix H.

Appendix F

1. This appendix is adapted from Richard C. Freed, "This Is a Pedagogical Essay on Voice," *Journal of Business and Technical Communication* 7, no. 4 (1993): 472–81.

2. Broadhead and Freed, *The Variables of Composition*, 103–4.

Appendix G

1. Given the rapid changes in Amazon's rankings, the results you see will likely be different from those I saw, though equally instructive.

2. Those buyers performing the procurement function are classic technical buyers. They focus on the measurable, quantifiable aspects of your proposal, namely price, using metrics like return on investment (ROI) and/or return on consulting investment (ROCI).

Index

Note: Page numbers followed by *f* refer to figures.